THE FIRST TEN YEARS OF THE WTO

This book was commissioned by the World Trade Organization (WTO) as a factual account of the first decade of its existence. It aims to cover the principal activities of the WTO as the successor to GATT and the steps taken to establish a global trading system.

PETER GALLAGHER is an independent trade analyst and consultant. He records here what might be regarded as the WTO's main achievements as well as describing the controversies that have arisen in its first ten years.

A useful reference book for policy makers, journalists, members of trade delegations and for everyone who requires a detailed understanding of the workings of the WTO.

THE FIRST TEN YEARS OF THE WTO

1995–2005

PETER GALLAGHER

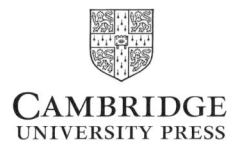

CAMBRIDGE
UNIVERSITY PRESS

CAMBRIDGE UNIVERSITY PRESS
Cambridge, New York, Melbourne, Madrid, Cape Town, Singapore, São Paulo

Cambridge University Press
The Edinburgh Building, Cambridge CB2 2RU, UK

Published in the United States of America by Cambridge University Press, New York

www.cambridge.org
Information on this title: www.cambridge.org/9780521862158

© World Trade Organization 2005

This publication is in copyright. Subject to statutory exception
and to the provisions of relevant collective licensing agreements,
no reproduction of any part may take place without
the written permission of Cambridge University Press.

First published 2005

Printed in the United Kingdom at the University Press, Cambridge

A catalogue record for this publication is available from the British Library

ISBN-13 978-0-521-86215-8 hardback
ISBN-10 0-521-86215-9 hardback

Cambridge University Press has no responsibility for
the persistence or accuracy of URLs for external or
third-party internet websites referred to in this publication,
and does not guarantee that any content on such
websites is, or will remain, accurate or appropriate.

CONTENTS

Preface   vii

1   Can it be true?   1
2   The GATT becomes the WTO, 1995   7
3   The first years: from Marrakesh to Singapore, 1995–1996   19
4   The road to Singapore, 1995–1996   32
5   Singapore to Geneva, 1996–1998   41
6   50th anniversary of the Multilateral Trading System (GATT–WTO), 1998   46
7   Geneva Ministerial Conference, 1998   52
8   Geneva to Seattle, 1998–1999   62
9   The Seattle Ministerial Conference–1999   69
10 The Road to Doha, 1999–2001   79
11 The Doha Ministerial Conference, 2001   96
12 Pursuing the Doha Mandate, 2001–2003   110
13 The aftermath of Cancún, 2003–2005   120
14 Looking back, looking forward   126

Annexes
A1 List of WTO Members and Observers (1 June 2005)   145
A2 Agreement Establishing the World Trade Organization (1995)   151
A3 Singapore Ministerial Declaration (1996)   167

v

- A4 Ministerial Declaration on Trade in Information Technology Products (1996)   181
- A5 Geneva Ministerial Declaration (1998)   204
- A6 Ministerial Declaration on Global Electronic Commerce (1998)   211
- A7 Doha Ministerial Declaration (2001)   215
- A8 Ministerial Declaration on the TRIPS Agreement and Public Health (2001)   233

PREFACE

This book has been commissioned by the WTO as a factual account of its first ten years. It covers the principal activities of the organization over the period of its establishment as the successor of GATT and the embodiment of the global trading system. I have tried to identify the main threads of what has been an important achievement without trying to avoid the controversies. But this book is not a complete record: for that, the reader might want to refer to the Annual Reports of the Organization. These are available as free downloads from the WTO website www.wto.org, in the Resources section, under Publications. All WTO documents and publications referred to in this publication can be downloaded from the same website. The official documents, whose codes are provided in this text, can be found in the Documents online database of the WTO website.

I would like to acknowledge the help of the WTO Secretariat in the preparation of this book.

Disclaimer
The opinions expressed in this book, and any errors of fact or omissions, are the author's. They are not to be attributed to the WTO or to the Secretariat of the WTO.

1

Can it be true?

In the early evening of 15 December 1993, the last Director-General of General Agreement on Tariffs and Trade (GATT), Peter Sutherland, gavelled through the final agreement on the Uruguay Round to 'huge applause'[1] from ministers gathered in the plenary hall of the Geneva Conference Centre.

For many, it was as much an expression of their relief that the Uruguay Round negotiations had finally reached a conclusion, as recognition of the momentous changes that had been made to the world trading system. Sutherland spoke of a 'major renewal' of the trading system; others talked of a momentous beginning and a new direction. *The Economist* magazine asked: 'Can it be true?'

One of the major results of the agreements concluded on that eventful day, which would come into effect on 1 January 1995, was the Agreement Establishing the World Trade Organization. Its articles included:

> **Article I**
> **Establishment of the Organization**
> The World Trade Organization (hereinafter referred to as 'the WTO') is hereby established.
>
> **Scope of the WTO**
> 1. The WTO shall provide the common institutional framework for the conduct of trade relations among its Members in matters related to the agreements and associated legal instruments included in the Annexes to this Agreement.
>
> **Article III**
> **Functions of the WTO**
> 1. The WTO shall facilitate the implementation, administration and operation, and further the objectives, of this Agreement and of the Multilateral

---

[1] John Croome, *Reshaping the World Trading System: A History of the Uruguay Round*, Geneva, 1998.

Trade Agreements, and shall also provide the framework for the implementation, administration and operation of the Plurilateral Trade Agreements.
2. The WTO shall provide the forum for negotiations among its Members concerning their multilateral trade relations in matters dealt with under the agreements in the Annexes to this Agreement. The WTO may also provide a forum for further negotiations among its Members concerning their multilateral trade relations, and a framework for the implementation of the results of such negotiations, as may be decided by the Ministerial Conference.

The agreement to create the WTO in 1995 stands in sharp contrast to the disagreements among countries over the proposal in the mid-1940s to create an International Trade Organization (ITO) that would be a complement to the World Bank and the International Monetary Fund. As the ITO proposal foundered, the GATT, created in 1948 as a preparatory measure for the new trade organization, lived on to provide the basis for the conduct of international trade relations for the next 50 years.

The establishment of the World Trade Organization, with a clear legal status and mandate was in itself the crossing of an important threshold in international trade relations.

Coming to grips with a globalizing economy

The world economy has experienced several periods of 'globalization', dating back to the end of the nineteenth century when vast trading empires made European wealth a function of the diverse supply of a global market. The period since the Second World War when those empires finally dissolved brought a new era of market globalization, with still broader horizons, greater flows of trade, investment and technology and many more economies that were potential beneficiaries of the market's wealth.

The General Agreement on Tariffs and Trade (GATT), formed provisionally at the start of this era (1947), had been successful in a task that had been framed by the experiences of the 1920s and 1930s. It ensured non-discrimination in the management of tariff-based trade barriers, reducing the impact of those barriers on merchandise trade (the average tariff of GATT Contracting Parties fell from double-digit levels to 4% through six negotiating rounds). But the governments who made up the membership of the GATT, known as Contracting Parties, had determined that it was not equipped to manage the multilateral trade system in a new era of globalization, much less to help its Members , both developed and developing countries, secure a share of the benefits of continuing growth in global trade.

The GATT concerned itself mainly with tariffs – in an era when commercial policies were expressed in new forms of trade regulation – and with merchandise alone: it ignored traded services (transport, communications, finance), which, by the mid-1980s, had grown to be a third of global trade in terms of value and underpinned all the rest.

For five decades following the creation of the GATT, the world saw an extraordinary increase in economic growth and prosperity. On an annual average basis, merchandise exports grew by 6% in real terms from 1948 to 1997. The large gains in income growth, job creation and overall prosperity in that period were in part attributable to the success of the multilateral trading system in lowering trade barriers. During this period of intense economic activity the GATT provided a forum where disputes over conflicting trade policies could be isolated and often resolved.

But well before its 40th anniversary, its Members concluded that the GATT system was already straining to adapt to the new realities of a globalizing world economy.

- There were 18 economies that were parties to GATT at its foundation. By 1985 there were 90 Contracting Parties. The membership was much more diverse industrially, economically and constitutionally than it had been when it comprised the major powers of the Second World War and their former empires and emerging colonies. 'North' and 'South' were concepts that had not existed in 1947 when the world had been divided 'East' and 'West'.
- Trade became much more important in relation to output (6.8% of GDP in 1950, 11.1% in 1973, 17.2% by 1998 at constant 1990 prices)[2] and its direction began to diversify away from the still predominant 'north-south' orientation set in the earlier era of globalization. The 'newly industrializing' economies of East Asia, especially, had expanded their share of trade and strengthened the growth of 'south-south' trade.[3] But even among the industrialized economies – now spread around the northern hemisphere – the waves of new industrial production in industries such as automobiles and steel created persistent peaks and troughs of trade imbalances.

[2] Angus Maddison, *Economic Progress: The Last Half Century in Historical Perspective*, Australian Academy of Social Sciences Annual Symposium, 1999.
[3] WTO, *World Trade Report*, 2003, p. 22ff.

- Technological change re-shaped production processes that had been devised around the time of the first era of globalization. This led to changes in scale, capital intensity and location that brought new competitors into light- and then heavy-industrial markets, creating new directions for trade and re-making the composition of imports and exports while dramatically increasing the importance of both in national accounts.
- In all quarters of the globe, governments were mid-wives or even parents of a new era of, first, industrial and then electronic development while managing – sometimes minutely – the pace and distribution of change in sectors such as agriculture. Many governments that had once taxed the 'old' source of wealth now subsidized it in the name of food security or in an effort to compensate for the redistribution of national wealth towards a more productive industrial and services sector. These actions, too, had spillover impacts on global trade of an order that the GATT was not designed to manage.
- The wealth that accompanied the new era of globalization itself brought consequences GATT could not manage. The rapid expansion of investment and of consumption possibilities in the new era of globalization saw the spread of designer and entertainment goods and the delivery of new communication and production technologies to vast new consumer markets in jurisdictions where the essential IP component of the goods was not secure. Consumer and producer put different values on the problem, at least in the short-term, creating tensions the GATT could not resolve.
- As the symbol of inter-governmental management of the trading system, the GATT's own structures were by the 1980's out of tune with the phenomenon then being called 'interdependence'; the network of exchange that linked each economy to every other and made the welfare of any individual country vulnerable to the policies of others. The fabric of Members' rights was patched by 'voluntary' codes that made their Members more equal than others; many smaller economies had been introduced into membership by former imperial powers without having to integrate a meaningful level of GATT disciplines into their trade policies; small groups managed internal GATT affairs with reference to the whole membership only at the last moment.
- Finally, the 'gold standard' that had been an icon of the first era of globalization broke, in the early 1970s, under the combined pressure of decades of fiscal expansion and speculation. The end of fixed exchange rates demanded more sophisticated economic strategies than many

governments were able to deploy and put unexpected pressures on economies with either surplus or deficits on their current accounts – including the world's largest economies – to resolve imbalances using crude trade barriers or some form of subsidy. Developing economies felt the challenges most keenly but found the multilateral institutions of the defunct Bretton Woods system still equipped only with harsh, anti-inflationary options.

Nowhere were the limits of the GATT more evident than in the Declaration following the turbulent 1982 Ministerial meeting of GATT's Contracting Parties. It catalogues the problems in language that conveys the dissatisfaction of the majority:

> The deep and prolonged crisis of the world economy has severely depressed levels of production and trade. In many countries growth rates are low or negative; there is growing unemployment and a climate of uncertainty, exacerbated by persistent inflation, high rates of interest and volatile exchange rates, which seriously inhibit investment and structural adjustment and intensify protectionist pressures. Many countries, and particularly developing countries, now face critical difficulties created by the combination of uncertain and limited access to export markets, declining external demand, a sharp fall in commodity prices and the high cost of borrowing...
>
> In the field of trade, the responses of governments to the challenges of the crisis have too often been inadequate and inward looking. Import restrictions have increased and a growing proportion of them have for various reasons been applied outside GATT disciplines, thus undermining the multilateral trading system. Trade patterns have also been adversely affected by certain forms of economic assistance for production and exports and by some restrictive trade measures applied for non-economic purposes... [leading to] delays... in necessary structural adjustment, increased economic uncertainty and discouraged productive investment.
>
> ... [D]espite the strength and resilience which it has shown, the stresses on the [trading] system, which are reflected in the growing number and intensity of disputes between contracting parties, many of which remain unresolved, have made more pronounced certain shortcomings in its functioning. Existing strains have been aggravated by differences of perception regarding the balance of rights and obligations under the GATT, the way in which these rights and obligations have been implemented and the extent to which the interests of different Contracting Parties have been met by the GATT... Disciplines governing the restriction of trade through safeguard measures are inadequate; there is widespread dissatisfaction with the application of GATT rules and the degree of liberalization in relation to

agricultural trade, even though such trade has continued to expand; trade in textiles and clothing continues to be treated under an Arrangement which is a major derogation from the General Agreement – a matter of critical importance to developing countries in particular. Such differences and imbalances are particularly detrimental to the stability of the international trading system when they concern access to the markets of major trading countries or when, through the use of export subsidies, competition among major suppliers is distorted.

(Paras 2–4 of the Declaration, 38th Session of Contracting Parties at Ministerial Level, Geneva, 29 November 1982)

2

The GATT becomes the WTO, 1995

The decades (1947–1994) in which the GATT organized the development of global trade in merchandise demonstrated that the concept could work and achieve results, while developing new methods to avoid or resolve trade disputes. The challenge that Members faced in the creation of the WTO was to build on the successes of the GATT system while overcoming its limitations.

The first thing that strikes us in comparing the GATT to the WTO is the obvious difference in size: ten agreements under the GATT (barely 80 pages in length) compared to 28 Uruguay Round agreements (26,000 pages, and 200 kilos in the originals, which include the national schedules). The WTO comprises more than 60 different formal councils and committees, compared to less than one third that number under GATT in its last years.

The increase in size is a symptom of the huge expansion in the scope of the agreements. Subjects covered by one or two articles of the GATT, such as agricultural trade, or only in passing, such as trade in textiles and clothing, have been spun out to individual agreements under the WTO with detailed schedules, footnotes and annexes. A single line in the GATT, such as Article XX(b) – which reads 'necessary to protect human, animal or plant life or health' – has been elaborated in the WTO into a complex, finely-balanced Agreement on Sanitary and Phytosanitary Measures (SPS) whose title alone is almost as long as the GATT provision.

In response to the problems identified in the 1982 Ministerial Declaration, the Uruguay Round agreements revised and expanded the GATT's rules on 'contingent' barriers such as anti-dumping, subsidies and safeguards, providing much more precise characterizations of GATT disciplines.

The approach adopted by the Uruguay Round negotiators was not merely to annotate, but to expand, define, explicate and consolidate the concepts and disciplines that already existed, combining them with new provisions that absorbed the experience of 40 years of the multilateral trading system. Some articles of the GATT were expanded – or rather 'complemented' since the original articles remain in force – to become entire agreements; paragraphs became articles; terms became lists and definitions.

It is worth remembering, for example, that the GATT did not define what it meant by an 'export subsidy' – although it had prohibited their use in non-primary products since the 1960s and weakly disciplined their use in agriculture. The Agreement on Subsidies and Countervailing Measures (SCM) filled this obvious gap.

The Agreement on Safeguards prohibits practices such as 'voluntary' export restrictions that obscured the use of unscheduled import barriers. But it also makes it possible to use safeguards more effectively as part of a legitimate trade adjustment program with expanded provisions for temporary, compensated use of import barriers, even on a discriminatory basis.

Governments extended the multilateral trading system to encompass the vast domain of trade in services. The General Agreement on Trade in Services (GATS) replicates the GATT principles for trade in 'intangibles' which make up an increasing percentage of world trade.[1]

The Agreement on Trade-Related Aspects of Intellectual Property Rights (TRIPS) specifies minimum standards of protection for intellectual property for all Members of WTO.

A capacity for reform

It is obvious that the WTO agreements introduced big changes. But there was much greater novelty in this revision of the trading system than even the explosion of numbers of agreements and topics indicates.

For the first time, The Uruguay Round Agreement gave the multilateral trading system a reform agenda. You'll search in vain for the word 'reform' in the text of GATT 1947, but it occurs ten times in the WTO Agreement on Agriculture alone, including in the first line. The WTO takes an intentional approach that more strongly implies policy choices and directions than anything found in the GATT.

The GATT avoided policy prescriptions. It was agnostic about the intention of commercial policies confining itself to regulating the impact

---

[1] Services represent the fastest growing sector of the global economy and as of 2004 accounted for 60% of global output, 30% of global employment and nearly 20% of global trade.

of commercial policies associated with cross-border movements of merchandise trade. It reached behind the border only to regulate internal taxes, levies or various 'advantages' that might circumvent or modify commitments given on border measures. It contained no directions to Members on the content of their laws and offered them no examples or templates that would help them to achieve conformance. Not until the last moment - more than 40 years after its creation - did the GATT show any interest in understanding the trade policies of its Members.[2]

GATT accommodated the policy objectives of its founding Members even to the point of inconsistency in the rules applying, for example, to the use of subsidies and quota barriers in the non-primary and primary sectors. It provided a waiver to allow many of the same countries to maintain tailored protection policies for their textile and clothing markets that were inconsistent with its non-discrimination objectives and its prohibition on quotas for manufactured products. But, these were merely inconsistencies in what were agreed sectoral objectives.

The WTO, too, avoids policy prescriptions, but not as thoroughly as the GATT. The Agreement on Trade-Related Aspects of Intellectual Property Rights (TRIPS), for example, sets out detailed requirements for Members' domestic laws on the protection of Intellectual Property (IP) and for the enforcement of those protections. The Agreement on the Application of Sanitary and Phytosanitary Measures (SPS) prefers standards and policies embodied in other multilateral agreements.[3] The Agreement on Technical Barriers to Trade (TBT) provides a template for best practice in the management of industrial standards. The GATS Annex on Telecommunications contains a 'reference paper' with specific standards for the regulation of complex market structures such as interconnection of telecom networks.

The WTO recognizes, more explicitly than the GATT, that trade measures are part of a larger environment of economic policies that serve many goals. The Trade Policy Review Mechanism (TPRM) offers an opportunity to observe that environment in Member economies.

But the most profound changes are found in the Agreement on Agriculture where the comprehensive and detailed provisions on the tariffication of non-tariff barriers, the opening of all markets to a

---

[2] At the Montreal Ministerial meeting in December 1988 the GATT Contracting Parties established the Trade Policy Review Mechanism, which retains a prominent role in WTO.

[3] Those of the Food and Agriculture Organization (FAO) and the World Organization for Animal Health (OIE).

minimum extent, the requirement for sector-wide bindings on border measures, the limits on the use of export supports and the value and character of domestic market support add up to a program for sectoral policy change on a global basis.

No global campaign on trade policy of this breadth had been attempted since the ill-fated Havana Charter (1947). However, this time the proposed reform of the global trading system was adopted and implemented. The Agreement on Textiles and Clothing, for example, matches the Agreement on Agriculture for its evident intention to bring about a sector-wide global policy reform; although in textiles and clothing the reform comprised merely a reversal of the anomalous waiver for quantitative border restrictions, without requirement for changes in the nature of domestic policies.

Everywhere, too, the new agreements provided for a much larger flow of information and reporting by each Member. Notifications that had been almost matters of courtesy under the GATT became obligatory and detailed under WTO agreements. Members are required to notify changes in circumstances and policies, or completion of obligations, under the agreements or national schedules. Committees established under the agreements created templates for notifications to ensure consistency and completeness.

Legal consistency

The GATT [1947] is a diplomat's agreement. Compared to the WTO Agreements, the articles of GATT are concise, but their terms are no more precise than they needed to be for the sake of agreement. Important differences that emerged during the 40 years in which the GATT was the guarantor of the multilateral trading system revealed ambiguities that 'papered over' imprecise concepts or seemed to create rights or obligations that, in practice, turned out to be unenforceable.

The Tokyo Round[4] 'Codes' attempted to improve the GATT in areas such as anti-dumping and countervailing duties that were frequently litigated in industrial markets and where greater forensic precision was essential. But the impact of the Codes was reduced by their limited membership and by their dependence, ultimately, on the enforcement powers of the main agreement whose vitality they sapped by undermining its central principle of non-discrimination.

[4] The Tokyo Round of trade negotiations took place from 1973 to 1979.

The enforcement and disputes resolution powers of GATT[1947] depended on consensus decisions to initiate and to decide a dispute. Thus, the GATT rules and principles were enforced only with the consent of the affected parties on a case-by-case basis. Conciliation was a preferred outcome of disputes but there was no necessary penalty for refusal to cooperate in the resolution of a dispute – other than the risk to overall relations.

Much effort was devoted in the Uruguay Round negotiations to dealing with these problems. The result is an updated disputes mechanism with characteristics that are unique among multilateral institutions:

- The right to a tribunal where a dispute was not conciliated.
- 'Automatic' progression from notification to assessment and decision.
- A right of review of the tribunal's assessment for legal soundness.
- Prior submission of all parties to the jurisdiction of the system and prior agreement to implement decisions.

The disputes system has been used intensively over the past ten years: Between 1 January 1995 and 31 December 2004, 324 complaints were filed with the Dispute Settlement Body (DSB), of which 159 resulted in the formation of panels. The Appellate Body has dealt with 64 appeals in that period.

Among the 10 biggest users of the dispute settlement system over the past ten years at least half are developing countries. Approximately two-thirds of all disputes in that period have been brought to the DSB by industrialized countries, and one-third by developing countries. The main users of the WTO dispute settlement mechanism, are in order of importance: the USA, the EC,[5] Canada, Brazil, India, Mexico, Japan, Korea, Thailand and Argentina/Chile.

The United States has brought 80 complaints and has been respondent in 88; the EC has brought 68 complaints and been respondent in 51; Canada has been involved in 26 cases as complainant and 13 as respondent; and Japan has been complainant in 12 cases and respondent in 14. Approximately 17% of the cases have occurred between the two largest users, the United States and the EC.

Among developing countries, the largest users have been Brazil (22 cases as complainant and 12 as respondent), India (16 cases as complainant and 17 as respondent), and Argentina (9 and 15 cases, respectively, as complainant and respondent).

---

[5] For legal reasons, the European Union (EU) is known officially as the European Communities (EC) in WTO business, a practice which is reflected in this book.

The percentage of panel reports appealed to the WTO Appellate Body has fluctuated over the years, but has averaged about 70% and so far has never gone below 50%. Over the last two years the percentage of panel reports appealed has shown an increasing trend and stood at 75% in 2004. If we include those Members that have appeared as third participants, the total number of WTO Members[6] that have participated in proceedings before the Appellate Body, either as appellant, appellee or third participant stands at 67 Members, of which 59 are developing countries.

The new system of legally reviewed panel recommendations has also had an impact on the agreements themselves. Although the Marrakesh Agreement Establishing the World Trade Organization (also known as the WTO Agreement) gives the right to interpret the agreements only to the Ministerial Conference, the reports of the Appellate Body have greatly refined the Members' understanding of the obligations and rights created in the agreements.

A single undertaking

'Singleness' is a function of the WTO Agreement that requires each Member to accept the full package of multilateral trade agreements that emerged from the Uruguay Round.[7]

> This Agreement shall be open for acceptance, by signature or otherwise, by Contracting Parties to GATT 1947, and the European Communities, which are eligible to become original Members of the WTO in accordance with Article XI of this Agreement. Such acceptance shall apply to this Agreement and the multilateral trade agreements annexed hereto.
>
> Article XIV.1 of the Agreement Establishing the WTO

The 'single undertaking' is an important asset of the WTO system, but it is not an entirely novel idea; it takes its cue from the requirement of unconditional non-discrimination embedded in Article I of the GATT. The GATT demands that every 'Contracting Party' apply the same 'advantage, favour, privilege or immunity granted . . . to any product originating in or destined for any other country . . . immediately and unconditionally to the like product originating in or destined for the territories of all other Contracting Parties'.

---

[6] The EC is counted as one Member in these statistics, representing its 25 member States.
[7] There were, also, three 'plurilateral' agreements not part of the 'single undertaking' to which a number of Members adhered: agreements on beef markets, on dairy markets and an agreement on government procurement.

That sweeping obligation created the basis for spectacular growth in global trade because it ensured predictability for traders, investors, producers and consumers. The WTO's single undertaking has the same effect on the much broader canvas now covered by the WTO Agreements because almost every government in the world now has precisely the same set of fundamental trade obligations toward every other government. No matter where goods or services originate or are destined (among the 148 economies in WTO), they are guaranteed the same basic rights to fair process.

The breadth of the 'single undertaking' mandate makes the WTO an indispensable institution for trade valued at nearly US$11 trillion in 2004. But what makes the WTO unique among intergovernmental organizations is that the obligations and the rights created by the multilateral agreements are applied and enforced in a coherent way by a single system of disputes conciliation and resolution without giving priority to one right or another or to one sector or another.

Its 'singleness' is what makes the WTO's undertaking global in more than merely geographical terms because the 'world' that the WTO surveys includes almost all the trade and trade-regulatory regimes of all its Members.

New Members

Of course, all WTO Members were new Members on the first day of 1995. Although the WTO absorbed the GATT and renewed its text (in GATT 1994), it is an entirely new legal entity that is not 'provisional' as the GATT was but an un-qualified intergovernmental agreement with the same status in the municipal jurisdictions of Members as any other treaty. All former Members of GATT were invited to join the new WTO by ratifying the Agreement Establishing the WTO to which all the other agreements and decisions and understandings adopted at Marrakesh are scheduled.

Several economies had joined the GATT in the closing years of the Uruguay Round with a view, possibly, to wielding some influence over the final package of agreements or with the objective of securing the expanded rights being created in the Round. The GATT had 100 or so Members in the early 1990s; by the time of the Marrakesh signing in 1994, it had 128 Members.

They were right to be 'early adopters'. More than 45 governments have applied to accede to the WTO since the Marrakesh Agreement

Establishing the WTO entered into force on 1 January 1995. Of these, 20 have completed their accession procedures and have become WTO Members, including (in the order they have become WTO Members): Ecuador, Bulgaria, Mongolia, Panama, Kyrgyz Republic, Latvia, Estonia, Jordan, Georgia, Albania, Oman, Croatia, Lithuania, Moldova, China, Chinese Taipei, Former Yugoslav Republic of Macedonia, Nepal and Cambodia.

The terms of entry for these economies included full acceptance of the obligations of the WTO agreements, but without automatic access to the implementation concessions that were available to developing country Members at the time of the WTO's establishment. Because other terms of accession are set in bilateral negotiations with WTO Members, they have sometimes been more exacting than those contained in the WTO agreements. For example, acceding economies have been asked to make broader tariff bindings or reduced access to *de minimis* agricultural support or 'allowable' agricultural export subsidies.

Thirty-one more governments are in the queue to negotiate accession (Afghanistan, Algeria, Andorra, Azerbaijan, Bahamas, Belarus, Bhutan, Bosnia and Herzegovina, Cape Verde, Ethiopia, Iran, Iraq, Kazakhstan, Lao PDR, Lebanon, Libya, Russian Federation, Samoa, Sao Tomé, Saudi Arabia, Serbia, Montenegro, Seychelles, Sudan, Tajikistan, Tonga, Ukraine, Uzbekistan, Vanuatu, Viet Nam, Yemen).

New structures and ministerial control

Many things about the management of the trading system remained much the same on 1 January 1995 as they had been the day before the WTO agreements entered into force.

- The organization remains 'inter-governmental' whose Members are governments – not necessarily independent or 'sovereign'[8] – that control a customs territory. There are no private interests recognized in the multilateral trading system.
- The WTO, like the GATT before it, remains 'Member-driven' compared to its Bretton Woods 'cousins', the World Bank (WB) and the International Monetary Fund (IMF). The WTO has a mandate of its own and is a forum for its Members' decisions.

---

[8] From the Agreement Establishing the WTO: 'The terms "country" or "countries" as used in this Agreement and the Multilateral Trade Agreements are to be understood to include any separate customs territory Member of the WTO.'

- The day-to-day running of the WTO remains in the hands of the ambassadors of Members and their staff who meet as the General Council of the WTO and in the many committees and working groups created by the agreements.

But three changes in the structure of control from the GATT to the WTO tell us much about the differences in the nature of the pre-1995 and post-1995 management of the trading system.

The first change is that ministers are now much more visibly and regularly in control. The Ministerial Conference, that alone has the power to interpret or add to the WTO agreements, meets every two years or more often as it decides. This is a much more frequent schedule than under the GATT, which recognizes both the greater contribution of trade to all economies and the policy reform objectives of the WTO agreements.

The second change is the creation of new subsidiary councils of the General Council: the Council on Goods to manage the agreements concerned with merchandise, the Council on Services for the GATS Agreement, and the Council on TRIPS for the intellectual property agreement. This structure has its origins in the compromise of separation of subjects in the Uruguay Round negotiations, to insulate economies from anticipated demands for 'cross concessions'. In the GATS, however, the size of the sector, the distinctness of the subject matter and of the language – 'national treatment', for example, means something different in GATS than it means in the other WTO agreements – make the separation convenient.

The General Council retains, however, oversight of the management of the agreements from one horizon to the other. As the senior 'plenary' body of Members, it also meets, when it considers a dispute, as the Dispute Settlement Body (DSB).

The third change is the embodiment of the Trade Policy Review exercise in a council-level body, the Trade Policy Review Body (TPRB),[9] that takes no substantive decisions, since it only discusses the reports of each Member and of the Secretariat in the review of that Member's trade policies. The elevation of this last-minute innovation in the GATT to the council level also reflects greater consciousness of the connections between the agreements, national policies and the task of implementing the WTO obligations. Although it makes no judgements, the Trade Policy Review Mechanism (TRPM) is recognition of the challenge of

---

[9] Actually the General Council sitting as the TPRB.

implementation for developing Members especially and that administrative and financial resources are needed in addition to political will to fully participate in the WTO.

Coherence of the multilateral financial and trading systems

The GATT was never part of the United Nations organization, having been planned separately by the US and the UK as part of the post-War arrangements they reached in the Atlantic Agreement of 1942. The GATT had obvious relationship to the Bretton Woods institutions of the IMF and IBRD (International Bank for Reconstruction and Development, the 'World Bank'). The Fund and Bank were designed to secure and maintain a stable system of international monetary exchange, to fund the reserves necessary to smooth out external imbalances and, to restart global growth, including by mobilizing the gold-standard United States dollar through reconstruction and development loans. Non-discriminatory trade policies and reduced barriers facilitated by the GATT were, naturally, a part of this same plan.

However, in time, the problems involved with regulating external balances would turn out to be almost the opposite of those for which solutions had been prepared. The IMF and IBRD emerged from the exchange turbulence of the late 1960s, which saw the end of dollar-gold convertibility and the re-basing of the global exchange controls, with the same responsibilities as those that had been planned at Bretton Woods but facing a different world. The IMF, as the final resort of governments in balance of payments crises and endowed with a mandate to prevent competitive devaluations and to fight any inflationary pressures with fiscal controls, established requirements that some governments considered they could meet only by breaching their GATT obligations to maintain open markets for imports. Although the IBRD accelerated its funding of structural adjustment programs to help developing countries build more productive economies, with the objective of escaping from a balance of payments constraint, its loans were also conditioned on acceptance of the exchange-stabilizing requirements of the IMF.

In principle, there was no reason that the objectives of all three institutions could not be reconciled. But none was endowed at the outset with a mandate to support or assist the development of developing economies, which had become the main economic pre-occupation of the global community from the 1960s on. Each institution had attempted separately to re-configure itself as necessary with the development objective in mind (although it remained a subordinate objective for the IMF). But, in practice, the reconciliation of their different but overlapping mandates had to be achieved, most of the time, on a case-by-case basis through the creation of programmes for economies in difficulty. Given the social and economic dimensions of the macro-economic challenges of developing countries these were the most difficult conditions in which to coordinate.

The Decision on Coherence adopted at Marrakesh, in the process of establishing the WTO, notes that greater exchange rate stability should contribute to 'the expansion of trade, sustainable growth and development, and the timely correction of external imbalances'. It recognizes that although macro-economic imbalances cannot be redressed through measures taken in the trade field alone, there are nevertheless links between the different aspects of economic policy, and it instructed the WTO Secretariat to examine the implications of the WTO's new responsibilities for its cooperation with the Bretton Woods institutions and to establish the basis for closer and more effective coordination in the future.

THE GOALS OF THE WTO

Critics of the WTO sometimes allege that it serves a radical trade liberalization ideology. Ministers set out their goals in the introductory paragraphs to the Agreement Establishing the WTO:

'The parties to this Agreement

Recognizing that their relations in the field of trade and economic endeavour should be conducted with a view to raising standards of living, ensuring full employment and a large and steadily growing volume of real income and effective demand, and expanding the production of and trade in goods and services, while allowing for the optimal use of the world's resources in accordance with the objective of sustainable development, seeking both to protect and preserve the environment and to enhance the means for doing so in a manner consistent with their respective needs and concerns at different levels of economic development,

Recognizing further that there is need for positive efforts designed to ensure that developing countries, and especially the least developed among them, secure a share in the growth in international trade commensurate with the needs of their economic development,

Being desirous of contributing to these objectives by entering into reciprocal and mutually advantageous arrangements directed to the substantial reduction of tariffs and other barriers to trade and to the elimination of discriminatory treatment in international trade relations,

Resolved, therefore, to develop an integrated, more viable and durable multilateral trading system encompassing the General Agreement on Tariffs and Trade, the results of past trade liberalization efforts, and all of the results of the Uruguay Round of Multilateral Trade Negotiations,

Determined to preserve the basic principles and to further the objectives underlying this multilateral trading system,

Agree as follows: . . .'

3

The first years: from Marrakesh to Singapore, 1995–1996

The Uruguay Round negotiations ended on 15 December 1993 with an exhausting rush to meet a deadline set, for the most part, by the expiry of the US President's negotiating authority. But the official end of negotiations was followed by months of hard work in Geneva and in the capitals of Members to get ready for the final signatures at Marrakesh in April 1994, and the entry into force of the WTO Agreements on 1 January 1995.

Many prospective Members of the WTO found that the task of completing the schedules of goods and services undertakings, based on the negotiations, and preparing changes to domestic laws and regulations necessary for the implementation of the agreements, stretched their administrative and law-making capacities. When the 1 January 1995 date for the launch of the WTO arrived, several developing countries had still not submitted their schedules for verification and were not ready, therefore, to take up the opportunity of original membership of WTO.

The WTO faced two sets of priorities. The first was to meet the immediate requirements of the new agreements: to appoint the officers of the new committees and the members of its new Appellate Body, set up an entity to manage conflicts over pre-shipment inspection, establish the system of notifications, verify the national schedules, and manage the accessions of 'original' and acceding Members.

The second priority was to organize and support the continuing negotiations on annexes to the GATS (financial, maritime and basic telecommunications) and to facilitate initiatives to extend market access negotiations on information technology goods and pharmaceutical products.

Many Members – but not all to the same degree, as it turned out – were also keen to use the momentum at last regained with the creation of the WTO to continue the elaboration of the new global framework of the trading system. In the industrialized countries especially, but also in the 'newly industrializing' developing world, the period 1994–1997 was one of spectacular growth in trade-led production and foreign direct investment. The promise of a globalized environment for investment, production and consumption never seemed more enticing. This enthusiasm was reflected in preparation of the agenda of the first WTO Ministerial Conference in Singapore (9–13 December, 1996) which included new items on competition policy, investment and the facilitation of trade as well as new attention to the relationship between environment and trade, labour conditions and trade and the ever-present problem of corruption.

New membership

From the start, WTO Members wanted the new multilateral trading system to be truly global in scope and application. The WTO rules constitute the 'trading system' to the extent that they are unique – no other rules govern the administration of global trade – and apply to the trade of all economies.

Any state or customs territory that has full autonomy in the conduct of its trade policies may become a Member of the WTO in one of two ways.

A Contracting Party to the GATT at the date of entry into force of the WTO (1 January 1995) could become an 'original' Member of the WTO if it accepted without reservations the WTO agreement and the 'single undertaking' row which it provides and had made concessions and commitments to the other Members on both goods and services, embodied in schedules that had been duly accepted and annexed, respectively, to the GATT 1994 and the GATS.

Seventy-six economies qualified on these terms as original members of the WTO on 1 January 1995 and an additional 36 Members had completed the processes – mostly the verification and acceptance of national schedules – that allowed them to accede by 13 December 1995, bringing the total membership to 112.

The second road to membership is by accession, which means negotiating the terms of membership with the governments that are already Members. Once an economy is a Member, however, it is on the same footing as all other Members vis-à-vis the WTO agreements, except for any special conditions negotiated as part of its acceptance into the WTO.

The WTO's vocation of universal membership was, and remains, a challenge that demands great efforts both from the WTO and from prospective Members. The process of accession has become much more complex than it was under the GATT, mostly because of the increased range and detail of obligations under the WTO agreements. Accession negotiations concern all aspects of the applicant's trade policies and practices, such as market access concessions and commitments on goods and services, legislation to enforce intellectual property rights, and all other measures which form a government's commercial policies. Applications for WTO membership are overseen by individual Working Parties that examine, comment and decide to accept or reject the reports (often voluminous) that prospective Members supply, detailing their commercial policies.

But in addition to committing themselves to comply with WTO rules, prospective Members must negotiate with their most important trading partners among existing WTO Members on the terms and conditions of bound market access rights for goods and services that are exchanged at the time of WTO membership. These bilateral negotiations may take years to complete.

The process is especially difficult for the governments of least-developed economies to manage. Those that became original Members of the WTO were subject to the same basic conditions as other original Members, but were asked to undertake commitments and concessions only to an extent consistent with their individual development, financial or trade needs or their administrative and institutional capabilities. The WTO's General Council approved the accession of 21 least-developed countries on this less demanding basis in 1995. The question soon arose, however, whether the provisions for accession by non-original Members of the WTO – those economies that had to negotiate accession – should be similarly adapted for least-developed economies.

Despite the formidable challenges, the demand for accession to WTO was strong from the outset. Many of the candidates for accession in the mid-1990s had recently begun a difficult transition from centrally-planned to market economies. For these, as for other economies today, accession to the WTO offered – in addition to the usual trade benefits – a way of underpinning their domestic economic and administrative reforms.

After only 18 months of operation, the WTO comprised 123 Members who accounted for more than 90% of world trade and most of the economies that remained outside the world trade system had requested accession to the WTO.

Setting up the WTO

The establishment phase of the WTO truly began in the months immediately after the Marrakesh meeting and before the formal entry into force of the agreements. During this period the GATT continued to function in parallel to the Preparatory Committee for the World Trade Organization.

Table 1. *Working parties on accession*

After Marrakesh →	After Singapore →	After Cancún
Albania	Albania	
Algeria	Algeria	Algeria
Armenia	Armenia	Andorra
	Azerbaijan	Azerbaijan
		Bahamas
Belarus	Belarus	Belarus
Bulgaria		
		Bhutan
		Bosnia-Herzegovina
		Cape Verde
Cambodia	Cambodia	
China	China	
Croatia	Croatia	
Estonia	Estonia	
		Ethiopia
Georgia	Georgia	
Jordan	Jordan	
Kazakhstan	Kazakhstan	Kazakhstan
Republic of Kyrgyz	Republic of Kyrgyz	
Latvia	Latvia	
		Lao PDR
Lithuania	Lithuania	
		Lebanon
Former Yugoslav Republic of Macedonia	Former Yugoslav Republic of Macedonia	
Moldova	Moldova	
Nepal	Nepal	
Mongolia		
Oman	Oman	
Panama		
Russian Federation	Russian Federation	Russian Federation
		Samoa
Saudi Arabia	Saudi Arabia	Saudi Arabia
		Serbia and Montenegro
Seychelles	Seychelles	Seychelles
Sudan	Sudan	Sudan

Table 1. *Working parties on accession (cont.)*

After Marrakesh →	After Singapore →	After Cancún
Chinese Taipei	Chinese Taipei	
		Tajikistan
Tonga	Tonga	Tonga
Ukraine	Ukraine	Ukraine
Uzbekistan	Uzbekistan	Uzbekistan
Vanuatu	Vanuatu	Vanuatu
Vietn Nam	Viet Nam	Viet Nam
		Yemen

The Committee concerned itself with the many administrative details needed to complete the transition from GATT to the WTO and with preparations for the Implementation Conference held in December, 1994, to decide on the membership of the WTO at the time of its entry into force.

The summaries in this section cannot capture all of the work that was done, but they list some matters that were important at the outset and continued to be important in the development of the organization over the decade that followed.

Notification requirements

The negotiators of the WTO agreements recognized that a system of rules is only as good as its implementation. They decided that the best way to ensure that the rules and other commitments are being respected is to give Members themselves the information necessary to undertake collective surveillance by requiring each Member to notify specific actions or changes in policies – or sometimes the absence of any action or change.

This transparency comes at the cost, however, of managing large flows of information. There are many obligations to notify – the Working Group on Notification Obligations and Procedures identified 175 notification requirements in the goods area alone – and they are scattered throughout the agreements. Members might fail to meet a notification requirement through error or from simple inadvertence. The WTO Secretariat noted that many Members were in arrears on some of their notification obligations almost immediately. For example, in the Agreement on Subsidies and Countervailing Measures (SCM), less than 10 % of the Members had notified subsidy programs under Article 25 of the Agreement and Article XVI:1 of GATT 1994 within the stipulated timeframe.

Under the GATS, measures recognizing foreign qualifications for service providers must be notified by a Member within 12 months from the date on which the WTO Agreement takes effect for that Member. Not one was received on time. Members also failed at first to meet the deadline to notify promptly, and at least annually, new or revised laws, regulations or administrative guidelines that significantly affect trade in services covered by a Member's specific commitments under GATS.

In other agreements the picture was brighter. Almost 90% of the Members subject to notification requirements under the Agreement on Textiles and Clothing had notified the first stage of their integration programs on time.

Developing countries faced the biggest problems with the expanded notification obligations as confirmed not only by defaults on notifications but also by their increasing requests for technical assistance with notifications. Developed countries too failed to make required notifications on issues such as state trading, customs valuation, subsidies, and preferential rules of origin.

The Working Group on Notification Obligations and Procedures has tried to overcome problems in the design of the notifications system by reducing duplication or overlap of notification obligations, simplifying data requirements and standardizing formats, improving the timing of the reporting process and by providing assistance to developing countries in meeting their notification obligations.

Because many notification requirements are linked to the implementation of substantive commitments, it was difficult at first to assess the degree of implementation of the agreements by the Members. But, according to the Annual Report (1995) of the first Director-General Peter Sutherland, notification appeared, broadly, to be satisfactory. His caution on this score was prudent, however. Implementation of the agreements remained a matter of controversy throughout the first ten years of WTO – in several different ways.

First, there were questions about the extent to which Members – especially the least-developed – had been able to implement agreements that demanded legislative, administrative or even judicial arrangements (e.g. in TRIPS) that sometimes exceeded their capacities. A number of Members found that they were unable to complete their obligations even within the extended deadlines contained in the Uruguay Round agreements and sought waivers for additional time to implement agreements such as TRIPS and the Agreement on Trade-Related Investment Measures (TRIMS). Controversial estimates of the costs – in terms of personnel, administrative and technical resources – of implementing some agreements such as TRIPS or Customs Valuation led to acrimonious exchanges both inside and outside the WTO about whether the agreements offered any net benefits to developing countries, at least in the short term.

A second aspect of what became known as 'the implementation problem' related to some uncertainties about what Members must do under the agreements. The clauses of the agreements describe governments' obligations to administer certain difficult domains in accordance with an objective or outcome. However, to allow governments the flexibility to achieve an outcome by means appropriate to their circumstances, the agreements rarely say what a Member must do, leading to some ambiguity in the definition of the obligation. Also, where a matter was controversial in the negotiations, the controversy was sometimes resolved by referring to the obligation in roundabout terms that smoothed the controversy but at the cost of precision. Where there was a doubt about the implementation of an obligation, Members were naturally inclined to interpret the agreements in accordance with whether implementation offered them a benefit or only a cost.

'Implementation' also meant the scheduling of the 'built-in' agenda. Some 74 provisions in the WTO agreements called for reviews, further negotiations, cooperation, and other decisions and declarations related to the implementation of the Results of the Uruguay Round. About half of this 'to do' list was scheduled for the first year after the WTO entered into force including the continuation of the negotiations on the Services annexes (maritime transport, financial services and telecommunications) and the establishment of the Appellate Body. But the precise boundaries of the 'built-in agenda' were not always clear. Decisions that, in the view of some Members, meant a commitment to achieve a result were considered by others to be no more than a commitment to undertake negotiations with a view to achieving a result.

Finally, 'implementation' also implied the fulfillment of promises that, although not obligations under the Uruguay Round agreements, coloured the overall result. Developing countries were particularly affected by such promises, including undertakings on increased technical assistance and food aid for net food-importing developing countries.

Some differences over implementation issues might have been expected after extended negotiations on a large number of detailed agreements, but these issues dogged the WTO throughout the period between

Marrakesh and Doha. Because the agreements are reciprocal, different interpretations of the obligations can upset the perception of an overall balance between benefits and costs. In those circumstances, the temperature of the debate on implementation among Members can rise quickly and the sense of injury over a bargain can persist.

Many of these 'implementation' problems were resolved by a lengthy series of negotiations following the Seattle Ministerial Conference (30 November – 3 December, 1999) that led, finally, to a decision taken at the Doha Ministerial Conference (9–14 November, 2001). Some of them were resolved by disputes such as the early dispute between the United States and India over the implementation of an aspect of the TRIPS Agreement[1] (see next Chapter). A few of these matters were referred to the negotiators in the Doha Development Agenda to renegotiate.

Openness

From the outset, the WTO has been caught in a dilemma on the issue of 'openness'. On one hand, the WTO is an inter-governmental, 'Member-driven' organization whose government Members know well that some things, including trade negotiation or the management of foreign policy, cannot be done efficiently before television cameras. On the other hand, most of those same governments are also committed to make decisions in their own administrations in the most transparent manner possible because to do otherwise is not only inconsistent with accountability but creates a refuge for inefficiency and corruption.

It is not always clear, even to Members of the WTO, where they should strike the balance. Although most governments are ready to consult closely with private interest groups on their management of trade relations, none believes that private interests should be a party to this management. National constitutions rarely make provision for private input into decision-making in foreign affairs policy.

For the WTO, achieving this balance is further complicated by the need to find practical solutions that attract the consensus support of all Member governments, who choose different approaches to openness in their own administrations.

Two big challenges occurred in the early months of the WTO's existence, concerning decisions to accept observers from other international

---

[1] India: Patent protection for pharmaceutical and agricultural chemical products (brought by US): 9 July 1996.

organizations and to de-restrict WTO documents. Both decisions proved to be more controversial and took longer than had been expected. Both were eventually adopted in July 1996, along with guidelines for relations with non-government organizations.

As a result of the decision on observers,[2] the WTO has extensive contact with other inter-governmental organizations interested in its activities. Relations have been established with relevant organizations in the United Nations system, the Bretton Woods organizations, or various regional bodies to ensure that the resources and expertise of the international community remain focused, coordinated and, most important, relevant to pressing global needs. Many of the organizations have observer status in one or more of the various WTO committees, councils or working groups. Some of them are also represented in the negotiating groups for trade in certain services sectors.

The 1996 decision[3] on de-restriction of WTO documents allowed the publication of a larger number of documents related to current and future decisions, while maintaining the more restrictive GATT approach, where no specific provisions were made for publication of official documents. The decision set a number of rules that could be characterized as a 'negative list' approach: some documents were to be 'automatically' de-restricted after their circulation and others would be de-restricted within a period of 2 to 9 months unless they were of a type scheduled for more restrictive treatment or if a Member objected to their de-restriction (objections were open to periodical review). It was a complex compromise that included long 'negative' lists of documents that were not subject to automatic or 'timed' de-restriction. Many outside commentators pointed out that, despite the de-restriction of many draft documents, the procedures did not shed much light on documents related to pending decisions.

Nevertheless, the overall experience of de-restriction and the accompanying wide access to official documents provided through the WTO's website was positive. In May 2002, Members revised and significantly extended the de-restriction procedures[4] from that point forward, making de-restriction automatic for almost all documents within 60 days of circulation (or 90 days if requested by a Member). A growing database of over 100,000 WTO documents is accessible to the public through the WTO internet site (www.wto.org).

---

[2] See WTO document WT/L/161, Annex 3.   [3] See WTO document WT/160/Rev. 1.
[4] See WTO document WT/L/452.

Over the first ten years of the WTO's history, decision-making in almost all areas of the WTO has become increasingly transparent. The WTO now publishes more information about the decisions made by its Members on the global trading system than many governments do in their national jurisdictions. It devotes significant resources (e.g. documentation, symposia, specific briefings and the time of senior Secretariat staff) to informing and exchanging views and information with international non-government organizations (NGOs) that play an important role in the dissemination of information and technical assistance related to trade, with trans-national corporations that mediate trade and even with individual citizens through a chat room on the WTO website. But it is safe to say that the demand for 'openness' remains a – probably permanent – challenge.

Dispute settlement

The new WTO dispute settlement procedures are a unified set of rules which provide 'automatic' access to compulsory adjudication of disputes over issues arising from all WTO agreements.

Dispute settlement activity began quietly but accelerated quickly as Members began to gather experience of the new system. From the outset, both developed and developing countries used their rights under the new procedures. By the end of the WTO's first year, the Dispute Settlement Body (DSB) had been notified of 21 requests for consultations – the step that marks the beginning of a WTO dispute – on 14 distinct matters. But almost a quarter of the requests (four) were withdrawn – presumably because the problem was resolved – and panels were established in four others. By mid-1996, the disputes notified had risen to 38 and in the following 12 months the number had grown to a total of 89 notifications.

In December 1996, the DSB adopted Rules of Conduct[5] for panellists, experts, Appellate Body members and Secretariat staff. These Rules of Conduct, the most elaborate and sophisticated rules applicable to participants in international dispute settlement, were the result of more than two years of negotiations initiated by the Preparatory Committee for the WTO in 1994. They seek to ensure the impartiality and independence of the persons involved in the WTO dispute settlement process as well as their obligation to maintain confidentiality and to avoid conflict of interest.

[5] See WTO document WT/DSB/RC/1.

The General Agreement on Trade in Services (GATS)

The Uruguay Round created a new legal framework for the liberalization of trade in services. The GATS Agreement required that Members negotiate a new series of scheduled commitments on access to markets through a variety of 'modes' (presence, movement of the provider or consumer or the temporary relocation of personnel). They could also choose to negotiate national treatment in markets where an access commitment was made. The GATS also provided, through a number of sub-sector protocols and annexes, a global framework for liberalizing the existing regulatory regimes for management of services markets such as finance, telecommunications and professional services.

When it entered into force on 1 January 1995, the new GATS Agreement was obviously underpowered. Members had scheduled only modest liberalization agreements on a small number of sectors. In part this limitation may have been due to the difficulty of the Uruguay Round negotiations, where the need to re-think and sometimes re-invent basic trade policy concepts and instruments required governments to put a great deal of effort into rule-making, partly at the expense of market-opening negotiations. Members may also have been reluctant to take on liberalization commitments where their own accompanying legal frameworks – governing for example quality standards, licensing requirements and regulatory supervision in a more open environment – had still to be created. Some participants also adopted a traditional bargaining stance under the new framework of rules, by deciding to wait for trading partners' requests, rather than using the provisions of the GATS as a framework for reform of their domestic services industries. As a result, the level of commitments undertaken for services in the Uruguay Round was generally modest, in terms of the number of services sectors actually included in the market access schedules of individual Members, and in terms of the quality of the market access they provided under the four GATS modes of supply.

WTO Members have been negotiating on services continuously since the end of the Uruguay Round in December 1993.

Continuing services negotiations

At the end of the Uruguay Round, Members had not completed negotiations on the annexes to the GATS on financial services, the movement of natural persons, basic telecommunications and maritime transport. Each covered a complex area of administration of national services markets to which concepts of multilateral trade liberalization had never applied but the reasons for non-completion varied. The negotiators on the Telecommunications Annex decided that the time was not 'ripe'; they could see imminent changes in global market conditions for the supply of telecommunications services in the late 1990s and decided to wait for those changes to take shape before settling on a new global regime of trade rules in the sector. In financial services, too, the global market was evolving rapidly but not in every sector of the industry and not in every economy. The biggest financial market economies (the USA, especially) held out at the end of the Uruguay Round for bigger access offers before they would consider approving a global GATS Annex.

Financial services

Negotiations on financial services were reopened in April 1997. Members again had an opportunity to improve, modify or withdraw their commitments in financial services and to take MFN exemptions in the sector from 1 November until 12 December 1997 (one year after the Singapore Ministerial in 1996). As a result of those negotiations, a new and improved set of commitments in financial services under the GATS was finally agreed on 12 December 1997.

With five countries making commitments in financial services for the first time, the total number of WTO Members with commitments in financial services rose to 102 upon the entry into force of the Protocol. As a result of the most recent negotiations, the United States, India and Thailand decided to withdraw their broad MFN exemptions based on reciprocity; only a small number of countries submitted limited MFN exemptions or maintained existing broad MFN exemptions.

Movements of natural persons

Six countries also improved their offers on the movement of natural persons, guaranteeing new opportunities for individual service suppliers – qualified professionals, computer specialists, experts in different fields – to work temporarily abroad.

Basic telecommunications

The success of negotiations on the liberalization of basic telecommunications became a touchstone of the services trade liberalization project of the WTO. They began in May 1994 – after the end of the Uruguay Round but before the WTO entered into operation – and were finally concluded in February 1997 after missing a mid-1996 deadline.

Sixty-nine governments made commitments to liberalize markets that accounted for more than 90% of global telecommunications (then worth more than $500 billion annually) at a time when the competitive conditions in those markets were changing rapidly. Technological change, economic growth and even the transition of centrally planned economies in Eastern Europe to market economies propelled a revolution in telecommunications markets at the end of the 1990s. It was a period marked around the world by the end – or at least the 'transition' – of former telecommunications monopolies and the entry of new competitors for the provision of basic telecommunications services.

There is an undertone of relief – as well as excitement – in the statement by the WTO Director-General Renato Ruggiero welcoming the conclusion of the negotiations, which extended the much more modest agreements already annexed to the GATS on value-added services.

> 'I want to congratulate governments for their determination and foresight in bringing this negotiation to a successful conclusion. Not all the decisions have been easy. But in the end, Member governments have put their faith in the multilateral process of the WTO, and the WTO has delivered.
>
> This Agreement promotes liberalization, and it enhances certainty, security and predictability through a clear set of rules. This is particularly valuable at a time when rapid growth and technological development are changing the face of the telecoms industry.'
>
> (WTO Press release, 17 February, 1997)

4

The road to Singapore, 1995–1996

The period immediately between the end of the Uruguay Round negotiations and opening of the Singapore Ministerial Conference in December 1996 was marked by considerable optimism among Members about growth, the world economy and the role of the WTO.

Although WTO Director-General Ruggiero identified some 'shadows' in the new organization's record – for example, the failure, up to then, to get beyond 'interim' results in the Financial Services or Basic Telecommunications Agreements – the outlook for further liberalization and integration of markets was encouraging and promised continued growth, more widespread prosperity, including through greater consumer choice in more open markets.

The WTO's Annual Report of 1997 reflected the view that a sort of revolution had taken place in trade policy over the preceding decade while Members had focused on completing the Uruguay Round negotiations.

> The essence of these far-reaching changes lies in the emergence of a virtual global consensus on the fundamental contribution to economic progress made by open trade policies. This in turn is reflected in the degree of trade liberalization achieved during and since the Uruguay Round, as well as the continuing consolidation and expansion since 1995 of the multilateral trading system embodied in the World Trade Organization. While Members continue to implement trade liberalization commitments made in the Uruguay Round, further multilateral, regional and autonomous liberalization efforts have proceeded . . .
>
> WTO Annual Report 1997, p. 3

This optimism was anchored in part in the success of the preparations for further liberalization of goods trade (information technology, pharmaceuticals: see below) and proposals for even broader sector-based acceleration of the Uruguay Round market access agreements. It reflected the conviction – proved well founded – that a breakthrough would be made in telecommunications and in financial services. It even found an echo in the spread of regional trade liberalization in Europe (the Association

Agreements promising extension of the European Communities), in North (NAFTA) and South America (MERCOSUR), in Asia (the acceleration of the ASEAN free trade area deadlines) and – the largest regional group of all – in the 1996 free trade resolutions of the economies of the Asia Pacific Economic Cooperation (APEC) group.

There were two consequences of this spirit that continued to have an impact throughout the WTO's first decade. The first was that the sudden jump in trade and economic growth rates during the period 1994–96, coinciding with the establishment of a broader, more inclusive WTO sharpened the contrast between those economies that were benefiting most from new globalized market opportunities and those poorest economies that continued to struggle with unacceptable levels of poverty and that remained only weakly connected to the global trade growth engine. The obligation of the WTO to take positive steps within its new mandate to address the needs of the least-developed economies was strongly expressed by WTO officials on Members' behalf and reflected in specific trade initiatives.

The second consequence was the creation of high expectations about the potential of the trading system embodied in the WTO to deal with the new and difficult issues of global cooperation on trade that would later become known as the 'Singapore issues'. The WTO would be asked to manage a startling volume of work over the next decade. Even as the preparations were being made for the First Ministerial Conference of the WTO at Singapore in December 1996, the committees and councils of the WTO, assisted by the Secretariat, were beginning to deal with the new agreements, including a substantial 'built-in agenda' – with commitments to new negotiations or continued negotiations stretching up to 2000 – they were being encouraged to prepare vast new areas of work on competition policy, investment, trade and labour standards, trade facilitation and the reduction of corruption.

In retrospect, this agenda was too much for the WTO to manage comfortably. Despite efforts of the Secretariat through the WTO's 'outreach' activities (charged with explaining and advocating the new agenda) many Members did not have the capacity to participate in negotiations on an expanded range of topics, while others questioned the priority of the additional agenda items for the majority of Members. In the end, as we will see, it was the single undertaking that forced retrenchment: when everything on the table forms part of the final 'package' of agreements, the stakes placed on the table at the start of negotiations are as crucial as the deals done at the end.

Although the WTO's agenda began to inflate right from the start, Ministers at Singapore decided to put limits on their consideration of two topics that had been under discussion within the GATT for several years: trade and environment and trade and labour standards.

Trade and environment

During the WTO's first two or three years the temperature of international debate over alleged conflicts between the management of the global environmental and the global trading system 'commons' rose sharply. One of the achievements of the Singapore Ministerial meeting was to 'cool' this debate.

The relationship between the objectives of international cooperation on the environment and the multilateral trading system began to attract critical attention from civil society organizations towards the end of the Uruguay Round, at the United Nations' Earth Summit in Rio De Janeiro in 1992. When governments were faced with deciding how the UN's sustainable development objectives were to be met, some representatives of international NGOs expressed concern over the clash, as they perceived it, between the objectives of some of the Multilateral Environment Agreements (MEAs) and the market opening objectives of the trading system that seemed to prohibit, for example, the use of trade-based sanctions to enforce an environmental standard related to trade.

One of the last, most controversial, and ultimately undecided, disputes in the GATT concerned United States legislation that banned imports of tuna from Mexico because Mexican tuna fisheries did not comply with a US law requiring the use of dolphin-safe fishing practices. The recommendations of a GATT Panel in 1991 that the US withdraw the ban caused an outcry in some environmental lobbies, directed at the alleged inconsistency of GATT rules with objectives of sustainable development and at the lack of sympathy, as they saw it, of trade administrations with objectives that lay outside the sphere of trade.

Several MEAs were 'best endeavour' agreements or, where they included specific obligations, lacked effective enforcement measures. After the entry into force of the WTO, many governments were under pressure from environmental lobbies to ensure, somehow, that the WTO – and specifically the WTO's ground-breaking disputes procedure – would be aligned with the objectives of the MEAs.

Since the same governments were Members of the MEAs and of the

WTO, there was every reason why there should be an alignment of Members' objectives in the management of the different global 'commons'. But what this meant for the management of the WTO and the rules of the trading system was less clear.

There had been a longstanding GATT Group on Environmental Measures and International Trade that had considered issues such as the relationship between WTO provisions and trade measures taken pursuant to multilateral environmental agreements (MEAs), eco-labeling and packaging requirements, and transparency. But the adoption of the Agreement Establishing the WTO, which for the first time identified support for sustainable development as one of the principal goals of the multilateral trading system, brought the relationship between environmental and trade policies new prominence within the WTO. Also, the wider perspective of the WTO, which extended to services as well as merchandise and to the security of intellectual property, allowed the new WTO Committee on Trade and Environment (CTE) – established as the successor to the GATT Group by a Decision annexed to the WTO agreements – to take a more comprehensive view of its mandate.

Early discussions in the CTE on the effect of environmental measures on market access, especially in relation to developing countries and the environmental benefits of removing trade restrictions and other distortions indicated widespread confidence in the complementarity between good environmental policy and good trade policy.

At the Singapore Ministerial, ministers resisted calls for a further expansion of the WTO's responsibility in multilateral environmental issues. They decided that the Committee on Trade and Environment should continue to examine the complementarity between trade liberalization, economic development and environmental protection and pointed out that the CTE's work had already identified the importance of policy coordination at the national level in the area of trade and environment. They concluded that the Committee should build on this work and report to the General Council under its existing terms of reference.

Labour standards

The debate on the interaction between trade and labour standards is in some ways similar to the debate on trade and environmental standards. Labour unions, among others in some industrial countries, contend that excessively low labour standards will impose downward pressure on standards everywhere, or give the low-standard countries an unwarranted competitive advantage. Developing countries, on the other hand, fear that this argument may be used as a surrogate form of protection.

As with environmental issues, the ministers at Singapore chose to avoid extending the WTO's activities into areas where existing international regimes provided sufficient guarantees, and chose instead to direct the WTO's efforts towards harmonizing its work and the work of existing competent organizations, such as the International Labour Organization (ILO). They reaffirmed their commitment to observance of internationally recognized standards. The Singapore Ministerial Declaration contained this article on labour standards:

> 4. We renew our commitment to the observance of internationally recognized core labour standards. The International Labour Organization (ILO) is the competent body to set and deal with these standards, and we affirm our support for its work in promoting them. We believe that economic growth and development fostered by increased trade and further trade liberalization contribute to the promotion of these standards. We reject the use of labour standards for protectionist purposes, and agree that the comparative advantage of countries, particularly low-wage developing countries, must in no way be put into question. In this regard, we note that the WTO and ILO Secretariats will continue their existing collaboration.

Members recognized the competence of the ILO to set and deal with these standards, while noting that economic growth and development, fostered by increased trade and trade liberalization, contribute to the promotion of such standards. Ministers rejected the use of labour standards for protectionist purposes, recognizing that the comparative advantage of countries, especially low-wage developing countries, must not be put in jeopardy.

The Information Technology Agreement and pharmaceuticals

The 'dot com' boom suffers from the selective memory of some of its survivors who remember its crash but forget its lasting achievements. One of those achievements was the Information Technology Agreement (ITA): still the largest, most rapidly negotiated and most successful market access deal done in the last decade.

Negotiations aimed at achieving the elimination of barriers to trade in information technology products including semiconductors, software and most hardware by the year 2000 were sponsored by the United States,

European Union, Canada and Japan with the target of reaching a deal at the Singapore Ministerial.

With the global market for information technology booming in the mid-1990s, the timing proved propitious. The Declaration on Trade in Information Technology Products (ITA), which came into force on 1 July 1997, committed participants to eliminating customs duties and other charges by 1 January 2000 (up to 2005 for some products from some developing countries).

Director-General Ruggiero welcomed the deal enthusiastically, putting it in the context, as he saw it, of WTO's broader contribution to enabling the benefits of globalization.

> Trade in information technology products amounts to more than $400 billion, roughly the same as global trade in agriculture. Just as significant, an ITA and an agreement on telecommunications trade . . . lay the foundation for trading into the future. These are the critical technologies of the 21st century, vital to the future competitiveness of every nation.
>
> By disseminating information so widely we can educate our peoples on a scale unimaginable 20, or even ten years ago. This is the human dimension of globalization and it offers an unprecedented opportunity not just for growth and development, but also for security and peace.
>
> WTO Press Release, December 1996

Also at Singapore, WTO Members agreed to eliminate tariffs on some 465 pharmaceutical products, adding to the list of more than 600 whose duties were eliminated by the Uruguay Round pharmaceutical initiative.

Four new agenda items

Ministers at Singapore agreed to establish three new working groups: one to examine the relationship between trade and investment, another to study issues raised by Members relating to the interaction between trade and competition policy, including anti-competitive practices, and a third on government procurement. The Ministerial Declaration[1] contained, however, a guarded provision on future work: the new working groups would explore the issues on the understanding that if negotiations were to take place in these areas, they would proceed on the basis of a consensus. Ministers left it to the General Council to take a decision before the 1998 Ministerial Conference (Geneva) on how work in these areas should proceed.

---

[1] See WTO document WT/MIN(96)/DEC.

Ministers also decided to direct the Council for Trade in Goods to undertake exploratory and analytical work on the simplification of trade procedures in order to assess the scope for WTO rules in this area.

Investment and competition policy

Member governments wanted to explore the extension of WTO concepts and rules to investment because they thought that greater coherence of policies across the domains of merchandise, services and financial exchanges might deliver economic benefits – a case argued strongly in the WTO's 1996 Annual Report.

The Director-General summed up the argument in his Sylvia Ostry Lecture in Ottawa early in 1996:

> 'As far as investment is concerned', he said, 'globalization has dramatically reduced the utility of distinctions that policy makers used to maintain between different forms of market access.'

He and others pointed out that the WTO agreements had already begun to blur these distinctions, especially in the GATS, which seeks to liberalize the terms of establishment of foreign service suppliers in a market, and in the Agreement on Trade-Related Investment Measures (TRIMS).

The argument for greater coherence applied at a multilateral level as well as in the policies of individual Members. The Director-General warned that a tangle of bilateral investment treaties would undermine the potential contribution of investment to growth:

> There is a risk, in the absence of a strong multilateral framework, of an accumulation of potentially inconsistent and even discriminatory regimes in regard to foreign investment. The question is how to ensure a truly multilateral dimension to this question that takes account not only of the role of investment within the international trading system, but also of the common interest that both industrial and developing countries have in ensuring a favourable investment climate. It is hard to imagine that an answer can be found outside the WTO. There are currently more than 900 bilateral investment treaties. And if all countries in the world were to participate in such agreements, we would need around 20,000 bilateral treaties. This fact provides a clear answer to those who preach the superiority of a bilateral approach. I cannot imagine that business would welcome such a bewildering variety of requirements. It is clearly preferable to have just one set, covering all countries, developed and developing

alike, under the same rules and disciplines and with just one enforcement procedure.

Renato Ruggiero, Fourth Annual Sylvia Ostry Lecture. Ottawa, 28 May 1996

As the proposal was put forward to ministers at Singapore for a work program on a possible future agreement on Investment, the 27 Members of the Organisation for Economic Co-operation and Development (OECD) were already engaged – for some of these same reasons – on the negotiation of a multilateral instrument on investment that would have been submitted to the 1997 OECD ministerial meeting. Ominously, the OECD agreement failed to attract the support of some of the largest OECD members, in part because of differences over the substance of the proposed agreement and in part because of the concerted opposition of NGO lobbies in OECD countries.

Simplification of trade procedures (trade facilitation)

Interest in WTO provisions for the simplification of trade procedures was undoubtedly piqued by the growing volume of trade in the early and mid-1990s as well as by the exposure of these administrative 'resistances' to trade as tariff levels fell. As new communications technology became available to significantly improve the management of cross-border trade and the distribution of goods, bottlenecks became more obvious. More than a dozen institutions including the United Nations Conference on Trade and Development (UNCTAD) and the World Customs Organization (WCO) as well as the World Bank had begun to collect both data and anecdotal evidence on the scale of the problems. Preliminary economic evaluation confirmed that businesses suffer losses through delays at borders, opaque and often-redundant documentation requirements and lack of automation of government-mandated trade procedures that can greatly exceed the tax impact of tariffs.

As was true of the Singapore proposals concerning environment, and investment – but to an even greater extent – the GATT and the WTO already had a history of activity in the simplification of trade procedures; for example in Articles V, VII, VIII, X of the GATT 1994 as well as in Agreements on Customs Valuation, Import Licensing, Preshipment Inspection, Rules of Origin, Technical Barriers to Trade, and the Agreement on the Application of Sanitary and Phytosanitary Measures.

The Singapore Ministerial Conference gave the WTO the mandate to take a more comprehensive look at trade facilitation, but not to begin any work to prepare for negotiations.

Plan of action for Least-Developed Countries (LDCs)

> The most obvious manifestation of the difficult situation of LDCs in the world trading system is their almost continuously declining share in world merchandise exports. This share was down to 0.4% in 1999, from 0.7% in 1980, while these countries accounted for 10.4% of the world's population. The decline largely reflects the continued importance of primary commodities in LDC exports, accounting for 80% or more of total merchandise exports in all but a handful of LDCs.
>
> WTO Annual Report 2001

The WTO has no mandate to address the declining share of world trade held by the poorest economies directly through aid. But the WTO gives high priority to assisting least-developed countries with trade administration and with accession to the WTO so they can enjoy the benefits of the trading system. Ministers at the Singapore Ministerial adopted a Plan of Action to assist least-developed Members, calling for positive trade measures to improve the capacity of least-developed countries to respond to the opportunities offered by the trading system. It also called for action aimed at enhancing conditions for investment, and export expansion and diversification. The main elements of the plan were to be market access and trade-related technical assistance, training and capacity building. Ministers instructed the WTO to organize a High Level Meeting involving a range of agencies that might be able to contribute to the objectives, including the International Trade Centre (ITC), UNCTAD, IMF, UNDP and the World Bank.

THE WTO LOGO

The design was adapted from a logo originally commissioned by the Government of Singapore for the Ministerial Conference in December 1996. In April 1997, the WTO General Council accepted Singapore's offer to donate the logo to the WTO. According to its designer, Ms Su Yeang, the logo represents 'A hint of the globe, suggested by the six graphic arcs symbolizing world trade with Members meeting to forge strategic alliances. Dynamism and optimism prevail as the swirls integrate, encapsulating the WTO's united spirit of promoting fair and open trade.'

5

Singapore to Geneva, 1996–1998

> The rise in global trade facilitated by trade liberalization within the rules-based system has created more and better-paid jobs in many countries. The achievements of the WTO during its first two years bear witness to our desire to work together to make the most of the possibilities that the multilateral system provides to promote sustainable growth and development while contributing to a more stable and secure climate in international relations.
>
> We believe that the scope and pace of change in the international economy, including the growth in trade in services and direct investment, and the increasing integration of economies offer unprecedented opportunities for improved growth, job creation, and development. These developments require adjustment by economies and societies. They also pose challenges to the trading system. We commit ourselves to address these challenges.
>
> Singapore Ministerial Declaration

The confidence expressed by the Singapore Declaration reflected the rapid pace at which output and trade had been growing in the first half of the 1990s (trade grew at an average of 6%) and the exciting prospects for still greater growth in the future. The development of new global information and exchange networks improved the productivity of existing industries as well as creating entirely new industries directed to satisfying new consumer needs. As productivity grew, wealth followed, investment boomed in both developed and developing countries and, thanks to rapid restructuring of their markets, opportunities appeared that were not previously visible in the transition economies. Director-General Ruggiero talked about progress towards a 'borderless economy'.

A sudden set-back

The slow-down in the financial sector in South East Asian countries in mid-1997 at first seemed to be a correction to the years of exceptionally good performance. But the financial crisis that affected the most rapidly growing economies of East Asia and then Russia quickly assumed much more serious dimensions. Growth of trade and output that soared in 1997 (with global averages of 10.5 and 4.5% respectively) crashed in 1998 to less than half those levels (4% and 1.5%). It seemed as if the crisis might spread and the retrenchment develop into a global recession. Trade in manufactures slowed from a record 12.7% in 1997 to only 3% in 1998. Growth in agricultural production stumbled to a halt – due to the collapse of agriculture in transition economies – and global agricultural markets shrank after growing more than 5% in 1997. Commodity prices, led by crude oil, plunged.

Businesses and consumers in Asia and Russia, especially, saw their assets shrink and jobs disappear during the global market retrenchment of 1997 and 1998. Developing countries as a group saw their share of world trade shrink for the first time in a decade. But, thanks to the continuation of a remarkable period of growth in the United States, and above average growth in Europe, global output growth stabilized at around 2% and world export growth at about 4% in 1998.

The transmission of growth from the industrialized countries to the rest of the world market was made possible, of course, by the openness of world markets and by the policy choices of the worst-affected economies. The determination to maintain open markets, to tackle structural reforms, and to trade their way out of recession held the key to the recovery of East Asia.

> Most of the countries most affected accepted severe macroeconomic disciplines, aggravating the short-term downturn in output, but probably helping to bolster market sentiment and confidence in the medium-term prospects. None of the countries involved in the financial crisis resorted to trade protectionism and indeed many took bold steps to continue to open their markets. Moreover, their trading partners also showed resolve in resisting protectionist pressures. The few trade measures that were taken by a small number of countries were not enough to dent the trend of continuing liberalization, flowing partly from the implementation of Uruguay Round results, and in some cases from autonomous action by governments. Rather than becoming part of the problem, as it did in the 1930s, trade made a crucial contribution to paving the way for recovery. Adherence to WTO principles and commitments has been a key element in this success story.
>
> WTO Annual Report 1999

The WTO believed with some justification that its principles were vindicated by the relative isolation of the problem, by the quick recovery of East Asia thanks to those countries' readiness to adjust, and by the continued access to open markets around the world for East Asian exports, which were made even more competitive by their exchange devaluation.

High-level meeting on LDCs

The WTO had focused early on ensuring that least-developed countries (LDCs) had access to WTO membership on a basis that took account of their limited capacity to implement the WTO Agreements. The Members established a Sub-Committee on Least-Developed Countries to help with the integration of WTO's 31 least-developed Members into the trading system. Immediately before the Singapore meeting, and with help from three OECD countries, the Director-General held a meeting with Ministers of Least-Developed countries to ensure that their concerns and interests were known and that they had an opportunity to prepare for the Singapore Ministerial.

On the basis of recommendations from the sub-Committee, the Singapore Ministerial Meeting had adopted a 'Comprehensive and Integrated WTO Plan of Action for the Least-Developed Countries'. The Plan of Action aimed to enhance LDCs' trading opportunities and their integration into the multilateral trading system by coordinating national efforts and those of technical assistance agencies and the international financial institutions. The focus would be on appropriate macro-economic policies, supply-side measures and improved market access and – from the WTO specifically – would include capacity building in trade policy administration and market access.

The Ministerial meeting directed the WTO to convene a High-Level Meeting, held in October 1997, which included the International Trade Centre (ITC) and UNCTAD, the IMF, UNDP and the World Bank. At this meeting the WTO laid the groundwork for the most prominent of its assistance programs – the Integrated Framework of assistance to least-developed countries – and for the special preference programs that are now a widespread feature of market access arrangements for LDCs.

The Integrated Framework, in its revised (2000) form remains one of the most important multilateral development assistance efforts for the 50 LDCs. The Framework began as an inventory of the international agencies' technical assistance and cooperation activities in support of trade of the least-developed countries. The Framework transformed this inventory into a comprehensive management tool for coordinating and rationalizing assistance that puts the recipient government at the center of the management process.

> ### THE INTEGRATED FRAMEWORK
>
> The restructured Integrated Framework (IF) brings together the IMF, ITC, UNCTAD, UNDP, World Bank, WTO and the governments of beneficiary countries to ensure that the trade related assistance needs of each country are included in the dialogue between governments and the multilateral agencies on the overall development policy to be implemented in each country.
>
> The aim of the IF is to incorporate trade policy into the heart of the LDCs' national development plans, including components aimed at reducing poverty in the country and to assist in the coordination and delivery of trade-related assistance as provided by each of the core agencies and by other development partners.
>
> The IF seeks to ensure country ownership, partnership, and coordination in the process to integrate trade into national development plans. It does this principally through such instruments as the Poverty Reduction Strategy Papers (PRSPs) and other national development plans.
>
> By the end of 2004, 35 least-developed countries were at different stages of the IF process or had requested access to the Framework, resulting in an expansion of the number of development projects with trade-related components.

The WTO and World Bank also took steps to implement new access for LDCs to the global information networks that many of them considered would be important for their closer integration with the global economy. The WTO established 'reference centers' in the trade ministries of least-developed countries, furnished with computers and internet connections to enable officials to access WTO documentation through the WTO website.

Several of the WTO's industrialized economy Member countries used the High Level Meeting to announce improvements and extensions of unilateral tariff preferences. Many of them noted, however, that preferences would be of limited value without complementary action by the LDCs themselves.

WTO's profile gets a boost

It seems fair to say that the importance governments attach to the open, multilateral trading system increased in the late 1990s as they developed a greater understanding and acceptance of the forces of economic globalization and the importance of a sound trade environment for the welfare of all economies. With that recognition came, gradually, a recognition of the crucial role of the WTO as the symbol and guardian of the system.

The impact of the new organization and the expanded system of trade rules it administers became more obvious in many domains after the Singapore Ministerial. For example:

a. The Agreements on Financial and Basic Telecommunications and the Information Technology Agreement brought impressive extensions of the global trading system hard on the heels of the Uruguay Round;
b. Members' implementation of their goods and services schedules drew the attention of global communities that had not previously paid the GATT much attention;
c. The shock of the Asian financial crisis demonstrated the safeguards that the multilateral trading system offered against the global spread of regional recession;
d. The management of important disputes in new areas such as patents on pharmaceuticals showed that the WTO rules could have obvious commercial impact;
e. The accession bids of China and Russia signalled that the WTO would succeed in achieving the global coverage that had eluded the GATT.

The first sign that WTO Member governments had recognized something new in the WTO might be dated to the Director-General's participation in the Lyon G7 Summit in 1996. In May 1998, the Director-General was invited to take part in the G8 Finance and Foreign Ministers Meeting in preparation for the Birmingham Summit, and immediately beforehand he addressed G15 Trade Ministers in Cairo. He attended the Summit of the Americas in Chile and was regularly invited to participate in ministerial meetings of major regional groupings, such as APEC and MERCOSUR.

The May Ministerial meeting and the 50th Anniversary of the GATT established, however, a pinnacle of this recognition – certainly in terms of media attention.

6

50th anniversary of the Multilateral Trading System (GATT–WTO), 1998

The 50th anniversary in May 1998 was, first of all, a marketing opportunity. US President Bill Clinton, British Prime Minister Tony Blair, Brazilian President Fernando Henrique Cardoso, South African President Nelson Mandela, EU Commission President Jacques Santer, Cuban President Fidel Castro Ruz, Swiss President Flavio Cotti, many prime ministers and other dignitaries hailed the strengths of the GATT system for the benefits that it had delivered to the world and highlighted the promise of the WTO as the GATT's successor.

It was an opportunity for the Members of WTO to talk about the direction, and even the detail, of future agreements in a way that – as it turned out – would be more optimistic and expansive than at any time since. It was also an opportunity to put the WTO's perspective on some concerns about the trading system that were attracting a higher public profile:

- The impact of the trading system on development, poverty and on the management of global environmental goals;
- The relevance of the multilateral system to globalized, increasingly digitalized commerce where borders seemed to lose importance;
- The balance of concessions and gains from the recent Uruguay Round agreements, not only in the poorest countries but even in the United States where the Congress, disaffected by its assessment of US concessions in the Uruguay Round – had refused to extend trade negotiating authority to President Clinton.

There was little doubt about the need to market the WTO. As heads of government and ministers met in the Palais des Nations, large sometimes-violent demonstrations were taking place outside the surrounding metal barricades and across the city of Geneva. The outrage expressed by the placards and attacks on cars and fast-food outlets was directed, however, at issues that were mostly in the hands of Member governments: especially at proposals for a new round of negotiations (the 'Millennium Round') that would cover investment and other 'new' issues, environmental policies and the impact of 'globalization' on employment, welfare and income equity in both developing and industrialized countries.

A misunderstanding of the WTO's constitution and activities led many people to believe that the WTO has global responsibilities and powers of coercion more extensive than they are in fact. Unfortunately, two events seemed to lend some credence to this misperception.

First, just a few days before the anniversary celebrations, news leaked out that the Panel Report[1] on Shrimp/Turtle (adopted by the DSB in November 1998) would find against United States regulations requiring shrimp boats in Asia and elsewhere to use devices to protect the endangered sea-turtle populations from their nets. This was an iconic case that, on Appeal some months later, produced two remarkable 'concessions' to the environmental NGOs who championed the US legislation.[2] First, the WTO provided room for 'exceptional' actions to enforce environmental goals. Second, NGOs could get their views before a disputes panel and before the Appellate Body of WTO. But that's not how the outcome appeared in the first instance to the groups protesting at the Palais des Nations: they were convinced that the Panel recommendation in Shrimp/Turtle showed the WTO to be an enemy of environmental protection.

A second contemporary event, however, probably held even more concerns for the participants, as they waited for President Clinton – the first guest to speak – to arrive at the Palais Des Nations. The GATT's founders knew that times of crisis would test the openness of the trading and financial system. Now just such a test – in the shape of the Asian financial crisis six months earlier and the subsequent sharp downturn in global trade growth – was creating political pressure for trade barriers to protect jobs, incomes and assets.

On both sides of the barricades outside the WTO Ministerial it seemed that the commitment to maintaining open markets and to embracing the costs as well as benefits of adjustment had just claimed a high-profile victim. The Suharto regime in Indonesia was being wiped away by mass popular protest directed not only at corruption and 'crony capitalism' but also at the impact on the poor of the economic collapse made many time worse, in the view of the protestors, by the program of reforms, including trade reforms, demanded by the IMF.

---

[1] United States: Import Prohibition of Certain Shrimp and Shrimp Products, November 1998.
[2] In a manner of speaking. They weren't real 'concessions', of course: one was a clarification of 50-year-old language in the GATT and the other was a procedural decision of the Panels and Appellate Body that was made for their own convenience.

Blaming the WTO rules might be one way that governments could shelter from the demands of protestors, but to do so would risk endorsing the mistaken view that the WTO was a source of the crisis, rather than part of the solution.

Not all of the protests were off-target. The attacks on both the WTO and its Member governments for the alleged secretiveness in WTO processes and decisions and for failure to respond to the demands of NGOs with claims to represent the opinion of civil society struck a chord with some Members.

> We must recognize that in this new economy, the way we make trade rules and conduct trade affects the lives, daily – and the livelihoods, and the health, and the safety of ordinary families all over the world. Therefore, our efforts to make the trading system more open must themselves be made more open . . . I propose the WTO for the first time, provide a consultative forum where business, and labour, and environmental, and consumer groups can provide regular and continuous input to help guide further evolution of the WTO.
>
> President Clinton's remarks at the 50th Anniversary celebrations.

Openness became a major preoccupation of the Director-General and the Secretariat in the period between Singapore and Geneva, to which they devoted an increasing amount of time and effort.[3] Thereafter it kept a high place on the WTO's agenda in the lead-up to the Seattle Ministerial and beyond.

The Organization took two immediate steps : in March 1999 it held symposia on trade and environment and trade and development in conjunction with a wide range of civil society groups, and it launched an extended programme of outreach to civil society especially in the build-up to the Seattle meeting, including specific briefings for NGOs by senior Secretariat staff, the development of a program of outreach for Parliamentarians and a range of publications and improvements to the WTO's website – made possible in part by a revised (2002) decision[4] on the de-restriction of documents – that broadened access to information on current WTO debates.

---

[3] For example, on the Saturday before the 50th Anniversary celebrations, Director-General Renato Ruggiero along with the heads of UNCTAD and the ILO had participated in a meeting with more than 90 representatives of NGOs from 33 countries in a conference organized by the International Federation of Free Trades Unions to discuss labour standards, environment, development and the impact of globalization. Such meetings have become a regular feature of WTO ministerials.   [4] WTO document WT/L/452.

50TH ANNIVERSARY OF THE MULTILATERAL TRADING SYSTEM 49

The WTO's contributions to the 50th Anniversary celebrations, as might be expected in such a politically-heated atmosphere, 'accentuated the positive'.

Director-General Ruggiero spoke convincingly about the success of the imaginative project that lay behind the GATT and the post-war evolution of the multilateral trading system and of the benefits that the system delivered. The official documents listed these benefits (in summary) as:

> First, the trading system had contributed to an extraordinary period of economic growth and increased prosperity. Trade had expanded faster than output by a significant margin over the last five decades. On an annual average basis, merchandise exports grew by 6% in real terms from 1948 to 1997, well ahead of total output at an annual average rate of 3.8%, or 1.9% in per capita terms. The significant gains in income growth, job creation and prosperity that underlie the statistics mentioned above are in part attributable to the success of the multilateral trading system in lowering trade barriers.
>
> Second, the system has widened the circle of participation in the global marketplace. While the early rounds of multilateral trade negotiations, up to the Dillon Round in 1961, typically involved some 20 to 30 countries, on the occasion of the 50th anniversary membership stood at 132 countries and those not yet Members, including the largest countries outside the system, China and Russia, had made WTO membership one of their key policy objectives.
>
> Third, the dispute settlement system has demonstrated the willingness of governments to respect the rules. The vast majority of cases brought before GATT or WTO had been settled, either on a bilateral basis before final multilateral determination, or through acceptance of a panel ruling. The new arrangements for the settlement of disputes under WTO had further strengthened the confidence of Members in the system. As of mid-March 1998, 120 cases have been presented to the WTO, compared to just over 300 cases throughout the life of the GATT. Moreover, increasing numbers of developing countries are making use of dispute settlement procedures.
>
> Fourth, the multilateral trading system had broadened and deepened its agenda to take account of new realities in international economic relations. The rules of the system had increasingly extended to the treatment of foreign persons and companies as well as foreign goods and services. New initiatives have been launched to examine the relationship between trade and investment, trade and competition policy and procurement.

The heads of government and state attending the celebrations spoke positively about the achievements and optimistically, for the most part, about the outlook for the multilateral system. Their projects for the WTO varied, however, from bullish – but significantly different – proposals from Europe and the United States for new WTO negotiations to pleas from Africa and elsewhere for the WTO to complete its current agenda and to deliver on the economic 'development' promise of the multilateral trading system.

The heads of government were in agreement that the biennial rhythm of Ministerial Conferences of the WTO created both an opportunity for review at a political level but also an occasion for the injection of political momentum. Many of them said they believed this momentum was important in mid-1998 as the extent of the setback in world trade growth, set off by the Asian region financial crisis, became evident.

European Commission President Jacques Santer told the WTO Ministerial that a new 'Millennium Round' – a name coined by the EU Trade Commissioner, Sir Leon Brittan – was 'the best way to move the multilateral liberalization process', and that experience had proved 'a global approach offers better prospects than a regional or sectoral approach': apparently a reference to the mandated 'continuing reform' negotiations on agriculture. President Santer said that the EU wanted a new round of negotiations to be launched in 1999 which should cover labour issues, the environment, industrial tariffs, non-tariff barriers, and the issues identified at the WTO's 1996 Singapore Ministerial (9–13 December, 1996).

President Clinton said: 'We took the first, vital step when we created the World Trade Organization in 1995 – a goal that had eluded our predecessors for nearly half a century. The Uruguay Round that founded the WTO amounted to the biggest tax cut in world history – $76 billion a year when fully implemented. And in just four years, world trade is up 25%.'

The US President did not directly endorse calls for a Millennium Round, preferring instead a sector by sector approach. He wanted to move quickly to open markets for farm and industrial goods as well as services and provide more protection for copyright and other intellectual property. He wanted the 'built-in agenda' negotiations on services and agriculture to begin in 1999 and he proposed adding new negotiations as agreement on them emerged. He did not think that the new, faster, more global markets would 'wait' for the decade or so it would take to produce comprehensive agreements where nothing was final until everything was final.

'We should explore whether there is a way to tear down barriers without waiting for every issue in every sector to be resolved before any issue in any sector is resolved', he said, adding that the Ministerial to launch the talks next year should take place in the US. President Clinton thought that the barriers in agriculture deserved special attention. 'We should aggressively begin negotiations to reduce tariffs, subsidies and other distortions that restrict productivity in agriculture,' he said, undoubtedly with European barriers in mind.

President Mandela said that for 47 of the 50 years in which the GATT had symbolized the attempt to free markets, raise standards of living and ensure full employment and steadily growing incomes, there had been no democratic vote in South Africa and little impact of the GATT's ideals on his country, continent or 'most of humanity'. President Mandela endorsed the multilateral rules-based system as 'fundamentally correct' and called for greater resolve to deliver on the promises of development through trade and investment:

> Fifty years ago, when the founders of the GATT evoked the link between trade, growth and a better life, few could have foreseen such poverty, homelessness and unemployment as the world now knows. Few would have imagined that the exploitation of the world's abundant resources and a prodigious growth in world trade would have seen the gap between rich and poor widening. And few could have anticipated the burden of debt on many poor nations.
>
> As we celebrate what has been achieved in shaping the world trading system, let us resolve to leave no stone unturned in working together to ensure that our shared principles are everywhere translated into reality. As we enter the new millennium, let us forge a partnership for development through trade and investment.

7

Geneva Ministerial Conference, 1998

The multilateral trading system celebrated its 50th anniversary at the Geneva Ministerial Conference in the warm glow of praise from international leaders and a general recognition of the system's benefits. There was also a sense shared in the WTO as well as among Members that the procedures and principles of the multilateral trading system were showing up well under test of the Asian financial crisis. The Director-General was justifiably proud of the business-like completion of the Singapore Ministerial just 17 months earlier and the conclusion of the agreements on telecommunications and information technology that together addressed the most vibrant international markets of the 1990s. Progress towards an agreement on financial services was also in prospect.

But the ceremonies of congratulation did not divert Ministers from the pressures of the WTO's current agenda for long. Contentious issues of implementation had begun to emerge as Members, especially from developing economies, sought to identify the benefits in the agreements that would compensate the costs of meeting their obligations. Members decided to ask a Special Session of the General Council – to begin in September 1998 and continue as necessary until the Seattle meeting – to make consensus recommendations on

- issues arising from the implementation of the Marrakesh Agreement;
- the 'built-in agenda' including the negotiations and reviews already mandated by the Marrakesh Agreement (including further negotiations on agriculture and services, a review of TRIPS and the review of the dispute settlement system);
- a possible work program on the new issues identified at the Singapore Ministerial; and
- a program to follow-up the recommendations of the High-Level Meeting on Least-Developed Countries.

Although the organization of such a large work program in a Special Session of the General Council did not formally comprise preparations for a future round of comprehensive negotiations, the breadth of the issues to be covered made it tantamount to such preparations. At the least, the specific co-location of these issues on the agenda of the Special Session shaped the preparations for the Third Ministerial at Seattle.

In retrospect, it might have been helpful, at this point, if ministers had tried to set some priorities among the many new and old issues – especially on implementation – that their brief Declaration[1] remitted to the care of the General Council. For example, ministers might have discussed whether, in light of the failure of the OECD countries to reach agreement on a Multilateral Investment Agreement on schedule in 1997 – and again at their second attempt in the month before the WTO Ministerial in Seattle – the WTO was quite ready to pursue the questions of trade and investment as a priority.

The 'implementation' problem

What does the developing world want – and need – from the multilateral trading system? First, the full implementation of existing liberalization commitments. This is of course a concern for all WTO Members, but for a number of developing countries in particular it is an issue which influences their attitude to further trade negotiations. These countries have stated that they have encountered unexpected problems with implementing existing Uruguay Round commitments, and furthermore that some of those agreements have deficiencies that have only become apparent during the implementation process. On the other hand, they claim that anticipated benefits have failed to materialize because, for example, industrialized countries have not lived up to the spirit of liberalizing agreements (such as textiles), made excessive use of anti-dumping measures, or failed to respect the principle of special and differential treatment. In short, these countries see an imbalance in the way existing agreements affect them, and they see this as a problem which needs a political solution, not just more technical assistance. They also argue that since this is a question of righting an existing imbalance, it should not become something they are expected to 'pay' for in a new Round.

WTO Director-General Mike Moore speaking to the European Parliament
REX Committee, January 1999

'Implementation' issues – especially the sense of differences between Members over the requirements of the agreements – had begun to take more time in the debates in councils and committees of the WTO.

[1] WTO document WT/MIN(98)/DEC/1.

Reviews of Members' fulfilment of their obligations under the agreements and adherence to the obligations accepted in their goods and services schedules had already thrown light on a number of differences of interpretation and on some imprecision in the agreements. The Ministers meeting in Geneva spent the first half of their meeting debating the complex problems thrown up under the broad heading of 'implementation' noting issues in some agreements that went so far as to adversely affect the balance of the agreements and broader problems of the administrative and legislative capacity of developing members to fulfil their obligations.

For example (from the record of the meeting):

> The representative of India said that the intention of the Uruguay Round negotiations had been to use trade as an instrument for development, to raise standards of living, and expand production, while keeping in view the needs of developing and least-developed countries. This was clear from the Preamble to the WTO Agreement. There was a need to study ways to ensure implementation of the objectives of the Preamble, which should not be merely left to 'best endeavours'.
>
> To address the needs of developing and least-developed countries, provisions for the special and differential treatment of such countries were built into various Agreements, but were not being implemented. This issue needed to be concretely examined in the Committee on Trade and Development.
>
> Furthermore, the Agreement on Textiles and Clothing was not being properly implemented. There had been absolutely minimum integration of restricted products into the GATT system, as a result of which textile exporting developing countries had not obtained the expected benefits from the Agreement. He urged developed countries maintaining quantitative restrictions on developing country textiles and clothing exports to speedily eliminate such restrictions in order to provide commercially meaningful market access for developing countries.
>
> On another matter, he said that India had agreed to the provisions of the TRIPS Agreement as part of the single undertaking of the Uruguay Round. However, it would seek to review the current status of implementation of this Agreement so as to restore the focus on its objectives, particularly the developmental and technological objectives . . .'
>
> From the summary minutes of the Geneva Ministerial meeting, WTO document WT/MIN(98)/WS/M/1

The ministers decided to take up the question again at their Third Ministerial in Seattle, after receiving advice from the Special Session of the Council: 'When we meet at the Third Session we shall further pursue our evaluation of the implementation of individual agreements and the realization of their objectives. Such evaluation would cover, inter alia, the problems encountered in implementation and the consequent impact on the trade and development prospects of Members. We reaffirm our commitment to respect the existing schedules for reviews, negotiations and other work to which we have already agreed.'

Declaration on electronic commerce

In March 1998, the WTO Secretariat produced a report on trade issues arising from the development of electronic commerce. That is, from the production, advertising, sale and distribution of products via digital networks: usually the Internet.

Electronic commerce was growing at a staggering rate. In 1991, there were less than five million Internet users. In 2003, UNCTAD estimated nearly 676 million people worldwide, had access to the Internet. E-commerce sales that had been projected in the WTO's study to reach $300 billion within two years are notoriously difficult to categorize and measure. According to UNCTAD they reached $430 billion in the EU alone by 2003 – and more than $1 trillion in the US – taking account of sales via EDI (electronic data interchange) networks as well as the Internet.

The WTO's study[2] emphasized the extraordinary expansion of opportunities that electronic commerce offered, including for developing countries. But it noted many challenges related to infrastructure and access as well as a host of regulatory problems.

Products which are bought and paid for over the Internet but are delivered physically would be subject to existing WTO rules on trade in goods such as the GATT. But the situation is more complicated for products that are delivered as digitalized information over the Internet, because a variety of issues arise relating to the appropriate policy regime. The study considered security and privacy questions, taxation, access to the Internet, market access for suppliers over the Internet, trade facilitation, public procurement, intellectual property questions, and regulation of content.

The Geneva Ministerial Conference in May 1998 issued a Declaration on Electronic Commerce[3] directing the General Council to explore how the World Trade Organization should deal with the question of electronic commerce. The Declaration stated that:

[2] WTO Special Study 'Electronic Commerce and the role of the WTO'.
[3] WTO document WT/MIN(98)/DEC/2.

> Without prejudice to the outcome of the work progamme or the rights and obligations of Members under the WTO Agreements, we also declare that Members will continue their current practice of not imposing customs duties on electronic transmissions.

This was in line with the decision adopted by the OECD governments at their ministerial meeting that year in which they decided that no special taxation should apply to e-commerce transactions and that 'the supply of digitized products should not be treated as a supply of goods'.

Openness

The protests at the 50th Anniversary and the Ministerial Meeting in Geneva had drawn sympathetic media commentary on the question of the transparency of WTO decision-making. But the issue now took two distinct forms: one concerned the access of the public to timely information on WTO debates and decisions and the other concerned access to the disputes system. Although superficially both are about the same 'openness' issue, the profound difference between them is suggested by (some of) the proposed remedies.

A legal decision and a work program answered the demand for greater public access to timely information. Members decided to de-restrict most documents in a short time frame and directed the Secretariat to distribute the documents and to undertake other significant information campaigns targeting different audiences and topics of special relevance to them.

The demand for greater transparency in disputes could also be answered (and has been answered in part) by a legal decision. In the Shrimp/Turtle case, the Appellate Body (and the Shrimp/Turtle Panel on its own behalf) opened the way for limited access to the disputes procedures at the initiative of disputes panels by specifying conditions under which panels and the Appellate Body could decide to accept briefs from non-government parties. Briefly, the Appellate Body noted that panels have wide discretion to determine for themselves what information they might need and from whom they should seek it. The Panel's decision in that case to accept a brief from an NGO that had been attached to the submission of one of the Parties (the United States) was within its discretion. The Appellate Body in its review of the same case also accepted a brief from an NGO after the United States had made the brief an attachment to its submission.

These decisions are broadly in line with the recommendation made by President Clinton in his address to the 50th Anniversary celebrations. But the President went further: challenging other WTO Members to join the US in offering to open up all of its legal briefs and panel sessions to public inspection and to publish immediately all panel recommendations. No other Member has accepted that challenge, in part because many of them believe that such a decision would bring a change in the nature of the WTO, from an organization that is inter-governmental and constitutionally beyond the reach of private interest to one that owes a duty of transparency to citizens, as the municipal courts do in many democracies.

In 2000, the Appellate Body further tested the boundary between private access and sovereigns' rights with a decision in EC-Asbestos[4] that it could decide for itself whether to accept or seek amicus curiae ('friend of the court') briefs that were not part of the brief from a Member government. But Members resisted this initiative and the Appellate Body did not pursue it.

WTO 50TH ANNIVERSARY

This was far more than a ceremonial occasion. It demonstrated how far the world has come towards constructing a truly global economic system. Even during this period of significant change and uncertainty, not a single speaker at the 50th anniversary meeting questioned the validity of multilateral trade or of the WTO. Even if each one had a different perspective, reflecting different backgrounds and historical experiences, all the leaders present saw the multilateral trading system as indispensable to growth and stability in our interdependent world. (Source: WTO Annual Report, 1998.)

At a birthday party in Geneva, revellers are celebrating the 50th anniversary of the General Agreement on Tariffs and Trade (GATT), and a local television crew is making a documentary about the World Trade Organisation (WTO), the GATT's successor. The film might have featured grey-suited trade ministers congratulating each other on 50 years of trade liberalisation, but instead the camera captures a colourful crowd of demonstrators on the far side of rolls of barbed wire. They denounce the organisation and all its works. Free trade, they claim, despoils the environment and enslaves dispossessed peoples. 'God is dead', reads one banner; 'The WTO has replaced Him.' Most of them protest peacefully, but a few start throwing stones and bottles, then overturn cars and set them ablaze.

The Economist magazine, Survey: World Trade, October 1998

---

[4] European Communities: Measures Affecting Asbestos and Asbestos-Containing Products.

FOUR KEY DISPUTES

United States shrimp/turtle

GATT [1994] 'exceptions' provisions allow governments to use trade measures to secure 'environmental' policy objectives, but only in accordance with WTO principles including non-discrimination. Under some conditions, non-government organizations' views may be considered by disputes panels and the Appellate Body.

On 25 February 1997, a Panel was established to consider complaints by Malaysia, Pakistan, Thailand and India (WT/DS58) concerning a ban on importation of shrimp and shrimp products from these countries imposed by the United States under Section 609 of US Public Law 101-162. In the course of the Panel proceedings, the Panel received two non-requested submissions from non-governmental organizations. The Panel found that, as it had not requested this information, it would be incompatible with the provisions of the DSU, as currently applied, for it to accept the information. However, the Panel gave the parties to the dispute the possibility to include these documents (or parts of them) as part of their own submissions to the Panel. The Panel found that Section 609 constituted 'unjustifiable discrimination between countries where the same conditions prevail' contrary to the provisions of the chapeau of Article XX, and thus was 'not within the scope of measures permitted under the chapeau of Article XX'. The report of the Panel was circulated to Members on 15 May 1998 (three days before the GATT 50th anniversary celebrations).

The Appellate Body reversed the Panel's finding that accepting non-requested information from non-governmental sources is incompatible with the provisions of the DSU. The Appellate Body observed that the DSU accords a panel extensive discretionary authority to control its information-gathering process, which includes the ability to accept non-requested information from non-governmental organizations. Concerning the Panel's actual treatment of the non-requested information submitted to it by the non-governmental organizations, the Appellate Body considered that the Panel had acted properly, and within the scope of its authority under the DSU, in allowing the parties to attach the briefs by non-governmental organizations, or parts of them, to their submissions. In addition, in the course of the appellate proceedings, the Appellate Body admitted briefs by non-governmental organizations that were attached to the US appellant's submission as part of that submission. The United States had clarified that it agreed with the legal arguments made in those submissions to the extent they concurred with the US arguments set out in its main submission.

The Appellate Body completed the analysis of the case by the Panel, considering the text of Article XX (g) that was not examined by the Panel. They found that sea turtles are an 'exhaustible natural resource', that a 'substantial relationship' existed between the general structure and design of Section 609 and the policy goal of protecting sea turtles and that Section 609 was made effective in conjunction with restrictions on domestic harvesting of shrimp. Consequently the Appellate Body determined that the US measures fell within the scope of Article XX(g). But they agreed with the Panel that the US measure was applied in a manner that amounts to a means of both 'arbitrary discrimination' and 'unjustifiable discrimination', and thus fails to meet the requirements of the chapeau of Article XX. The DSB adopted the Appellate Body report and the Panel report, as modified by the Appellate Body report, on 6 November 1998.

EC Hormones

Clarified the application of the SPS provisions.

In their reports of 18 August 1997, the Panel found that the EC ban on imports of meat and meat products from cattle treated with any of six specific hormones for growth promotion purposes was inconsistent with Articles 3.1, 5.1 and 5.5 of the Agreement on Sanitary and Phytosanitary Standards (the 'SPS Agreement'). The Panel found that the EC violated Article 5.1 because its import ban was not based on a 'risk assessment', that is, an evaluation of the potential for adverse effects on human health arising from the presence of certain hormones in meat. In its report of 16 January 1998, the Appellate Body upheld the Panels' finding that the EC import prohibition was inconsistent with Article 5.1 of the SPS Agreement. In so doing, the Appellate Body clarified that for an SPS measure to be 'based on' a risk assessment within the meaning of Article 5.1, there had to be a 'rational' or 'objective' relationship between the measure and the risk assessment. The Appellate Body further clarified that the risk that is to be evaluated in a risk assessment under Article 5.1 is not only risk ascertainable in a science laboratory operating under strict controlled conditions, but also risk in human societies as they actually exist. Therefore, risks resulting from the abusive use of hormones and the difficulty of controlling the use of hormones were also relevant to a risk assessment under Article 5.1.

EC Bananas

A wide-ranging case concerning quotas, discrimination, regional agreements and more.

On 8 May 1996, a Panel was established to consider complaints by Ecuador, Guatemala, Honduras, Mexico and the United States regarding the EC's regime for the importation, sale and distribution of bananas. The essence of the claims was that the EC's banana regime granted preferential treatment to EC and African, Caribbean and Pacific (ACP) bananas at the expense of non-EC, non-ACP bananas. In its reports of 22 May 1997, the Panel found that the EC's banana import regime was inconsistent with the EC's obligations under GATT and GATS. The Panel found that the EC's tariff quota allocations violated Article XIII:1 of GATT, because import quotas were allocated to certain countries not having a substantial interest in supplying bananas to the EC (e.g., Nicaragua and certain ACP countries), but not to other similarly situated countries (e.g., Guatemala). Concurrently, the Panel found that the quota reallocation rules under the EC's market-sharing Framework Agreement on Bananas (BFA) were inconsistent with Article XIII:1. The Panel further noted that neither the negotiation of the BFA and its inclusion in the EC's Schedule, nor the Agreement on Agriculture, permits the EC to act inconsistently with Article XIII's requirements. The Panel also found that the EC's import licensing procedures were inconsistent with MFN and national treatment obligations under both GATT (Articles I:1 and III:4) and GATS (Articles II and XVII). The Appellate Body upheld the Panel's principal findings on violations of Articles I, III and XIII of GATT, and Articles II and XVII of GATS.

India Patent Protection for pharmaceutical and chemical products

Detailed obligations on the implementation of the TRIPS agreement and the meaning of a Member's 'expectations' of an agreement.

On 20 November 1996, the DSB established a Panel at the request of the United States to consider the alleged failure of India to meet its obligations under the Agreement on Trade-Related Aspects of Intellectual Property Rights (the 'TRIPS Agreement') regarding patent protection for pharmaceutical and agricultural chemical products. Under the transitional provisions of the TRIPS Agreement, India was entitled as a developing country to delay providing patent protection for these products until 1 January 2005. However, the Panel found that India did not comply with the transitional provisions of the TRIPS Agreement. The Panel found that India had failed to implement its obligation to establish a mechanism (a so-called 'mailbox system') that preserves the novelty and priority of the patent applications for pharmaceutical and agricultural products after the expiry of the transitional period available to developing countries for implementing new pharmaceutical and chemical protection systems. The Appellate Body agreed with the Panel's principal conclusions.

8

Geneva to Seattle, 1998–1999

The timing of the Second Ministerial Conference of the WTO at Geneva in 1998, coinciding with the 50th anniversary of the GATT, divided the three years between the Singapore and Seattle meetings neatly in two. This was a greater frequency of ministerial meetings than planned, but there was a great deal of work to do to manage the huge WTO agenda, and issues in the public debate surrounding 'globalization' were becoming politically more sensitive all the time.

For the WTO, the summer of 1998 was the start of three years of confusion, delayed decisions and bitter, but often misdirected, criticism from elements of civil society. From the sunny heights of the 50th Anniversary of the GATT offering vistas of unique achievement and bright horizons shaped by growing commitment to a further round of comprehensive trade negotiations, the multilateral system descended into what seemed like a mire of debates on difficult issues in the trading system – including persistent questions about the impact and value of the agreements reached in the Uruguay Round. Many of these debates were resolved by decisions on implementation taken in the year following the Seattle Ministerial, but some continued up to and beyond the launch of the Doha Development Agenda negotiations in 2001.

Member governments also faced a period – brief, as it turned out, for most – of uncertainty in their growth outlook and a sharp slowdown in their trade. Most economies saw a fall in both exports and imports of merchandise in 1998–99. This was especially true in Asia, and in the transition economies of the former Soviet Union and Eastern Europe but also elsewhere, including Brazil. Lower global demand and a weaker US dollar led to a sharp fall in commodity prices that affected plans in many developing economies, while sharply lower private capital flows – reflecting the impact of the Asian crisis on confidence in emerging markets – meant that governments had to focus on controlling their external liabilities.

By the middle of 1999, however, the global economy began to recover. Renewed growth was due both to the recovery of confidence and growth in the Asian economies (except Japan) affected by the financial crisis of late 1997 and to the continued strength of a prolonged period of economic growth in the United States. But the growth was unbalanced, on a global scale. The US economy was sucking up both imports and investment, resulting in current account surpluses for developing countries that really needed to spend, rather than save. US growth also sustained a higher oil price that depressed the prices of both manufactures and some commodities important to developing country exporters (especially coffee and cocoa) still further. By January 2000, the prices of non-fuel commodities were at less than 70% of their pre-Asian-crisis levels. Growth in African economies reached the lowest levels of the 1990s.

Towards a new round of negotiations

The Uruguay Round agreements contained commitments to continued negotiations on agriculture and services after 1999. When they agreed on the package to be put to ministers in Marrakesh, it was clear to the negotiators that these agreements, more than any others, created dynamic frameworks for future reform (of agriculture trade) and future expansion (of scheduled services commitments).

It was unclear, however, how the 'continuing' negotiations within these frameworks would fit into the discussions of a new comprehensive round of negotiations. At the end of the Geneva Ministerial there were three more-or-less-incompatible approaches on the table.

The European Commission was looking for a broad package of agreements that would balance continued liberalization of agriculture trade against progress in other areas and would pick up the proposals that the EC strongly supported at Singapore for negotiations on investment disciplines, competition policy, trade administration and transparency in government procurement.

The United States, too, wanted a broad agenda but didn't want to tie progress in one area to progress in another. The US wanted continuing negotiations and more rapid progress than had been achieved in the eight-year Uruguay Round negotiations, but on the basis of deals balanced within each sector. The Clinton administration may have wished to avoid asking Congress for a comprehensive negotiating mandate, but opportunities for a 'self-balancing' deal in sectors such as agriculture seemed small. Furthermore, it was likely that the US and EC would need to find some balancing opportunities for developing countries if they were to win support for their proposals for negotiations on the 'Singapore issues', in a round.

Many developing country ministers however, warned the Geneva Ministerial against any plans for new negotiations while the implementation of the current agreements was incomplete – meaning, among other things, that they were not satisfied they had received full value for their concessions.

The 1998 Geneva Ministerial Declaration,[1] inevitably therefore, struck a compromise. Paragraph eight reaffirmed the ministers' commitment to 'full and faithful implementation of the WTO Agreement' and maintained the issue of implementation on the agenda of the next Ministerial meeting (Seattle, 1999): 'When we meet at the Third Session we shall further pursue our evaluation of the implementation of individual agreements and the realization of their objectives.'

The following paragraph (nine) decided to establish a series of Special Sessions of the General Council to prepare a decision at the Seattle meeting 'regarding the WTO's work programme, including further liberalization sufficiently broad-based to respond to the range of interests and concerns of all Members, within the WTO framework . . .'

The Declaration then listed under six headings the nature of the recommendations to be made including implementation issues, the mandated negotiations of the 'built-in agenda', the 'Singapore' issues, the follow-up to the High Level meeting on Least-Developed countries and anything else that Members considered important.

Did this amount to a commitment to a Millennium Round of comprehensive negotiations? Not formally. The Ministers requested 'recommendations' on a work program, avoiding the word 'negotiations'. Also, the degree to which such a program would be considered a comprehensive 'package' depended on a re-working of the already-mandated negotiations of the 'built-in' agenda, especially on agriculture and services. Since these negotiations had no specific mandate other than the 'continuation' of the Uruguay Round programme after 1999, it would have been necessary at Seattle to give the ministers mandated objectives as part of a balanced outcome in a comprehensive 'package'.

Despite the differences of approach, therefore, between the United States and Europe and despite the many misgivings expressed by ministers from developing countries – not to mention the clamour of opposition from NGOs – there was a widespread expectation that the Seattle Ministerial would launch the first WTO 'Round'.

---

[1] WTO document WT/MIN(98)/DEC/1.

Preparations for Seattle

> #### HOW TO PREPARE A MINISTERIAL MEETING
>
> There have been five Ministerial Conferences in the WTO's first ten years. If they have demonstrated anything it is the crucial role of preparation. The model is a familiar one from any collective decision context. There are three steps
>
> (a) **Expansion**: Sometimes called a 'stocktaking'. Every Member has an opportunity to put issues, proposals and information on the table. The process is transparent, inclusive and can be endless unless circumscribed.
> (b) **Condensation**: Summarize, set priorities, agree to drop issues that have low priority or are not ready for agreement. The process must be transparent but inclusiveness may be sacrificed to time.
> (c) **Mapping**: The condensed set of issues is mapped to an agenda of decisions that can be feasibly taken by ministers. This process is typically in the hands of the Council Chairman alone but on the basis of his consultations.
>
> Neither (b) nor (c) was effective before Seattle. Cancún failed principally over (c). The preparations for Doha scored on all three counts.

The General Council, however, failed to complete its preparations for the Seattle Ministerial and the lack of preparation largely explains the failure of the meeting. Members' representatives began by expanding their focus to a wide range of problems, disappointments, challenges and ambitions. During the 14-month preparatory period more than 800 detailed proposals, recommendations and submissions were put forward for consideration.[2] But Members were unable, in the end, to condense their recommendations into a draft decision for ministers to debate and adopt at the Seattle Ministerial.

The work that was done was valuable, but its full value was not realized until after Seattle, when the councils and workgroups were able to build

---

[2] According to the record at http://www.wto.org/english/thewto_e/minist_e/min99_e/min99_e.htm. The summary of proposals in Job(99)/4797/Rev.3 lists about 280 different documentary sources but the 'background' briefing document at http://www.wto.org/english/thewto_e/minist_e/min99_e/english/about_e/03bgd_e.htm says only that 'more than 150 proposals' had been tabled.

on the earlier debates and the summaries produced by the Secretariat to arrive at more expeditious decisions resolving most of the implementation debates and clearing the decks for the Doha Development Agenda negotiations.

The work in the Special Session of the General Council was divided into three phases:

Phase 1 of the preparatory process encompassed four meetings of the General Council – the WTO's top decision-making body between sessions of the Ministerial Conference – during which WTO Members addressed the issues referred to in the 1998 Ministerial Declaration. A large number of detailed papers and statements outlining specific issues and concerns in each of these areas were submitted by delegations. While Phase 1 essentially served the purpose of issue identification and a basis for more focused work to follow, Phase 2 – between August 1998 and August 1999 – was intended to bring forward specific proposals on recommendations to ministers on the future WTO work programme: especially on the growing list of 'implementation' issues.

In **Phase 2**, developing countries pointed repeatedly to two broad categories of concerns on implementation:

(a) Difficulties, costs and challenges in implementing the WTO agreements that were not foreseen at the time they signed the agreements; and
(b) Absence or small size of the benefits that they had expected from these agreements, because of the way in which some other Members had implemented the agreements.

Many were worried, too, by the demands of the notifications system, the difficulty of finding technical assistance and by the provisions of special and differential treatment in the rules on regional trade agreements.

The proposals and discussions on the negotiations in agriculture mandated in the Uruguay Round Agreement revealed a wide range of differences on the scope, structure and timeframe of the talks. A number of countries called for the agricultural sector to be fully integrated into WTO disciplines and placed on an equal footing with other areas of trade, placing agricultural subsidies, for example, under the Agreement on Subsidies and Countervailing measures or applying the GATT rules to quotas to the use of agricultural tariff quotas. Others called for a more gradual approach, taking due account of the 'multifunctionality' of agriculture, food security concerns, and the need to support rural employment.

Members broadly shared the objective of comprehensive negotiations on all issues within the services sector. They agreed there should be no general exclusions in a substantial liberalization package and that there should be no major changes in the architecture of the existing agreement. There was similarly general agreement on the need for the negotiations to begin on time at the end of 1999, with a clear time frame for completion.

Some developing countries argued that the reviews and examinations mandated for other Agreements such as TRIPS, TRIMS and dispute settlement should not become pro forma exercises but should provide the opportunity to redress shortcomings in the agreements highlighted by Members. Other countries argued that although some implementation problems revealed during the reviews and examinations might be settled within the competent WTO bodies, substantive problems affecting the balance of rights and obligations could be resolved only in broad-based negotiations.

There were surprisingly few proposals on the four Singapore issues (investment, competition, transparency in government procurement, and trade facilitation) in Phase 2 revealing, probably, a low level of engagement by most Members. Submissions and co-sponsored submissions from only eight non-OECD countries – Kenya, Hong Kong, Singapore, Venezuela and Costa Rica among the developing economies and Poland and Hungary among the transition countries – figure in the Secretariat's compilation of proposals. The submissions and the subsequent discussions revealed divergent views about what recommendations, if any, should be made to Ministers on further work after the Seattle meeting.

Phase 3 of the Special Session program began in September 1999, but with only weeks to go before the Seattle meeting at the end of November it was no longer clear whether the wide differences canvassed in the debates of Phase 2 could be bridged. The Chairman of the Council, the new Director-General Mike Moore and the Secretariat worked hard to help Members refine a feasible agenda for future negotiations to be put to ministers. But to no avail: it was not possible to create a list of issues that could be feasibly discussed by ministers in three or four days. Much less was it possible clearly to identify key differences on each issue that were ready for ministerial decision.

Appointing a Director-General

The process of selecting a Director-General of the WTO has been difficult. The last Director-General of the GATT, Peter Sutherland, became Director-General of the WTO in an acting capacity for the first months after the creation of the WTO on 1 January 1995.

Renato Ruggiero, the former Italian Minister for Trade, was selected by Members to become Director-General and took up the position in May, 1995, for a four-year term to end in April 1999.

Developing countries insisted that the person to succeed Mr Ruggiero should be a non-European, and many of them probably expected to see overwhelming support for a developing country candidate since developing countries dominate WTO's membership.

The process of selecting a successor to Mr Ruggiero started immediately after the Geneva Ministerial in May 1998 . But it was almost a year before agreement was reached on the appointment of Mr Mike Moore, former Prime Minister of New Zealand, in a split-term arrangement with Dr Supachai Panitchpakdi – former Deputy Prime Minister of Thailand. Each was appointed to serve a term of three years without extension or reappointment, a unique arrangement to bridge divisions between Members that had become entrenched by the end of a long campaign.

Members agreed that the three-year terms for the Directors-General appointed at that time would not form a precedent and that the normal term of office would be four years. They also proposed to spare themselves the future embarrassment of a lengthy behind-the-scenes wrangle over selections by adopting[3] new procedures for the appointment of Directors-General.

[3] Director-General selection procedure WTO document WT/L/509.

9

The Seattle Ministerial Conference, 1999

The principal lesson from the failure of the talks at the Seattle Ministerial in November 1999 was that ministers could not possibly negotiate on the broad agenda, covering many sensitive topics, that was now before the WTO (and would continue until Cancún) without detailed preparation at the WTO in Geneva. This advance preparation would need to clarify the extent of the commitments that might be required when the negotiations were concluded. The various distractions and disagreements which arose during the preparatory period for the Ministerial Conference had hindered this process of preparation to the extent that ministers did not feel confident about launching negotiations.

The challenge facing the ministers at Seattle was to reach agreement on a round of negotiations that would follow the ground rules laid down in the WTO Agreement. Any agreements reached in these negotiations would be based on a 'single undertaking' for all WTO Members. The final 'package' would be constructed on a broad front to ensure the potential for a 'balanced' outcome addressing all Members' interests; it would include potentially expensive implementation requirements and would be locked in place by a solid disputes procedure. It is understandable that ministers approached the prospect of such wide-ranging and binding agreements cautiously. Their caution extended to keeping a careful watch on the potential domestic impact of the agreements and on the political backwash from campaigns by international NGOs.

Ministers and delegations convened at Seattle on 30 November 1999 against the backdrop of sometimes violent street demonstrations against the WTO by non-governmental organizations and other civil society groups representing labour, the environment and other interests. The demonstrations hampered the start of the talks and made logistics difficult for the duration of the Ministerial.

Ministers adopted a four-point agenda for the Conference under which they agreed to

(i) Review WTO activities and evaluate implementation of past agreements;
(ii) Adopt a Ministerial text and take any other action necessary for the future work of the WTO;
(iii) Elect officers for the next Conference; and
(iv) Decide on the date and venue of the next Conference.

In the course of that afternoon and the two following days, Ministers devoted 21 hours in formal plenary meetings, including late-evening sessions, to the overview of WTO activities under the first agenda item. One hundred and twenty-two Member governments, 24 observer governments and five observer international organizations delivered statements under this item. While the plenary business got under way, and in order to make maximum use of the limited time as well as to give all delegations the opportunity to participate in the continued work of drafting a Ministerial text for adoption under the second agenda item, US Trade Representative Ambassador Charlene Barshefsky, as Chair of the Ministerial, announced in the afternoon of the first day the establishment of four open ended informal Working Groups that focused on key issues in parallel to the work of the plenary meeting.

Ultimately, however, faced with the need to condense the still-wide-ranging debates and to create their own frameworks for decision, the working groups failed to generate the necessary consensus. By early evening on 3 December it was clear that too little time remained to complete the work of narrowing gaps, bringing the resulting texts back to the plenary working groups, making any additional changes and approving the declaration by consensus at the formal plenary meeting of the Conference.

At the concluding plenary session held late in the evening on Friday, the Chair informed ministers that divergences of opinion remained at the end of the process that could not be resolved rapidly. Her own judgment, shared by WTO Director-General Mike Moore, the working group Chairs and co-Chairs and by the Members generally, was that it would be best to suspend the work of the Ministerial Conference and to allow the Director-General time to consult with delegations and discuss creative ways to bridge the remaining differences, as well as to develop improved rules and processes that would respond to the demands by many Members for a more inclusive, more transparent negotiating process.

While the demonstrations and police action in the streets of Seattle were the media's focus of attention, the real obstacle to reaching agreement at the Ministerial proved once again to be the big gaps in negotiating positions between WTO Members.

Accessions

There is no truer testament to the difficulty of implementing WTO obligations than the slow progress at this time (1999) of the Working Parties on Accession of new WTO Members.

Thirty governments were negotiating the terms of their WTO accession by the time of the Seattle meeting, one more applicant than at the time of the Geneva Ministerial. But the WTO membership grew by only seven (Bulgaria, Ecuador, Estonia, Kyrgyz Republic, Latvia, Mongolia, and Panama) between 1995 and 1999; three of the accessions taking place in the Geneva–Seattle inter-Ministerial period.

The accession process had become more complex because of the WTO's increased coverage compared to GATT but also because many acceding countries were undergoing transition from centrally planned to market economies. Although accession to the WTO was compatible with this transition, it 'raised the bar' by requiring the government to make explicit commitments in policy domains where the role of markets and the role of government were still being defined by municipal law or practice.

Electronic commerce

In addition to its huge work program in the Special Session, the General Council now took up the mandate from the Geneva Ministerial to examine all issues relating to trade and global electronic commerce. It commissioned reports on the work programme from the Goods Council, the Services Council, the TRIPS (Intellectual Property) Council and the Trade and Development Committee.

Members considered that the vast majority of transactions on the Internet are services that are covered by GATS and that all the provisions of the GATS apply to trade in services that takes place electronically. They did not agree on the classification of a small number of products made available on the Internet such as books and software; whether they were services or goods or perhaps some distinct form of exchange. Consequently there was no consensus on whether GATS or some other provision of the WTO might apply to this trade. Members also considered, without concluding, whether Internet Service Providers might be subject to obligations under the GATS Annex on telecommunications, for example with respect to interconnection.

Electronic commerce remains on the agendas of the General Council and its subsidiary councils, although the decision of most governments not to impose customs duties on Internet transactions specifically has reduced the potential for conflict of policies over e-commerce exchanges; the considerations of the Council have not yet resulted in any recommendations for cross-cutting negotiations on e-commerce.

Review of the Dispute Settlement Understanding (DSU)

The Dispute Settlement Understanding (DSU) was a major component of the agreements signed in Marrakesh in 1994 that established groundbreaking new procedures for the management of disputes under any of the other agreements. Ministers also adopted in Marrakesh a Decision on the Review of the Understanding on Rules and Procedures Governing the Settlement of Disputes in which they invite themselves (the Ministerial Conference) to complete a full review of the DSU within four years after the entry into force of the WTO.

Members considered that the dispute settlement system had worked reasonably well but that experience had shown that the disputes procedures could be clarified or improved in a number of areas. These included the length of time allowed for compliance with a Dispute Settlement Body (DSB) decision and an ambiguity about whether a successful complainant might pursue non-compliance before the expiry of this 'reasonable period of time'. Some Members wished to clarify the procedures for objecting to the authorized suspension of obligations in the case of non-compliance. Other matters raised by Members included access for private parties to the disputes processes and greater transparency of processes in the panels and in the Appellate Body.

The Dispute Settlement Body (the WTO General Council in one of its guises) began to prepare the review in early 1998 but, by their self-imposed deadline of July 1999 had not reached agreement on recommendations to make to the Seattle Ministerial and ultimately had to inform ministers that no agreement had been possible. A group of 15 Members forwarded their own proposal to the Ministerial, but as it turned out, the matter was not discussed in Seattle and the review of the DSB remained on the table when ministers re-convened at the Doha Ministerial Conference two years later.

Trade Policy Review Mechanism (TPRM)

The Marrakesh Agreement also required a review of the Trade Policy Review Mechanism that had begun before the entry into force of the WTO. It was probably an indication of the general satisfaction of Members with the Reviews that this item on the Seattle agenda did not attract much attention.

Trade policy reviews reported by the Secretariat and by Member governments separately aim to achieve greater transparency in, and understanding of, the policies and practices of Members, including by their own civil society. The discussion by the General Council, meeting as the Trade Policy Review Mechanism, provides for a collective appreciation and evaluation of policies and practices in all areas covered by the WTO agreements, and their impact on the functioning of the multilateral trading system. Reviews take account of the wider economic and developmental needs and objectives of the Member concerned and of the external trading environment. They are not intended to serve as a basis for the enforcement of obligations, for dispute settlement procedures, or to impose new policy commitments.

By the end of 1999, a total of 120 reviews had been conducted, covering 71 WTO Members (counting EU–15 as one), with Canada and the United States having been reviewed five times; the EU and Japan four times; four Members (Australia; Indonesia; Hong Kong, China; and Thailand) three times and 26 Members twice. By the time of the Seattle meeting, ten of the 28 least-developed economies that were WTO Members had been reviewed.

NGO access to the WTO

The WTO is one of a small number of inter-governmental organizations whose founding document refers explicitly to relations with non-governmental organizations.

The Marrakesh Agreement Establishing the World Trade Organization (article V:2) says '. . . the General Council may make appropriate arrangements for consultation and cooperation with non-governmental organizations concerned with matters related to those of the WTO'. Relations with non-governmental organizations were also the subject of a set of guidelines adopted by the General Council in July 1996[1] to '. . . recognize

---

[1] WTO document WT/L/162.

the role NGOs can play to increase the awareness of the public in respect of WTO activities . . .'

The Director-General, his deputies and other Secretariat staff meet routinely with NGO representatives – both in Geneva and in other venues. Members of civil society and NGO representatives are in almost daily contact with External Relations Division and, in addition, Secretariat officials frequently participate in meetings where trade-related subjects are discussed with civil society organizations. The Secretariat organizes regular briefings for Geneva-based NGO representatives on WTO issues and NGOs are also invited to attend issue-specific symposia such as the WTO's annual public symposium which provides a platform for dialogue among all stakeholders of the multilateral trading system.

As well as being informed, NGOs can be present at WTO Ministerial Conferences. Under procedures agreed by the General Council, NGOs may attend plenary sessions of the Conference, and now do so in large numbers. There were 235 participants representing 108 NGOs at the first WTO Ministerial Conference in Singapore, 686 NGOs were represented at Seattle and 795 NGOs (1578 participants) at the 2003 Fifth Ministerial Conference in Cancún, Mexico – a near seven-fold increase in the first decade of the WTO's existence.

In Seattle and at every Ministerial thereafter, a special NGO Center was set up by the WTO to provide registered NGOs with a large number of meeting rooms, computer facilities and documentation from the official event. The available facilities are used intensively.

Throughout the Seattle Conference more than 160 meetings (workshops, seminars, private meetings) took place in the NGO Center. WTO officials briefed NGOs on a daily basis on the progress of the working sessions. Additionally, NGOs had full access to the Press Center located in the official Conference venue. NGOs have welcomed these efforts as genuine signs of commitment to ensure transparency.

The WTO now also invites NGOs to present policy research and analysis directly to WTO Members; NGO position papers are compiled and circulated to WTO Members on a regular basis and they are posted on the WTO website to make NGO views accessible to the public.

LANDMARK DISPUTE CASES

US – Cotton underwear

An early case bought by a small developing country.

In March 1996, a Panel was established to consider Costa Rica's claim that the United States had imposed quantitative restrictions on cotton and man-made fibre underwear from Costa Rica in a manner inconsistent with the requirements of the Agreement on Textiles and Clothing (ATC). Under the ATC, the United States was required to show 'serious damage' or 'actual threat of serious damage' to its industry in order to impose such restrictions. The Panel found, among other things, that the United States had failed to comply with its obligations under the ATC by imposing a restriction on imports of Costa Rican underwear without making an adequate attribution of serious damage to Costa Rican imports, as distinct from other imports. Costa Rica appealed the Panel's conclusions relating to the permissible effective date of application of the United States' transitional safeguard measure and the Appellate Body agreed, saying that the ATC does not permit the retroactive application of transitional safeguard measures. In April 1997, the United States informed the DSB that the contested measure had expired.

EC – Beef hormones

A case that helped establish the meaning of risk assessment under SPS. Implementation remains incomplete.

On 20 May 1996, a Panel was established to consider a complaint by the United States regarding the EC import prohibition on meat and meat products from livestock that has been treated with certain hormones for growth promotion purposes. Similar complaints from other meat exporters were joined to the same Panel. The Panel found – among other things – that the EC violated SPS Article 5.1 because its import ban was not based on a 'risk assessment', that is, an evaluation of the potential for adverse effects on human health arising from the presence of certain hormones in meat. In January 1998, the Appellate Body upheld this finding (although it reversed other Panel findings). In so doing, the Appellate Body clarified that for an SPS measure to be 'based on' a risk assessment there had to be a 'rational' or 'objective' relationship between the measure and the risk assessment. The Appellate Body further clarified that the risk that is to be evaluated in a risk assessment is not only risk ascertainable in a science laboratory operating under strict controlled conditions, but also risk in human societies as they actually exist. Therefore, risks resulting from the abusive use of hormones and the difficulty of controlling the use of hormones were also relevant to a risk assessment under Article 5.1. On 13 February 1998, the DSB adopted the Appellate Body report and the Panel reports, as modified by the Appellate Body report. In May 1998, an arbitrator appointed under Article 21.3(c) of the DSU determined the 'reasonable period of time' for implementation to be 15 months from the date of adoption.

EC – Bananas (II)

The second of three major cases concerning quotas, preferences and discrimination in the valuable banana trade.

On 8 May 1996, a Panel was established to consider a revised complaint by Ecuador, Guatemala, Honduras, Mexico and the United States (with a large number of other American and Caribbean countries participating as interested parties) regarding the EC regime for the importation, sale and distribution of bananas. The essence of the claims was that the EC banana regime granted preferential treatment to EC and African, Caribbean and Pacific (ACP) bananas at the expense of non-EC, non-ACP bananas.

The EC common market organization for bananas, instituted in 1993, allocated import quotas based on the origin of the bananas and allocates import licenses – which are linked to specific quotas – according to the importing practices of licensees. The terms of entry varied widely. Bananas from traditional ACP suppliers entered duty-free up to a maximum quota allocated for each country. Imports of non-traditional ACP bananas entered the EC market duty-free within the limits of their tariff-rate quota ('TRQ'), and beyond that subject to a preference of ECU 100 on the out-of-quota tariff. Imports from third countries were subject to an in-quota duty of ECU 75 per tonne, and were assessed an out-of-quota tariff rate of ECU 793 per tonne in 1997. The quotas for countries other than the traditional ACP suppliers were further subdivided in to a range of functional and 'operator' categories. The EC had entered a 'framework agreement on bananas' (BFA) that favoured a subset of central American suppliers and relied on a temporary GATT waiver to maintain preferences for ACP states that were not available to other developing country suppliers.

The Panel rejected challenges under Article I:1 of GATT to the EC tariff preferences granted to traditional as well as non-traditional ACP banana imports. Rather, it accepted the EC argument that the Lomé waiver permitted such an inconsistency with its MFN obligations. But the Panel found that the EC import licensing procedures were inconsistent with MFN and national treatment obligations under both GATT (Articles I:1 and III:4) and GATS (Articles II and XVII). The Appellate Body endorsed these findings (although it reversed or modified others). The DSB adopted the reports in September 1997 and the period for implementation by the EC was set to expire in January, 1999.

India – Patent protection for pharmaceutical and agricultural chemical products

A test of 'implementation' under the TRIPS agreement and clarification of some interpretative principles.

On 20 November 1996, the DSB established a Panel at the request of the United States to consider the alleged failure of India to meet its obligations under the Agreement on Trade-Related Aspects of Intellectual Property Rights (the 'TRIPS Agreement') regarding patent protection for pharmaceutical and agricultural chemical products. Under the transitional provisions of the TRIPS Agreement, India was entitled as a developing country to delay providing patent protection for these products until 1 January 2005. However, the Panel found that India had failed to implement its obligation under Article 70.8(a) of the TRIPS Agreement to establish a mechanism (a so-called 'mailbox system') that preserves the novelty and priority of the patent applications for pharmaceutical and agricultural products and had failed to make the specific terms and provisions of such a system available to governments and rights holders.

The Appellate Body upheld the Panel's conclusion that India had not complied with its obligations but disagreed with certain elements of the Panel's reasoning leading to that conclusion. They found fault with the Panel's invocation of a general interpretative principle that the 'legitimate expectations' of WTO Members must be taken into account in interpreting the TRIPS Agreement. The Panel had stated that protection of legitimate expectations of Members regarding the conditions of competition is a well-established GATT principle, and argued that it was merely applying this principle in the context of the TRIPS Agreement. The Appellate Body concluded, however, that the Panel's reasoning did not accurately reflect GATT/WTO practice which distinguished between 'violation' and 'non-violation' complaints.

The Appellate Body stressed that, in interpreting the TRIPS Agreement, the Panel should not have gone beyond the general principles of agreement interpretation set out in the Vienna Convention on the Law of Treaties. In addition, the Appellate Body reversed some other Panel findings on the grounds that the claim was excluded from the Panel's 'jurisdiction' because the United States had submitted it during the Panel's first substantive meeting with the parties – rather than in its original Panel request. At the DSB meeting on 16 January 1998, the Appellate Body report and the Panel report, as modified by the Appellate Body report, were adopted. At the DSB meeting on 22 April 1998, India and the United States jointly announced that they had agreed on an implementation period of 15 months, whereby India would introduce the necessary legislation to ensure that the new procedure would be in place and operational no later than 19 April 1999.

10

The Road to Doha, 1999–2001

> The suspension of talks is not unprecedented in the history of the multilateral trading system. But what is vital is that we maintain and consolidate what has already been achieved. The progress made must not be lost.
>
> I feel particular disappointment because the postponement of our deliberations means the benefits that would have accrued to developing and least-developed countries will now be delayed, while the problems facing these countries will not be allayed. A package of results is within reach.
>
> Statement by WTO Director-General Mike Moore, 7 December 1999

After Seattle, it took two years to put together the comprehensive negotiations that had been considered, first, at the Geneva Ministerial Conference in 1998. During that time the WTO had to recover its balance, maintain progress in the directions established at Marrakesh, Singapore and Geneva and demonstrate to its Members and civil society that the trading system would be an essential part of the answer to global challenges, not part of the problem.

Most of the activities of the WTO were unaffected by the events in Seattle in December 1999. The councils and committees continued as before to manage relations between Member governments under the WTO agreements. Dispute settlement activity increased as the potential of the new system was realized. The outreach and technical assistance activities of the WTO continued to grow and accessions remained a high priority for governments not yet Members as well as for the WTO itself (there were five new Members in 2000: Albania, Croatia, Georgia, Jordan and Oman – with progress being made rapidly on the accession of others including China and Chinese Taipei).

But the confidence of Members had been dented. It was not so much the highly visible protests and their disruption of the Seattle Ministerial that was depressing; it was the management failure of the WTO in the face of the huge agenda Members had adopted for themselves.

Over the five years since the WTO entered into force, Members had aggressively expanded the number of subjects under debate, driven, mostly, by the ambitions of the industrialized countries. They had done this while struggling with a growing list of outstanding questions – some of them quite fundamental, most from developing countries – grouped under the heading of 'implementation issues' related to the agreements already in place.

Eighteen months of preparations had not made it possible to answer these questions or to bring together in a balanced package an agreed program of work that united the mandated negotiations (agriculture, services) and the 'new' issues identified at Singapore. In retrospect, the urgent work of the open-ended Ministerial Working Groups at Seattle seemed a desperate measure that had always been unlikely to succeed.

The work program that the General Council set for itself reflected the WTO's determination to re-gain its balance and re-start progress towards the new round of negotiations that had gone off the rails even before Seattle. It had four parts:

First, the negotiations in services and agriculture that were already mandated by the Agreement on Agriculture and the GATS were set in motion, as planned, at the end of 1999. They were essentially open-ended negotiations aimed at 'continuation' of the liberalization achieved in the Uruguay Round within each sector, without reference to others.

The mandate for 'continuing reform' in the agriculture negotiations opened up a wide range of possible approaches and subjects for discussion. Initially, the Agriculture Committee in Special Session undertook a 'stock taking' phase in 2000 to allow Members to discuss priorities. The mandate implied a continuation of the reductions in domestic support, market access barriers and the use of export subsidies that had begun in the Agreement on Agriculture. But some Members wanted to temper the pace of any further reforms with consideration of the broader or 'multifunctional' nature of support to the sector, notably the situation of rural communities. Forty proposals were tabled in time for a stocktaking review held in a Special Session of the Committee on Agriculture in March 2001 before the start of a second phase, intended to include negotiations.

The negotiations on services were intended to address further rule-making in matters such as safeguards, government procurement and subsidies and to 'achieve a progressively higher level of liberalization' (GATS Article XIX), building on the market-access commitments already contained in the schedules. In 2000, WTO Members agreed on a 'roadmap' for the first phase of negotiations and that the second phase of these negotiations would begin with a stocktaking exercise by a Special Session of the GATS Council in March 2001, to consider progress made and how to move forward.

The mandated reviews under the TRIPS Agreement were also launched, as were the negotiations required on a possible multilateral register for Geographical Indications for wines and spirits.

A second part of the post-Seattle work program involved the Director-General and the General Council Chairman in a program of consultations with Member governments. The purpose was to progress a range of issues not resolved at Seattle where, nonetheless, agreement had seemed almost within grasp. They included

- measures in favour of least-developed countries – part of the continuing follow-up to the 1997 High Level meeting on LDCs;
- improving the funding and planning of WTO technical cooperation activities;
- differences on issues such as the extension of transition periods for developing countries facing problems with their obligations under the Uruguay Round agreements and other implementation issues; and
- improving internal transparency and the fuller participation of WTO Members in the process of making decisions.

The third objective for the program, aimed primarily at developing country Members, was to reach agreement on implementation issues, especially on the transition periods under various WTO agreements which were expiring or had expired, such as deadlines on the implementation of the TRIMS agreement. The Special Sessions of the General Council leading to the Seattle Ministerial had identified many problems and also many solutions, but now it was important to take decisions that would address Members' concerns and resolve the matter. It was even more evident after Seattle than it had been before that, without progress on these issues, most countries would not be prepared to work on the more ambitious aspects of WTO's agenda.

The fourth element in the post-Seattle work program concerned transparency and participation. Members seemed to acknowledge that the biggest problems in Seattle were differences over the substance of proposals rather than over non-inclusive decision-procedures (such as the 'working groups' which posed a difficult coverage task for small delegations). Many Members were, nonetheless, highly critical of the way the WTO's procedures for consultation and decision-making had operated before and at Seattle. The WTO realized that it had to learn from Seattle and sought submissions from Members on improvements to decision-making.

The 2000 work programme included a series of discussions aimed at finding ways to ensure the fuller participation of all Members in the work of the WTO and to improve consultative procedures. A majority of Members saw no need for radical changes and strongly supported the practice of reaching decisions by consensus. Members thought that informal consultations would continue to be a useful tool, provided that improvements were made in the inclusiveness and transparency of the consultations. A number of innovations were made including improved use of Internet communications, an annual week-long seminar for non-resident delegations ('Geneva Week') and the installation of an increasing number of WTO Reference Centres in developing and least-developed countries.

Global growth and recession

> The blow to the world from a slowdown in America could be many times greater if harder times stoke up protectionist pressures. Even during the good times, there has been a worrying surge in anti-dumping and anti-subsidy investigations in both developed and developing countries. Over 400 were launched in 1999, up from only 166 in 1995. And the OECD has noted that producer support estimates for agriculture are rising again. Support for agriculture in OECD countries amounts to a billion dollars a day.
>
> Things could get much worse if companies squeezed by falling profits convince governments that they need protection from foreign competition. The virtuous circle of trade liberalisation and economic growth could all too easily become a vicious spiral of protectionism and stagnation.
>
> Director-General Mike Moore, at the European Business School, London, March 2001

The second half of 1999 had already seen the world economy picking up from the retrenchment of 1998–99 and the year 2000 saw the strongest global trade and output growth in more than a decade. North America and Western Europe, which together account for about 60% of global output and trade, recorded in 2000 their fastest annual GDP growth for a decade. The economies of North America, especially, continued to grow strongly, pumped up by the higher levels of productivity and exuberant consumer demand flowing from the information technology revolution. Developing Asia had begun to recover from the reversals in its financial markets, sharing in the North American growth. There was a recovery, too, from output stagnation in South America and Russia and a pickup in economic activity in other regions.

More open markets paid off by spreading the growth to every region. In addition to the outstanding overall levels of global growth, the dispersion of regional growth rates was low in 2000, indicating that the growth was broadly based. Stronger output was associated with trade expansion in 2000 that matched – in volume terms – the best rates observed over the last five decades. For most regions, merchandise trade growth ranged between 10 and 15%.

Non-fuel commodity prices recovered somewhat, but both they and manufactures prices were overshadowed by a sharp increase in oil prices, reflecting rapid output growth.

These rapid rates of growth could not be sustained and by the second half of 2001 and into 2002 growth in the OECD countries ground to a halt and their trade started to contract both on the import and export sides of the external balance sheets. The simultaneous deterioration of trade and output in the United States, Japan and Europe, and the continuing slump in Japan, reflected the sluggishness of the economies of Western Europe, the bursting of the IT 'bubble' and, to a smaller extent, a loss of confidence following the attacks on the United States in September of 2001.

Regional agreements

It is never easy to discern, from a close distance, the significance of trends in a complex domain such as trade policy. From the late 1990s one of the most controversial trends has been the spread of regional trade agreements (RTAs).

As the rate of creation of these discriminatory agreements has increased, more and more analysts have expressed concern that the predominant character of global trade policy may be reverting to discrimination: the policy that had marked the darkest period of modern international trade relations between the two World Wars of the twentieth century.

As of mid-2000, the WTO Secretariat counted 114 RTAs that were in effect and had been notified to the WTO by one or more Members. By mid-2004 the number notified was approaching 200. All WTO Members apart from Mongolia were partners in at least one RTA by the end of 2004, and many were partners in two or more. Most RTAs were 'free trade' areas based on an exchange of preferential market access among the members without the creation of common external barriers to trade with the rest of the world (that sort of RTA is called a 'customs union').

The highest number of preferential trade agreements connected the European Union with economies across Europe, Africa, the Middle East, Asia and Latin America. The expansion of the EU – initially through RTAs and proceeding sometimes to full accession by contiguous states – accounted for much of the spurt in the growth of the number of RTAs in the period of the late 1990s. Since then, there has been strong growth of RTAs, too, in the Pacific region where China has established new regional agreements as have, to a lesser extent, the United States and Japan.

WTO rules on the creation of RTAs require Members strictly to limit the degree of discrimination and to move quickly to full liberalization. Behind this rule is the hope that the growth of trade within the region due to the elimination of barriers would have positive 'ripple' effects on global demand levels, offsetting any adverse impact from discriminatory policies. But the Committee on Regional Trade Agreements, appointed to review Members' compliance, has issued few final determinations on the compliance of RTAs with the WTO rules and has a heavy backlog of agreements under examination. The lack of decisions is due to a 'stand-off' among WTO Members who decline to ratify the discriminatory policies of any other Member[1]. This 'rolling deadlock' in the verification and approval process has rendered the WTO rules on regional agreements, at best, ineffective.

The decision adopted at Doha to clarify and improve the existing WTO provisions on RTAs reflects Members' concern to preserve the non-discriminatory global trading system while pursuing the advantages they obviously see in discriminatory agreements.

Trade and poverty: action on least-developed countries

The most obvious evidence of the difficulties of LDCs in the world trading system is their declining share in world merchandise exports. Although these countries account for 10.4% of the world's population, their share of exports was only 0.7% in 1980 and had fallen to 0.4% twenty years later. The decline largely reflects the continued dominance of primary commodities in the export profiles of almost all LDCs and the continuing fall in the value of commodities over that period.

At the General Council in May 2000, Canada, the European Union, Japan, and the United States announced that they would implement

---

[1] Just one RTA has been ratified by WTO Members: that between the Czech and Slovak Republics after the dissolution of Czechoslovakia in 1998.

'both tariff-free and quota-free treatment, consistent with domestic requirements and international agreements, under their preferential schemes, for essentially all products originating in LDCs'. Nine other Members either joined this pledge or had already granted duty free and quota free access to LDCs. The WTO estimated that these actions – some of which imposed conditions and limits on free access – combined with existing programmes and MFN tariffs, resulted in duty-free access for approximately 75% of LDC exports to their 30 main markets.

In response to the evident plight of the poorest countries, the WTO pursued improvements to the Integrated Framework (IF) for assistance to least-developed countries. Established in October of 1997, following the Singapore-mandated High Level Meeting on Least Developed Countries, the IF combined the efforts of six multilateral institutions (IMF, ITC, UNCTAD, UNDP, World Bank and the WTO) in an effort to deliver greater development dividends for least-developed countries in the multilateral trading system.

In the year following Seattle, the WTO participated in a review of the Integrated Framework which had made some modest progress but had been criticized for administrative inefficiencies, under-funding, slow disbursement and a lack of coherence between the objectives of donors and recipients. The partner agencies decided on a number of steps to help the LDCs make trade an important contributor to their development strategies: to include beneficiaries in the strategic planning for the program; to upgrade the program administration and to seek a larger pool of funds from which to draw.

The WTO also joined with the World Bank and IMF in turning its focus and outreach efforts to a public discussion with civil society and government donors on the connection between trade and poverty. If there were benefits to be gained from the IF objective of 'mainstreaming trade' in the development policies of the poorest countries then poverty alleviation should be one of them. At the least, the accusations thrown around by the protest organizations at Seattle – and the even more violent demonstrators at the Prague World Bank/IMF meetings in September 2000 – that WTO rules and activities were somehow increasing poverty, would be answered.

In June the WTO published a major study[2] on trade and poverty that found – consistently with work being pursued separately in the Bank and Fund – that trade liberalization helps poor countries to catch up with rich ones and that this faster economic growth helps to alleviate poverty.

---

[2] WTO Special Study 'Trade, Income Disparity and Poverty'.

> **TRADE AND POVERTY STUDY**
>
> The WTO study 'Trade, Income Disparity and Poverty' found that living standards in many developing countries were not catching up with those in developed countries. But some developing countries were catching up. What distinguished the latter group was openness to trade; and the more open their economy the faster they converged. The study also found that poor people within a country generally gain from trade liberalization. It concluded that 'trade liberalization is generally a strongly positive contributor to poverty alleviation, allowing people to exploit their productive potential, assists economic growth, curtails arbitrary policy interventions and helps to insulate against shocks'. The authors acknowledged that some people do lose in the short run from trade liberalization. Some are well off, others not. The report argues that the plight of the losers should not be ignored, but that the right way to alleviate their hardship is through social safety nets and job retraining rather than by abandoning reforms that benefit most people.

By May 2001, at the Third UN Conference on Least-Developed Countries, the WTO Director-General was able to report on 'deliverables' resulting from the WTO's commitment to assist the least-developed countries. These deliverables included the pledged improvements in access and improvement and extension of the Integrated Framework of assistance. The Director-General detailed efforts being made in the WTO to accelerate the process of accession for least-developed countries and to improve the operations of a number of WTO programs of interest to the least-developed, including the expanded program for Members and Observers without Geneva Missions – such as the 'Geneva Week' programs. The WTO had also improved the Trade Policy Review mechanism to include help for LDCs with trade policy capacity-building; it had expanded its trade policy training courses, developed a program of WTO Reference Centres designed to connect capitals of least-developed countries with the WTO through the Internet, and launched a program to fund interns within country missions in Geneva.

Technical assistance program

Although the WTO is not primarily a technical assistance organization, it maintains a substantial technical assistance program intended to assist

Members, especially least-developed countries, to get full benefit from their participation in the multilateral trading system.

Assistance and training activities have burgeoned in the first ten years of the WTO. Starting with 85 activities in 1995, the WTO now sponsors more than 500 events each year including short and longer (three-month) training courses for officials, training publications and software, 130 'Reference Centres' in 87 countries (including some in countries that are not yet WTO Members), distance-learning across the World Wide Web and 'Geneva Weeks'. Training is overseen by the Committee on Trade and Development.

Technical cooperation funds

In his consultations with Members following the collapse of the Seattle meeting, Director-General Mike Moore pushed for an increase in the 'core' WTO budget for technical cooperation, less than CHF 1 million, to more than CHF 10 million, to be phased-in over three years from 2000. His efforts were partly successful. Members did not question the importance of WTO technical assistance efforts, because 'voluntary' contributions, supplementing the regular budget, rose rapidly after the Seattle Ministerial from about CHF 6 million in 1999 to about CHF 25 million in 2003.

But, perhaps reflecting the dominance of developing countries (i.e. potential beneficiaries) in the membership or possibly their view that WTO is not a technical assistance agency, Members have not agreed to the increase in the regular technical assistance budget sought by the Director-General. The 'core' technical assistance budget rose after 2002 to more than CHF 5 million: a level at which it has remained since.

An implementation mechanism

By the end of 2000, Members were, at last, reaching decisions on the bundle of issues collected under the heading of 'implementation'. The pressure for decisions had been growing as several deadlines built-in to the Uruguay Round agreements expired at the end of 1999, shortly after the Seattle Ministerial.

For the most part, Members were meeting the deadlines. By 1999 the bulk of the tariff cuts of the Uruguay Round were completed. Consequently, the customs duty collected on imports decreased between 1994 and 1999 by 10% to US$ 39.4 billion for the US, the EU and Japan, which combined account for nearly one half of world imports. As their imports increased over the same period by 40%, the ratio of duties collected to the value of imports decreased by about one third to 2.5% for the US, 2.3% for Japan and to 1.7% for the EU.[3]

Developed countries had implemented their GATS and TRIPS obligations in the first year after entry into force of the WTO, but developing countries were allowed five years for implementation of many obligations. Some obligations (such as TRIMS, see below) remained incomplete at the end of five years. But most developing countries were able to meet their obligations on time.

Members with obligations under the Agreement on Agriculture to cut trade-distorting support to production had achieved their obligations, and obligations to cut export subsidy use were also being fully met. Market access obligations in agriculture were being met by reducing all agricultural tariffs, including those resulting from the tariffication exercise, by an average 36% over 1995–2000 in the case of developed countries (developing countries would cut their agricultural tariffs by an average of 24% by 2004).

Developing countries were allowed extended periods for the implementation of certain obligations under the agreements. For example, deadlines for compliance with provisions on intellectual property protection, the elimination of trade-related investment measures that depart from the GATT national treatment obligation, such as local-content requirements, the adoption of certain methods of customs valuation, and on subsidies. But some developing countries had not met their obligations in time.

In May 2000, the General Council set up a series of Special Sessions to work through the implementation issues listed by Members before Seattle. It was a long list containing matters of different degrees of urgency and requiring different types of decision. Some, for example, required a simple extension of time for an implementation period: several developing countries that had missed the deadline related, for example, to the TRIMS agreement were given additional time by agreement at the General Council. Other issues, however, required more consultation among Members and some could be resolved only by negotiation and amendments to the agreements – a power that resides only with ministers, not with the General Council.

The General Council took decisions in December 2000 that relied both on the wide-ranging informal consultations by the Director-General and his staff as well as on reports and suggestions from subsidiary committees

---

[3] The averages are not a ranking of 'openness'. Tariff lines in which 'peak' rates mean few if any imports, and therefore few or no duty collections, affect the ratio of collections to lines.

of the Council on matters referred to them on agriculture, sanitary and phytosanitary measures, technical barriers to trade, customs valuation, and intellectual property. The General Council Chairman admitted that the decisions were 'modest' but they progressed outstanding matters and took some of the heat out of the debate. For the most part the decisions clarified a small number of existing obligations and recommended further work leading up to the Fourth Ministerial, at Doha, Qatar in 2001.

TRIPS and public health

Concern about the scale of the epidemic of HIV/AIDS, malaria and other diseases in developing regions, and legal action in 2000 by a group of pharmaceutical companies against possible infringements of their patents on HIV/AIDS drugs in South Africa prompted a vigorous debate in the United Nations, the World Health Organization and in the WTO on the availability of essential medicines in developing countries. The WHO estimated at the time that, although the number of people with access to essential drugs has doubled in the last 20 years, one-third of the world's population – more than 50% of the populations of Asia and Africa – still lacked such access. Two out of every three deaths of children and young adults in regions such as Africa and South East Asia were attributable to one of just seven causes, according to the WHO, most of which are treatable – or curable – by drugs.

It was not clear to what extent TRIPS provisions that required governments to provide patent owners the right to protect their patents, but also provided exceptions to that protection, contributed to this problem. Many activists and some Member governments claimed that the protection of patents on essential drugs raised the price of the medicines to a point where they were unavailable to poor people. Among the solutions advanced was the compulsory licensing of these patents to manufacturers who would supply low-priced drugs. Under this plan, however, some countries that lacked the manufacturing capacity to produce their own versions of the patented drugs would have to import them from compulsorily licensed manufacturers in other countries. Although TRIPS provides for compulsory licensing under certain conditions, it appeared to prohibit the export of drugs made under these licences.

In 2001, the TRIPS Council held a special discussion on intellectual property and access to medicines, as part of its weeklong regular meeting. Much of the discussion concerned the flexibility available in the TRIPS Agreement for governments to adopt appropriate public health policies while complying with the provisions of the Agreement. The discussion turned again and again around the provisions of the TRIPS Agreement dealing with compulsory licensing and parallel imports.

Many delegations held that the TRIPS Agreement can provide sufficient flexibility to enable public health needs to be met, if it is properly interpreted and applied. However, some developing country delegations expressed concern that these provisions could sometimes be interpreted too narrowly and that countries might be pressured not to make full use of the flexibility that the TRIPS Agreement provides them.

The claims of NGOs, some Member governments and the drug lobbies fanned the flames of a debate that ranged much further than the WTO perspective, which necessarily focused on the extent of TRIPS obligations. Matters such as the role of patents in medical research, the management of public health resources in developing countries and equity of access to medical services that lay at the heart of the controversy were beyond the mandate of the WTO and the provisions of the Agreement.

But the WTO provided a familiar target and the provisions of the TRIPS Agreement were too complex to allow most citizens to evaluate the real impact of its provisions for themselves. Members agreed that a statement from ministers should clarify the meaning and objectives of the TRIPS Agreement as it affected the supply of drugs (the WTO Agreement reserves the power to make such interpretive statements to the Ministerial Conference).

Finding a basis for consensus

> The mandated negotiations [on Services and Agriculture] are going well. But we must guard against the stock-taking exercise . . . becoming a roadblock. It is also disturbing that over 400 anti-dumping and countervailing investigations were initiated last year, up from only 166 in 1995. It is worrying that, according to the OECD, producer support estimates for agriculture are rising again. It is disappointing that the benefits of eliminating the Multifibre Arrangement are taking so long to be realized. And there is a growing danger that bilateral and plurilateral trade deals, whose huge rise is detailed in my report, could come to be seen as a substitute for multilateral liberalization rather than a complement to it.
>
> Director-General Mike Moore introducing his Annual Report on the trading system, December 2000

The objective of launching comprehensive negotiations was 'postponed' at Seattle; Members expected a further attempt at the Fourth Ministerial in Doha, Qatar, scheduled for November 2001.

The re-engagement of negotiations on agriculture and services, as mandated, posed the question whether agreement to further reforms and liberalization in these sectors could be 'self balancing' within each sector. The 'stock taking' in March 2001 suggested that even if services market access negotiations could achieve this, agriculture was unlikely to be 'self-balancing' because some Members that had high levels of protection for their agricultural markets or used large export subsidies to dispose of surpluses on export markets were more vulnerable to change than others as a result of continued reform. These Members would want to see changes in their agriculture policies matched by changes in the policies of their trading partners in non-agriculture sectors in which they had a trading interest.

There was little prospect of further big steps in agriculture reform except in the context of a 'balanced' comprehensive agreement on trade reforms in a wide range of sectors, including services.

Work to develop a better understanding of the 'Singapore issues' restarted at the point where it had been left before Seattle; but there was little consensus. Working Groups on Competition Policy, Investment and Transparency in Government Procurement established by the Singapore Ministerial held meetings and considered a small number of proposals but, essentially, 'marked time'. Progress there, too, seemed to depend on balancing any new commitments with further progress on matters of priority concern to developing countries, on implementation but also on progress in agriculture and on the elimination of textile and garment quotas.

A new negotiating mandate was needed for the further liberalization of markets for manufactured products, the sector with the biggest potential trade benefit for developing countries. By the end of the 1990s, manufactures comprised four-fifths of developing country exports by value. Average tariffs on manufactures are low in industrialized economies but there are many 'peak' tariffs in the tariff schedules that are concentrated in those product areas of most export interest to developing countries. One World Bank study estimated that barriers to manufacturing exports accounted for around 70% of the total export barriers faced by developing countries and that 75% of the gains from further manufacturing liberalization would go to developing countries. Since the ITA Agreement in 1997, however, there had been no negotiations on the liberalization of markets for manufactured goods.

As the WTO Director-General and senior members of the Secretariat pursued a process of consultations, speeches and information activities in 2001, building awareness of, and public support for, an attempt to launch negotiations at the Fourth Ministerial, some issues began to fall off the agenda for the meeting. It was apparent that there was not sufficiently broad support for negotiations on labour standards and trade; demand for further agreements on e-commerce or an extension of the International Technology Agreement had cooled with the bursting of the dot-com bubble in 2000; there seemed to be little prospect of an extended protocol on the movement of natural persons under GATS or new commitments on Maritime Services.

Agriculture

The Agreement on Agriculture required that the negotiations on continuing the reform programme should begin one year before the end of the implementation period; that is, by the start of 2000. The first phase of these negotiations began in March 2000, comprising a year-long survey of the reforms that had been achieved in each of the 'three pillars' of domestic supports, export competition and market access. Almost all WTO Members (126 countries) were associated with at least one submission during these discussions that were the visible evidence of deeper technical analysis in capitals.

Members analyzed achievements, promise, and shortcomings of the Uruguay Round Agreement during its first five years and made recommendations for further negotiations that would be made more specific in the second phase of the talks beginning in March 2001. These included recommendations on tariff quota administration, tariffs, deprecated ('amber box') forms of domestic supports, export subsidies, export credits, state trading enterprises, export restrictions, food security, food safety, and rural development.

The meetings in the Second Phase were largely 'informal', which meant that the Members' submissions were not official documents of the WTO (they are described as 'non-papers') and remained restricted. The only record of discussions was the summary released by the Special Session Chairman that nominated topics without details. The discussions were intended, however, to allow Members to develop specific proposals and ultimately reach a consensus agreement on changes to rules and commitments in agriculture.

Members were, of course, aware that their Special Session overlapped the proposed November dates for the Fourth Ministerial meeting in Doha so that their focus was on preparing the way for a mandate from ministers that would be much broader than the mandate for the 'continuing negotiations' process in which they were engaged.

Services

The text of the GATS Agreement calls for successive rounds of trade negotiations, the first of which was to start five years after the Agreement entered into force. After some preliminary 'stock-taking', a Special Session of the Services Council approved guidelines for negotiations in March 2001.

The negotiations would take as their starting point the scheduled obligations of Members and seek to improve on them by bilateral and multilateral negotiation. This was broadly in line with the usual GATT procedure of starting from the bound levels when negotiating tariff cuts. But it suffered from the same deficiency as the GATT procedure: it failed to capture actual levels of protection in services markets, which were frequently much less than the scheduled obligations implied, including in sectors where Members had undertaken no market access obligations at all (implying a prohibition of imports).

The Members also decided that no sectors would be withheld from liberalization in principle and that the interests of developing countries – especially the least-developed who were to enjoy 'maximum flexibility' – would be taken in to account in the negotiations.

There was, in effect, no further progress in the negotiations beyond these preliminaries until the comprehensive Round was launched nine months later in Doha.

TRIPS

Members might have forecast more controversy arising from the TRIPS Agreement than actually occurred. The Agreement was out of the ordinary for the WTO – involving the creation of a new legal framework of obligations that are much more specific than those in most WTO agreements – and was controversial because it seemed to favour the interests of exporters (mostly industrialized countries) more than the interests of importers (most developing countries).

But by the 2000 deadline, most obligations had been met with the exception of some new areas of IP administration (such as plant variety protection and integrated circuits) and some in which many developing countries had hitherto not maintained patent protection, such as in pharmaceuticals. The great majority of the disputes arising in TRIPS were between industrialized countries and only two panels were created to adjudicate a complaint against a developing country.

There were only small matters that required further negotiation. Some of these, such as the proposed international register of Geographical Indications (GI) for wines and spirits and the possible extension of GI protection, arose out of 'implementation' debates. Others arose because of changes in the global IP environment such as the relationship between TRIPS and the Convention on Biological Diversity.

The 'Harbinson/Moore' texts

Everyone involved in preparations for the Fourth Ministerial in Doha (2001) wanted to be better prepared than they had been for the Third in Seattle (1999). The Special Sessions of the General Council before Seattle had not been programmed to allow time for a convergence of views before the ministers met and, once at Seattle, the necessity of managing a still too-broad agenda in three days had posed an insurmountable hurdle, especially to small delegations, and contributed to a sense among some Members that decisions were being prepared behind their backs.

The General Council of the WTO under its chairman, Hong Kong China Permanent Representative Stuart Harbinson, began the formal preparations in February 2001, nine months before the Doha meeting, calling on the input of the subsidiary Councils for Goods, Services and TRIPS. By April, the Chairman was circulating a list of items that should figure on the agenda for ministers. These issues became the focus of meetings with senior officials from capitals in June and July 2001 where Director-General and the General Council Chairman identified the many gaps still remaining between Members on each issue, and where they pressed for flexibility.

In June, too, a small group of Members building on the work of the General Council in the implementation mechanism put forward a framework for decisions on the wide range of implementation issues that formed the basis of a Chairman's proposal in mid-July and a first draft Decision on implementation by late September. The suggested Decision split the long list of implementation issues into two parts: the first, a list of issues for decision by the General Council in October for immediate implementation. A second list was to be submitted to ministers for decision in Doha. Eventually, a single list of implementation issues was sent to ministers at Doha with most issues flagged for immediate decision and implementation and some for further negotiation as part of the Doha Development Agenda.

By September, just a month ahead of the Ministerial Conference, the consultations on the agenda had moved to considering cross-cutting issues, rather than single agenda items, in a search for trade-offs and concessions that would narrow the breadth of ministerial debate still further. By the end of the month the Director-General and the General Council Chairman could issue a first draft of a Ministerial Declaration that suggested where the areas of likely agreement would be found, where more ideas were needed (agriculture, TRIPS and public health) and where there were options that required ministers to make a choice. Revised drafts of the Declaration and of a Decision on TRIPS and public health were issued at the end of October, which, the Chairman said represented the farthest that the WTO could take the matters, pending judgements to be made by ministers in Doha.

The techniques employed in the General Council in 2001 had the effect of narrowing the post-Singapore agenda to proportions that could be presented to ministers before they arrived at Doha and that were arranged as priorities for decision.

11

The Doha Ministerial Conference, 2001

In 2001 global production and trade recorded their weakest performance in more than a decade. The fall in IT investment and the run-down of inventories added to the weakening of consumption. As the IT sector had a larger share in international trade (15%) than in global output (5%) trade suffered more as a result of the bursting of the IT 'bubble' than did output. International transaction costs also rose due, in large part, to the fallout from the terrorist attacks of 11 September 2001, which further dented confidence in the growth dividends of globalized markets.

Merchandise trade volumes that contracted 1% in 2001 recovered to 2.5% growth in 2002, but this was less than half of the average levels of the 1990s. Services transactions also picked up again to 5% growth in value terms. But economic growth was unevenly spread; the US economy recovered its recent role as the key engine of global economic demand although its markets were burdened by a series of corporate and accounting scandals – as were European and other markets over the next year or two – when the slump exposed the underside commercial activity during the 'roaring nineties'. China, too, sustained remarkable levels of year-to-year growth, recalling levels achieved by Japan during the 1960s. Japan itself remained in a recession while economic and political turmoil in some of the largest economies in Latin America contributed to a sharp contraction in the trade and capital flows to the region.

Those most vulnerable to the slump in trade-led growth were the poorest. The World Bank estimated the cost of all trade barriers to global income at about US$2.8 trillion and estimated that about 320 million people could have escaped poverty by 2015 had all barriers been abolished. Plausible estimates indicated that removing all subsidies to agriculture in OECD countries alone could return to developing and least-developed countries – the poorest of the poor – three times more than all the overseas development assistance (ODA) they currently received.

WTO Director-General Mike Moore reminded Member governments that achieving such liberalization was within their power and suggested that it had become a moral imperative in light of the IMF/World Bank estimate that reaching all seven of the Millennium Development Goals set by the United Nations would require additional transfers of US$50 billion annually; a sum that would be far less than the increment to income in the rich countries which trade liberalization would generate.

Achieving consensus

At Doha, the process of decision-making was similar to that employed in Seattle: six open-ended groups of heads of delegation were formed to work on the main elements of the draft declaration (Agriculture, Implementation, Trade and Environment, WTO Rules, Singapore issues, TRIPS – to handle the drugs and public health controversy – and Other Issues). But in Doha, the six groups met sequentially so that even small delegations could participate in all of the groups. 'Friends of the Chair' attempted to resolve specific controversies in smaller, open-ended groups that fed back to the main groups. Even so, the final decision was not reached without difficulty. The final session of the heads of delegation took most of the night of 12–13 November 2001 to reach a consensus.

What made the difference? How did Doha achieve what Seattle could not – that is, an agreement on an ambitious mandate for comprehensive negotiations under the 'single undertaking' procedure – and reach it in a relatively short time and with little dissent even from the most outspoken critics of the WTO among civil society organizations? Among the reasons:

- The issues were much better prepared by the 'continuing negotiations' on agriculture and services,
- The list of outstanding implementation questions had been shortened and there was a plan to deal with remaining implementation questions that required negotiation,
- Ministers were well aware of the potential damage to the organization should a second Ministerial Conference end in failure,
- The political environment had changed: there was a strong desire to affirm common interests and signal stability in the global trading system following the sharp downturn in global trade growth and the terrorist attacks weeks earlier in the United States,
- Even greater efforts were made in the lead-up to Doha to include the views of NGOs in the preparatory process and to ensure that NGOs with an interest in trade were kept informed of WTO activities,

- The management skills of the Chairmen of the councils and of the Secretariat and the acquired experience of the Members in understanding and navigating options in the broader and more complex WTO agenda contributed to this hard-won result.

Decision-making in the WTO

The difficult task facing most Chairs in WTO Ministerial Conferences, councils, committees and groups is to find a way through a long list of issues under consideration by a large group of participants with divergent views to a decision that will be subscribed by consensus. Most of the techniques for doing this rely at some point on cutting down the number of 'core' participants in a decision-making step to save time on formal interventions and to reduce the tendency to oppose a measure merely to block progress.

In a consensus-based decision-making process like that of the WTO, and its predecessor the GATT, it is doubly important to make sure that every Member is sufficiently informed about progress on, and sufficiently engaged in, a proposed decision to consider that its views contributed to the final consensus. Otherwise, in the absence of a vote, dissenting Members will have had neither an opportunity to register their disagreement nor an opportunity to barter their acceptance of a less-preferred result against concessions on their priorities elsewhere.

Many Members, particularly developing countries with small WTO delegations, do not have the resources to participate in a number of such 'core' groups simultaneously and are, naturally, sensitive to the risk that they may be excluded from full participation in a consensus on that basis. But each Member has, by definition, the power to hold up a consensus, so the degree to which the use of such consultations speeds up the process of consensus decision-making depends often on the capacity of the least-resourced Members to keep in touch with the decision-making process.

There have been many different attempts to overcome these procedural problems by adding a 'transparency' step to the consultation process. For example small-group consultations by the chairman of a group and the Secretariat would be followed at intervals by reports from the chairman to a plenary meeting of his 'summary understanding' of the views of Members that could then be debated and decided among the full group of Members. The GATT's CG-18 ('Consultative Group of 18') and the Director-General's 'green room' consultations used this format as do several of the most active negotiating groups in the Doha Development Agenda negotiations.

Informal 'groups' of Members such as the G-20 or the G-10 on agricultural issues can provide an important sounding board for a committee chair. These groups are formed to advocate common approaches to a topic under negotiation; their views can often be conveyed to the chair in one consultation. Also, partners in some regional trade agreements tend to coordinate their positions, so the group's internal processes can supplement the 'transparency' reporting by committee chairs for a member of the EC or ASEAN, for example.

Another technique currently being used in the Doha Development Agenda negotiations involves 'scaling' a meeting so that a 'first reading' of Members views or of a proposal is held at a plenary level. A 'second' reading may then be held among a smaller, self-selected but still open-ended sub-set of those Members most interested in the issue. If necessary, a third meeting could take place among a group selected by the chairman which will try to broker a decision among those with the most strongly-held or influential positions. This decision will then be brought back to a plenary meeting for discussion and adoption.

Other variations exist. But none is guaranteed to minimize procedural delay while maximising transparency of decision-making for all Members. Any technique runs the risk of taking just as long and being just as contentious as the 'traditional' practice of debating an issue to exhaustion in a plenary meeting.

The 'Development' Round

> It is no secret that our aim is to come away from Doha with a mandate to start broad trade negotiations. The economic argument is strong. Already current trade rules permit world trade in goods and services to be successfully conducted at the rate of close to US$1 billion per hour every hour of every day. If we cut by a third remaining barriers to trade in agriculture, manufacturing and services, this would boost the world economy by $613 billion, according to one study from Michigan University. That is equivalent to adding an economy the size of Canada to the world economy . . . The development argument is equally compelling. Notwithstanding the advances in living standards over the last 50 years, 1.2 billion people are still living on less than $1 a day. Another 1.6 billion are living on less than $2 a day . . . Poor countries need to grow their way out of poverty. Trade is a key engine for growth but currently products of developing countries face many obstacles in entering the markets of rich

countries including high tariffs, mainly in agriculture, textiles, clothing and leather.

Director-General Mike Moore at Winconference, Interlaken, Switzerland, July 2001

The Doha Declaration

The 52 detailed paragraphs of the Doha Ministerial Declaration[1] encompass a broad and ambitious work program, organized as a 'single undertaking' that ministers decided should be concluded within four years (by 1 January, 2005). It was the first comprehensive negotiating mandate in the global trading system since 1986: a fifteen-year gap.

Implementation-related issues and concerns

Ministers agreed to adopt around 50 Decisions that had been prepared by the intensive work in the General Council in preparation for the Ministerial Conference. These Decisions clarified the obligations of developing country Members on matters including agriculture, subsidies, textiles and clothing, technical barriers to trade, trade-related investment measures and rules of origin.

Other implementation issues of concern to developing countries had been included in the work programme. Issues for which there was an agreed negotiating mandate in the Declaration – for example on a registration system for Geographical Indications – would be dealt with under the terms of that mandate. Implementation issues without a mandate to negotiate would be taken up as 'a matter of priority' by relevant WTO councils and committees. These bodies were to report on their progress to the Trade Negotiations Committee by the end of 2002 for 'appropriate action'.

Agriculture

Negotiations begun in early 2000 were continued, within the new 'single undertaking' mandate given by the Doha Declaration, which also included a series of deadlines.

The Declaration reconfirms the long-term objective already agreed in the WTO Agreement: to establish a fair and market-oriented trading

---

[1] WTO document WT/MIN(01)/DEC/1.

system through a programme of fundamental reform. Member governments committed themselves to comprehensive negotiations aimed at substantial reductions in market access barriers, 'reductions of, with a view to phasing out' all forms of export subsidies and substantial reductions in production supports that distort trade.

The declaration makes special and differential treatment for developing countries integral throughout the agriculture negotiations, both in countries' new commitments and in any relevant new or revised rules and disciplines. It says the outcome should be effective in practice and should enable developing countries to meet their needs, especially in food security and rural development.

Services

Negotiations on services had been re-launched almost two years before the adoption of the Doha Agenda. The Doha Declaration noted the large number of proposals submitted by Members on a wide range of sectors and several horizontal issues, as well as on movement of natural persons, endorsed the modest progress that had been made in the Special Session of the GATS Council on this Agenda and established a new timetable for the conclusion of the negotiations as part of a single undertaking, including the submission of requests and initial offers before the Fifth Ministerial meeting in Cancún.

Market access for non-agricultural products

The ministers agreed to launch tariff-cutting negotiations on all non-agricultural products. The aim was 'to reduce, or as appropriate eliminate tariffs, including the reduction or elimination of tariff peaks, high tariffs, and tariff escalation, as well as non-tariff barriers, on products of export interest to developing countries'.

There is no fixed procedure ('modality') for tariff-cutting in the WTO: in the Tokyo Round, the participants used an agreed mathematical formula to cut tariffs across the board; in the Uruguay Round, participants negotiated cuts product by product. The Doha Declaration required participants to first agree on the procedures and to undertake studies and capacity-building measures that would help least-developed countries participate effectively in the negotiations, before the Fifth Ministerial Conference in Cancún (2003).

Trade-related aspects of intellectual property rights (TRIPS)

Ministers issued a separate declaration on TRIPS and public health designed to respond to concerns about the possible implications of the TRIPS Agreement for access to medicines. They stressed it is important to implement and interpret the TRIPS Agreement in a way that supports public health – by promoting access to existing medicines and the creation of new medicines – and that the TRIPS Agreement does not and should not prevent Member governments from acting to protect public health.

Ministers affirmed governments' right to use the agreement's flexibility such as compulsory licensing and parallel importing and set the TRIPS Council two specific tasks: to find a solution to the problems countries may face in making use of compulsory licensing if they have too little or no pharmaceutical manufacturing capacity and to extend the deadline for least-developed countries to apply provisions on pharmaceutical patents until 1 January 2016.

The Declaration set the Fifth Ministerial Conference as the deadline for completing negotiations on a multilateral register of Geographical Indications (GIs) for wines and spirits and noted that the TRIPS Council would handle the matter of launching negotiations on an extension of the additional protection given to GIs for wines and spirits to other products. This issue was sent back to the TRIPS Council for further work because no consensus was reached on whether there was an existing mandate to negotiate on this extension.

The Declaration also says that the TRIPS Council should examine the relationship between the TRIPS Agreement and the UN Convention on Biodiversity, and the protection of traditional knowledge and folklore.

The 'Singapore issues'

The Doha Declaration did not launch negotiations immediately on any of the Singapore issues (i.e. WTO Members at the Singapore Ministerial added these issues to the work program: trade and investment, trade and competition policy, trade facilitation and transparency in government procurement). It states 'negotiations will take place after the Fifth Session of the Ministerial Conference on the basis of a decision to be taken, by explicit consensus at that session, on modalities of negotiations'.

The Declaration instructed the committees and working groups that had been working on these issues since 1997 to continue detailed preparatory work in the period up to the 2003 Ministerial Conference. This work should identify the specific matters to be considered including the interests of developing countries and the ways in which future agreements might be constructed.

WTO rules: anti-dumping and subsidies

The ministers agreed to negotiations on the Anti-dumping (GATT Article VI) and the Subsidies and Countervailing Measures Agreements. The aim was to clarify and improve disciplines while preserving the basic concepts, principles and effectiveness of these Agreements, and taking into account the needs of developing and least-developed participants. Participants in the negotiations would indicate which provisions of these two Agreements they want clarified and improved, but the Ministers mentioned specifically fisheries subsidies, a subject of special interest to a number of developing countries.

WTO rules: regional trade agreements

The Declaration mandated negotiations aimed at 'clarifying and improving disciplines and procedures under the existing WTO provisions applying to regional trade agreements. The negotiations were to be concluded within the general timetable for the negotiations; that is, by 1 January 2005.

Dispute Settlement Understanding

The Declaration instructs negotiators to complete the review that ministers called for in Marrakesh, but which had stalled in 1998–99, by May 2003. The early deadline meant that negotiations on the Dispute Settlement Understanding would not be part of the single undertaking – i.e. that they would not be tied to the overall success or failure of the other negotiations mandated by the Declaration.

Trade and environment

The Declaration mandated both new negotiations on this long-standing topic of the WTO/GATT agenda and an initiative on regular information exchange between secretariats of multilateral environmental agreements and the WTO.

Ministers agreed to launch negotiations on the relationship between existing WTO rules and specific trade obligations set out in the 200 or so multilateral environmental agreements (MEAs) that are in force. Although only 20 of these contain trade provisions, some Members expressed concern that there could be a conflict between their WTO obligations and the trade provisions of the MEAs – including, possibly, sanctions mandated by an MEA. Negotiations then address how WTO rules apply to WTO Members that are parties to environmental agreements.

Ministers also agreed to negotiations on the reduction or elimination of tariff and non-tariff barriers to environmental goods and services and to clarify and improve WTO rules that apply to fisheries subsidies. The issue of fisheries subsidies has been studied in the Trade and Environment Committee for several years. Some studies demonstrate these subsidies can be environmentally damaging if they lead to overfishing.

Least-developed countries

In the Doha Declaration, WTO Members commit themselves to the objective of duty-free, quota-free market access for LDC exports and to consider additional measures to improve market access for these products.

Special and differential treatment

The WTO agreements contain special provisions that give developing countries special rights. These special provisions include, for example, longer time periods for implementing agreements and commitments or measures to increase trading opportunities for developing countries.

In the Doha Declaration, Member governments agree that all special and differential treatment provisions in the WTO agreements should be reviewed with a view to strengthening and making them more precise.

The Declaration and the Decision on Implementation-Related Issues and Concerns mandate the Committee on Trade and Development to identify which of those special and differential treatment provisions are mandatory, and to consider the implications of making mandatory those which are currently non-binding.

Other issues

The Declaration also broadens the WTO's regular work program by including, continuing or expanding work on electronic commerce, small economies, debt and finance, technology transfer and technical cooperation and capacity building (Members decided to significantly expand the 'core budget' for these activities immediately after the Ministerial meeting in December 2001).

Accession of China and Chinese Taipei

China and Chinese Taipei finally acceded to the WTO during the Doha meeting, following Lithuania and Moldova who joined earlier in 2001.

In the long run, China's membership could be the most enduring legacy of the Doha Ministerial Conference because China committed, as part of its Accession Protocol to implement far-reaching legal and domestic policy reforms that guaranteed new economic opportunities for its own 1.5 billion citizens, as well as for the other three-fourths of the world's population.

For other WTO Members, China's membership will cement and accelerate the benefits of the liberalization undertaken in China over the last 20 years. After implementing its commitments, China's average bound-tariff level will fall to 15% for agricultural products, and to 8.9% for industrial goods. In Chinese Taipei, tariffs will fall an average of just over 4% for industrial goods and to an average of just under 13% for agricultural items.

NGOs at Doha

Almost as many NGOs were registered to attend Doha as had been present in Seattle. The WTO offered credentials for the conference to 647 NGO organizations (there were 686 represented two years earlier) although only 365 actually attended, due in part to the security situation following the September 11 terrorist attacks. NGOs were offered office and workshop facilities for conferences including press conferences in an NGO centre adjacent to the main conference centre. They were briefed daily by senior WTO officials, and by some ministers on progress in the discussions.

In the months leading to the Conference, the WTO organized presentations by selected NGOs to Members in Geneva, held briefings and workshops with NGOs, established a public discussions forum (still in place) on its website for organized and self-initiated discussion, circulated NGO views and papers to Members and published a monthly bulletin on NGO/WTO contacts and events of interest to NGOs.

LANDMARK DISPUTE CASES

United States – Anti-dumping Act of 1916

Members can challenge the validity of an anti-dumping law without reference to a specific case.

The European Communities and Japan complained that the United States Anti-dumping Act of 1916 ('1916 Act') civil actions and even criminal proceedings to be brought against importers who have sold foreign-produced goods in the United States at prices which are 'substantially less' than the prices at which the same products are sold in a relevant foreign market. The complaining countries argued that the 1916 Act authorized remedies for 'dumping' other than the imposition of anti-dumping duties, and did not respect the procedural requirements or the injury test set out in the relevant provisions of the Anti-Dumping Agreement. The Panel found that the 1916 Act violated certain anti-dumping provisions of the GATT 1994, as well as certain provisions of the AD Agreement. The Appellate Body agreed and said that it did not accept the United States' argument that Members may not challenge the consistency of legislation with the AD Agreement without reference to a dispute under a specific anti-dumping case.

United States Copyright Act

A copyright abuse finding against the United States

The European Communities complained that Section 110(5) of the US Copyright Act permits bars, shops, restaurants, etc to play radio and television music in public places without the payment of a royalty fee. The European Communities considered that this statute is inconsistent with United States obligations under Article 9(1) of the TRIPS Agreement, which requires Members to comply with Articles 1 to 21 of the Berne Convention. The so-called 'business' exemption in the US Copyright Act allowed the amplification of music broadcasts, without an authorization and a payment of a fee, by food service and drinking establishments and by retail establishments, provided that their size does not exceed a certain square footage limit. The so-called 'homestyle' exemption allows small restaurants and retail outlets to amplify music broadcasts without an authorization of the right holders and without the payment of a fee, provided that they use only homestyle equipment (i.e. equipment of a kind commonly used in private homes). The Panel found that the 'business' exemption was inconsistent with the Berne Convention (1971) on Copyright as incorporated into the TRIPS Agreement by Article 9.1 of that Agreement. The Panel noted, inter alia, that a substantial majority of eating and drinking establishments and close to half of retail establishments were covered by the business exemption. The Panel found, however, that the 'homestyle' exemption met the requirements of Article 13 of the TRIPS Agreement and was thus consistent with the Berne Convention (1971) as incorporated into the TRIPS Agreement.

European Communities – Measures affecting asbestos products

When is a dangerous product 'like' an innocuous substitute: the Appellate Body offers and then declines to consider amicus curiae submissions from non-Members on this topic. The Appellate Body establishes procedural rules for the application for authorization to submit an amicus curiae brief, and substantive rules for the authorized brief itself. No authorization to submit a brief was granted.

A French government Decree of 24 December 1996 imposed prohibitions on the manufacture, processing, sale, import, etc. of asbestos and products containing asbestos. Canada claimed that this Decree violated a number of WTO provisions because – among other reasons – the restrictions banned the import of one type of asbestos, namely chrysotile (or white) asbestos and products containing chrysotile. The Panel examined, and upheld, Canada's claim that the measure was inconsistent with Article III of the GATT 1994, which prohibits WTO Members from treating imported products 'less favourably' than 'like' domestic products. The Panel concluded that chrysotile asbestos fibres are 'like' polyvinyl alcohol, cellulose and glass fibres ('PCG fibres') and, also, that cement-based products containing chrysotile asbestos fibres are 'like' cement-based products containing PCG fibres. However, since chrysotile asbestos is carcinogenic, the Panel found that the French ban was justified by the exception provided in Article XX(b) of the GATT 1994 for actions 'necessary to protect human . . . life or health'. The Appellate Body agreed that Canada had not shown that the French Decree was inconsistent with its obligations under the WTO agreements. But it reversed the Panel's findings with respect to 'like products'; chrysotile asbestos was not 'like' the other substitute products because of the health risks associated with asbestos. The health risks were relevant to 'likeness', so the Appellate Body reversed the Panel's conclusion that the measure was inconsistent with Article III of the GATT 1994. The Appellate Body itself examined Canada's claims under Article III of the GATT 1994 and ruled that Canada had not satisfied its burden of proving the existence of 'like products' under that provision. Finally, the Appellate Body upheld the Panel's conclusion, under Article XX(b) of the GATT 1994, that the French Decree was 'necessary to protect human . . . life or health'. In this appeal, the Appellate Body adopted an additional procedure 'for the purposes of this appeal only' to deal with amicus curiae submissions. The Appellate Body received 17 applications to file such a submission. All these applications were rejected. It also refused to accept 14 unsolicited submissions from non-governmental organizations that were not submitted under the additional procedure.

United States – Transitional safeguard measure on combed cotton yarn

A developing country exporter uses the Disputes system to enforce its rights under the Agreement on Textiles and Clothing

The United States had notified the Textiles Monitory Body (TMB) on 5 March 1999 that it had decided to unilaterally impose a 'transitional safeguard' quota on imports of combed cotton yarn, after consultations as to whether the situation called for a restraint had failed to produce a mutually satisfactory solution. In April 1999, the TMB examined the United States restraint pursuant to Article 6.10 of the ATC and recommended that the United States restraint should be rescinded but the USA declined to do so, despite repeated recommendations from the TMB. Pakistan sought a Panel to resolve the dispute and, in May 2001, the Panel concluded that the transitional safeguard (quantitative restriction) imposed by the United States was inconsistent with the provisions of Article 6 of the ATC. The Appellate Body subsequently upheld the Panel's overall conclusion that the transitional safeguard measure taken by the United States with respect to imports of combed cotton yarn ('yarn') from Pakistan was inconsistent with the ATC because the United States had failed to define properly the relevant 'domestic industry' producing yarn; and had failed to examine the effect of imports of yarn from other major suppliers (e.g. Mexico) when attributing serious damage to imports from Pakistan.

12

Pursuing the Doha Mandate, 2001–2003

The Doha Declaration set out the deadlines in this way:

- Deadline for clarifying flexibility in the TRIPS rules: December 2002
- Deadline for Dispute Settlement Understanding negotiations: May 2003
- Deadline for negotiations on registration system for geographical indications: 5th Ministerial Conference in 2003 (in Cancún)
- Stock taking: 5th Ministerial Conference in 2003 (in Cancún)
- Deadline for other negotiations: by 1 January 2005 as single undertaking.

None of these deadlines has been met for reasons that will be the focus of the next chapters. The only decision taken was the Decision on TRIPS and drugs, which was finally agreed at the end of August 2003. There has been no 'stocktaking' decision, although as the result of a failure to reach decisions at the Fifth Ministerial Conference, Members have narrowed the focus of debates on possible modalities (adopted in a Framework agreement in July 2004).

The WTO adopted several decision-making tracks arising from the Doha mandate.

TRIPS and public health

A decision on Drugs and Public Health was on the fastest track emerging from Doha. The draft that had already been prepared in the General Council before Doha helped to ensure agreement on a firm statement of ministers' intentions.

> The TRIPS Agreement does not and should not prevent Members from taking measures to protect public health. Accordingly, while reiterating our commitment to the TRIPS Agreement, we affirm that the Agreement can and should be interpreted and implemented in a manner supportive of WTO Members' right to protect public health and to promote access to

medicines for all. In this connection, we reaffirm the right of WTO Members to use, to the full, the provisions in the TRIPS Agreement, which provide flexibility for this purpose.

From Article 4, Declaration on TRIPS and public health, 14 November 2001

Ministers said that each government retained the right to determine for itself the grounds for compulsory licensing of a patent within its territory and the basis on which patent rights would be 'exhausted', subject to non-discrimination and the national-treatment principles of the TRIPS agreement. Ministers instructed the TRIPS Council to find, before the end of 2002, a way to resolve the dilemma facing developing countries without manufacturing capacity who, under a strict construction of the TRIPS provisions, did not have the right to designate a compulsory licensee in another country to undertake manufacturing..

The Ministers' statement demonstrated their political will to cut any legal 'red tape' holding up a humanitarian response to public health emergencies. Had that been all that was required the matter would have been quickly resolved. But legitimate private rights were also at stake in this decision and were not so easily set aside. Widespread use of this flexibility in TRIPS over extended periods of time or in non-emergency situations would defeat the market segmentation and price discrimination among markets that the territorial basis of IP rights enables. These practices by the drugs companies – and by many other global firms – are difficult to defend from attack on equity grounds where a humanitarian need is identified. But in most commercial contexts they are not only legitimate business practices, they are also essential for commercial success. In many global industries – from automobiles to publishing, retailing and tourism – firms use such segmentation and price-discrimination in different markets as a matter of course. The question faced in this case was about the degree to which governments should secure, through the TRIPS rules, an opportunity for private firms to engage in price-discrimination. The companies and some Members feared that the principles of global patent protection in pharmaceutical markets could unravel if 'flexibility' became the general rule rather than the exception and could lead to large-scale exports of 'exceptionally sourced' drugs in competition with drugs sourced from fully licensed manufacturers.

The President of the Federation of Pharmaceutical Manufacturers Associations argued, for example, that it would be a 'gross exaggeration and a gross distortion' to give more advanced countries such as India and China the same rights as 'poor states like Haiti, Namibia or Bangladesh'.

The Ministers' statement affirmed the good will of Members, but it left the more difficult issue for the WTO to sort out over the next 12 months.

A new Director-General

On 1 September 2002, less than a year after Doha, Dr Supachai Panitchpakdi succeeded Mr Mike Moore as Director-General of the WTO. Dr Supachai emphasized his commitment to reaching a successful conclusion to the Doha Development Agenda by the mandated deadline of 1 January 2005. He also outlined four pillars which would be core priorities during his tenure: further strengthening the WTO's legal framework; developing a long-term strategy for technical assistance and capacity building; promoting greater coherence in international economic policy-making between the WTO and other international agencies; and strengthening the WTO as an institution, and as a Secretariat.

In one of this first speeches as head of the WTO he focused on the stakes for the Doha Round:

> There is great expectation about the results of these negotiations and for good reason. The World Bank's Global Economic Prospects 2002, estimates that abolishing all trade barriers could boost global income over a ten year period by US$2.8 trillion. Of this, developing countries stand to reap more than half of these gains and an additional reduction in global poverty of 320 million people by 2015. These are rough estimates, but they provide us with a clear indication; freer trade, accompanied by appropriate domestic macroeconomic policies and a sound legal framework, is vital in helping poor countries grow their way out of poverty and move on to the path of sustainable development.

Breaking the TRIPS deadlock

WTO Members broke their deadlock over this issue by an agreement in the General Council on 30 August, 2003 in Geneva. Director-General Supachai welcomed the agreement with these words:

> This is a historic agreement for the WTO . . . The final piece of the jigsaw has fallen into place, allowing poorer countries to make full use of the flexibilities in the WTO's intellectual property rules in order to deal with the diseases that ravage their people.

The Decision[1] of the General Council waives the TRIPS Agreement restrictions on the export of drugs manufactured under compulsory licenses to the extent necessary to enable the exporting Member to meet the (emergency) public health requirements of the importing Member. There are a number of conditions in the decision intended to ensure that the waiver is used appropriately. Regional agreements comprising mostly least-developed countries are enabled to use this flexibility regionally to increase economies of scale so as to obtain a better price for the drugs. Members are not required to seek advance authorization, as is the usual waiver procedure, but only to notify their intentions to use the export or import side of this waiver. A page has been created on the WTO website to record such notifications to ensure transparency. As the 10th anniversary of the WTO approaches, there have been no notifications from either importing or exporting countries.

Special and differential treatment

A second decision-making track was established by the Doha Decision on Implementation-Related Issues and Concerns which required, among other things, the Committee on Trade and Development (CTD) to 'consider the legal and practical implications for developed and developing Members of converting special and differential treatment measures into mandatory provisions ... and to report to the General Council with clear recommendations for a decision by July 2002'. The General Council later extended the deadline to December 2002 and again to February 2003.

Taken at face value, the decision to consider making S&D mandatory – that is, obliging discrimination in favour of the majority of WTO Members as one of the pillars of the 'non-discriminatory' trading system – was one of the most fundamental, even revolutionary, proposals made by the ministers. It would have required Members to rewrite the WTO agreements including for example Part IV of the GATT that in 1965 established the principle – but not an obligation – of less than complete reciprocity for developing countries.

The project turned out to be unfeasible. Fourteen formal meetings and a large number of informal meetings took place during 2002 on both cross-cutting and agreement-specific proposals on this mandate. Many

---

[1] WTO document WT/L/540: Decision on implementation of paragraph 6 of the Doha Declaration on the TRIPS aspects of public health.

implied, to some extent, a change in the balance of rights and obligations under the agreements or implied new obligations that went beyond the provisions of the Doha mandate. Work intensified as the initial deadline for the recommendation to the General Council passed with a number of 'back-to-back' Special Sessions of the CTD.

But Members were unable to reach agreement on the large number of proposals (88 agreement-specific proposals alone) even with a second extension in the deadline. The General Council suspended the work of the CTD special session and the Chairman appointed 'friends of the Chair' to attempt to broker a recommendation to ministers at the Cancún Ministerial. After protracted consultations Members were able to agree on recommendations for specific action on 26 agreement-specific proposals. These recommendations were attached to the draft texts of decisions for ministers at Cancún but, like other decisions prepared for that meeting, were not adopted. As a result of their decision in December 2003 to focus on achieving progress on a restricted range of subjects, the Members did not revert to these recommendations in 2004 and, to date, the recommendations remain inactive.

Dispute settlement

A third track from Doha (2001) to Cancún (2003) detoured via the incomplete Review of the Understanding on Dispute Settlement that had first been mandated in Marrakesh (1994) for completion before Seattle (1999), but was still not complete by the time of Doha. The Ministers had called for agreement, outside the single understanding, to be reached in the Dispute Settlement Body by May 2003. When, by July 2003 as the Cancún meeting dates approached, it was clear agreement was still not in prospect the General Council postponed the deadline yet again to May 2004.

One matter of contention concerns implementation of the DSB's recommendations and rulings following the adoption of a panel and/or Appellate Body report. Although Members have either complied with or expressed their intention to comply with every recommendation and ruling, compliance has still not occurred in several cases and in other cases has only occurred after lengthy delays. Developing countries have complained, too, that it has been difficult for them, in certain circumstances, to ensure compliance with DSB recommendations on the part of larger trading partners given that developing countries have little economic leverage that they can apply in such cases (even where retaliation has been authorized by the DSB).

The centre ring

All other negotiations mandated by Doha followed a fourth track which saw 2002 given over mostly to producing – or in agriculture and services, refining – proposals in response to the Doha mandate. The goal was to produce first drafts of modalities prepared in each of the negotiating groups by the second quarter of 2003.

The idea was that these draft decisions would be further refined around mid-2003 in the Trade Negotiations Committee (TNC), the oversight body created to manage the flow of work in the negotiations separately from the day-to-day workflow of the WTO. They would then be presented to Ministers at the Fifth Ministerial meeting (Cancún) in September 2003, either for decisions on 'modalities' or for 'stock taking' as required by the different subject mandates.

The Director-General, in ex officio capacity, was appointed Chairman of the Trade Negotiations Committee, and negotiating groups were set up as subsidiaries of the TNC. Members were able to move swiftly into an intensive phase of substantial work in all areas of the Doha Work Programme.

Deadlines were short, but as none of the issues was new to the WTO, there was confidence that they could be achieved. Some of the issues had been on the WTO's table since at least Singapore (i.e. the 'Singapore issues', trade and environment, electronic commerce), most of the others since Marrakesh (i.e. agriculture, services, TRIPS-GI's, action in favour of least-developed), and at least one was the perennial subject of multilateral negotiations, Non- Agricultural Market Access (NAMA).

There was no shortage of preparatory work on which negotiators could call. On complex subjects such as agriculture, tens of thousands of pages of proposals and analysis produced by the pre-Doha negotiating phase (not to mention parallel work in the World Bank, the OECD, the FAO, in regional development banks, from government and private research organizations and from the NGOs). On cross-cutting topics such as market access, the Secretariat had produced detailed analysis and research, in its ground-breaking study 'Market Access: Unfinished Business' and again in a comprehensive discussion paper 'Industrial Tariffs and the Doha Development Agenda' issued in May 2003. In services, too, there had been extensive reviews of the GATS Agreement, of its annexes and of potential extensions of the Agreement in the Services Council and its subsidiary bodies since 1995 with almost two years of pre-Doha experience of negotiations on the extension of GATS and the Members' schedules.

In 2002 and 2003 Members made a number of efforts to give discussions on difficult matters greater political guidance in ministerial meetings held outside Geneva. Between November 2002 and August 2003, a score of ministerial gatherings that were designed either to move the process forward or to provide an opportunity for consultations that would help do so took place. Four so-called 'mini-ministerial' meetings involving groups of ministers invited by the host country were convened in Sydney (November, 2002), Tokyo (February, 2003), Sharm el-Sheikh (June, 2003) and Montreal (July, 2003). In addition, ministerial level meetings of international organizations and regional groups – such as the G8, the OECD, the World Bank and IMF, APEC, ASEAN, the Commonwealth of Nations, the governments involved in the FTAA negotiations, the African Union and the Second LDC Trade Ministers' conference and the ACP Trade Ministers' Conference – devoted items on their agenda or in the margins of their regular program in 2003 to the Doha mandate.

In Geneva, the plan for managing negotiations emulated the successful recipe followed after Seattle. A year of expanded discussion on Members' proposals (February 2002 – March 2003) was followed by an ever-more-intense process designed to reduce the broader exchanges to potential decisions in the negotiating committees (Agriculture, NAMA, Services, TRIPS etc) followed by an attempt to extract consensus recommendations to ministers usually on the basis of a draft text proposed by the Chair of the discussions on his own responsibility.

THE SIGNIFICANCE OF AGRICULTURE

The negotiations on Agriculture were potentially the most contentious and the most significant for the largest number of WTO Members. The chairman of the Agriculture Negotiating Group (the former Chair of the General Council) Stuart Harbinson, prepared a first draft of the modalities decision required by the Doha mandate in February 2003. Following comments from participants, this was revised in March, but Mr Harbinson noted that negotiators had tended to stick to their starting positions and had given him little guidance on how to narrow the wide gaps between them.

In May 2003 Director-General Supachai Panitchpakdi as ex-officio chair of the Trade Negotiations Committee felt obliged to remind heads of delegations and ministers at the World Bank/IMF meetings that there was a danger that missed deadlines would merely postpone 'gridlock' to the Cancún meeting.

Dr Supachai was careful to point out that this ninth round of negotiations was more difficult than earlier GATT rounds, with important extenuating circumstances for delays. First, these negotiations had produced full engagement from almost all Members, developed and developing alike, including in services negotiations. Second, the proposals were more ambitious than they had been in the past: for example the possible elimination of export subsidies on agricultural products and proposals aimed at achieving zero tariffs on industrial products. Third, a comprehensive round deals not only with market access negotiations – as the GATT rounds had done – but also with negotiations on trade rules, subsidy rules, trade remedy rules, countervailing duty rules, and also the new rules foreshadowed at Singapore.

Dr Supachai also drew attention to the WTO's good record in trade-related technical assistance; by mid-2003 all the programs that Members had mandated were on track with expanded resources. The WTO was delivering more than 400 technical assistance activities each year to developing countries.

Between May and August, 2003, Director-General Supachai Panitchpakdi and the General Council Chairman, Ambassador Perez del Castillo, of Uruguay, employed the techniques that had been used leading up to Doha to 'crunch' agreement on a draft text of decisions for ministers, bearing in mind the lesson of Seattle that without a set of draft decisions at a fairly advanced stage there was little prospect that ministers would be able to reach agreement within three or four days.

A revised draft ministerial text was discussed at length over several days at the General Council meeting in August and subsequently forwarded under the Chairman's own responsibility to the Fifth Ministerial Conference (Cancún). The text had a number of weaknesses, however, that were tested to breaking point in the Ministerial Conference.

The Cancún Ministerial Conference, 2003

Once again, as in Seattle and Doha, the meeting began with the designation of 'facilitators' to conduct consultations in five groups on the main issues (agriculture, Singapore issues, NAMA, Development issues, other issues) plus an additional consultation group on the cotton initiative. The groups were to operate in parallel (rather than sequentially as at Doha) and to report to an open-ended Heads of Delegation meeting. For three days the consultations attempted to bridge some significant differences that remained between Members.

Probably the most obvious differences were those on agriculture. Because Members had not 'picked up' the draft texts brokered by the Committee Chairman, Stuart Harbinson, the United States and the European Communities, jointly put forward a 'draft' text in July that they considered could be the basis for a Ministerial Declaration. It was incorporated in Ambassador Perez del Castillo's draft for Ministers but even as the Ministerial Conference convened, an emergent group of developing countries (the G-20) including some of the largest and most influential WTO Members, rejected the draft.

A revised draft text of a decision – which included further progress on agriculture, although much less on NAMA or other issues – was put to the heads of delegation on the third day by the Conference Chairman, Mexican Foreign Minister, Luis Ernesto Derbez. But in the heads of delegation meeting one developing country minister after another criticized the draft for lack of progress on the Cotton initiative and referred to still stronger concerns about the suggestions for a consensus decision launching negotiations on the Singapore issues.

The Singapore issues had been discussed in dedicated working groups in the lead-up to the August General Council meeting. But the groups had held just two meetings each in 2003. The 'Castillo' draft text for a decision by Ministers contained options to begin negotiations on each of the issues on the basis of separate (annexed) provisions with different degrees of detailed direction or to continue the process of consultation. It was apparent even before the Ministerial, however, that there was no consensus on launching negotiations. In August, a statement[2] circulated on behalf of a number of African countries (Benin, Botswana, Kenya, Mauritius, Nigeria, Senegal, Sierra Leone, Tanzania, Uganda, Zambia, and Zimbabwe) calling for work to continue on clarifying the issues rather than launching new negotiations. Then, in the days immediately before the Ministerial Conference a still wider group of Least-Developed, African, Asian and Latin American countries had objected to the annexes on the Singapore issues.

> Annexes D, E, F and G to the Draft Ministerial text, that reflect the view of proponents on the modalities, give a distorted view, that the Annexes have been discussed by Members. It would be recalled that the text on transparency in government procurement was introduced by the proponents in

[2] WTO document WT/GC/W/510.

a small group meeting. We are not aware of any text having been put forward by the proponents on trade facilitation. The text on competition policy was discussed only in a small group meeting. Only the proponents' paper on investment was introduced and discussed inconclusively in the HOD level meeting. Thus, Members did not have an opportunity to discuss the modalities identified by the proponents in all the Annexes to the Draft Ministerial text.

WTO document WT/MIN(03)/W/4

Attempts at the Ministerial itself to broker a consensus agreement between the proponents of the 'Singapore issues' negotiations, especially the EC, and a large number of developing countries including the African, Caribbean and Pacific (ACP) group failed. A last minute gesture from the EC attempted to create a consensus on further negotiations by offering to abridge the agenda for the Singapore issues. But it appeared that the 'explicit consensus' required for further negotiations was out of reach. On the fifth day, the Conference Chairman decided that the meeting no longer had time to complete its agenda and brought it to a conclusion without deciding any of the issues in the draft negotiating text.

13

The aftermath of Cancún, 2003–2005

As we conclude our Fifth Ministerial Conference in Cancún, we would like to express our deep appreciation to the Government and people of Mexico for the excellent organization and warm hospitality we have received in Cancún.

At this meeting we have welcomed Cambodia and Nepal as the first least-developed countries to accede to the WTO since its establishment.

All participants have worked hard and constructively to make progress as required under the Doha mandates. We have, indeed, made considerable progress. However, more work needs to be done in some key areas to enable us to proceed towards the conclusion of the negotiations in fulfilment of the commitments we took at Doha.

We therefore instruct our officials to continue working on outstanding issues with a renewed sense of urgency and purpose and taking fully into account all the views we have expressed in this Conference. We ask the Chairman of the General Council, working in close co-operation with the Director-General, to coordinate this work and to convene a meeting of the General Council at Senior Officials level no later than 15 December 2003 to take the action necessary at that stage to enable us to move towards a successful and timely conclusion of the negotiations. We shall continue to exercise close personal supervision of this process.

We will bring with us into this new phase all the valuable work that has been done at this Conference. In those areas where we have reached a high level of convergence on texts, we undertake to maintain this convergence while working for an acceptable overall outcome.

Notwithstanding this setback, we reaffirm all our Doha Declarations and Decisions and recommit ourselves to working to implement them fully and faithfully.

Ministerial statement, Cancún, 14 September 2003

As their predecessors had done after Seattle, the Chairman of the General Council, Ambassador Carlos Perez del Castillo and Director-General Supachai Panitchpakdi attempted to keep the position reached in the

Ministerial Conference prior to the suspension of talks on 'life support'. Despite the criticism levelled at the text on the night of 14 September, it seemed from early consultation in capitals that many Members might have been prepared to keep the Conference Chairman's latest text (the 'Derbez text') before them as the basis for resuming talks and, potentially, reaching agreements.

But there were deeper problems that prevented early re-engagement. For many Members, the disappointment was sharper than it had been at Seattle when the Ministerial Conference had last ended without agreement. The stakes had been higher in Cancún because Members were no longer on the threshold of a Round; they were supposedly halfway through negotiations that they promised would finish in January 2005. Their chagrin showed in the recriminations that followed: the US Trade Representative Robert Zoellick spoke of pursuing bilateral deals and not having to 'wait for the won't-do countries'. The EC's Trade Commissioner Pascal Lamy, who had taken a lot of the heat of the debates over the Singapore issues at Cancún thought that more time was needed to reflect on the meaning of the setback and on what it said about the WTO's agenda, its processes and its objectives.

Some developing country observers and NGOs claimed that the result was a slap in the face for the industrialized countries that had championed the Singapore issues. Others expressed the view that the stalemate was a setback for developing countries.

At Cancún, Members had been conscious of their responsibility to live up to the ambitious timetable for the Doha Development Agenda, that mandated an end to the negotiations by 1 January 2005. Without a successful 'stock taking' in Cancún, a consensus decision on whether to negotiate on the Singapore issues and some essential Ministerial decisions on modalities in key areas such as agriculture, industrial market access and services it was unlikely that the Doha Round of negotiations would finish on time.

At the WTO General Council meeting in December, after multiple rounds of consultations with Ministers on a bilateral basis and in other multilateral forums, with Heads of Delegation in Geneva and with senior capitals-based officials, the General Council Chairman and Director-General were able to report Members' agreement that negotiations should continue with a focus on four key topics identified at Cancún: Agriculture, NAMA, Singapore issues – probably 'unbundled' so that each could be treated individually on its own merits – and the Cotton Initiative. But neither the Chairman nor the Director-General could report any convergence among Members' views on these issues since

Cancún. The outlook for 2004 – a year filled with other distractions including Presidential elections in the USA and the appointment of a new European Commission – was not good.

Doha's mid-point finally reached

The US Trade Representative Robert Zoellick had a New Year surprise for his colleagues. On 11 January he wrote to all ministers urging that they should not give up on progress in 2004 and proposing what he believed was the basis for moving forward on the group of topics enumerated by the Council chair, which he described as the 'market access agenda'. Ambassador Zoellick offered some detailed suggestions for finding agreement, indicating areas where the US could move. He suggested limiting negotiations on the Singapore issues to trade facilitation, asked for movement from others including on the elimination of export subsidies on agriculture and went so far as to suggest bringing the next Ministerial Conference (scheduled for Hong Kong in 2005) forward to the end of 2004. The reaction from Members was positive but, in response to the US call for concessions the EC asked for 'more flexibility' from all sides.

As proposed by the Council Chairman in December 2003, all of the negotiating groups resumed their work in early 2004. But, by April, at the first Trade Negotiations Committee in almost eight months, there was still little evidence of movement. This stalemate occurred in spite of the adoption of a self-imposed July 2004 deadline to reach agreement on the 'modalities' that should have been agreed at the Ministerial Conference (on agriculture, NAMA and on negotiations on trade facilitation) and on a suitable response to the Cotton Initiative.

A letter to all ministers from the EC Commissioners for Trade and for Agriculture on 9 May 2004 reinvigorated the talks. Like the US the EC offered movement on its negotiating positions notably by agreeing, conditionally, to the elimination of agricultural export subsidies and by proposing the 'unbundling' of the Singapore issues – leaving only trade facilitation and possibly government procurement inside the 'single undertaking'. The EC proposed, too, offering the 'Round for free' to the poorest countries, who would not be asked for reciprocity in any of the market access negotiations or in the development of new WTO rules.

The US and EC offers, combined with the willingness of all other Members to re-engage on the now-reduced 'core' agenda, laid the grounds for a variety of informal processes in Geneva, frequently involving capitals-based officials, that prepared a series of texts for consideration

> ### THE SIGNIFICANCE OF AGRICULTURE
>
> Why is agriculture a 'lynch pin' of the negotiations? On average it is much less significant now than it has ever been, representing less than 10% of world merchandise trade and less than 20% of developing country exports (less than 15% of African exports). However, farming is still the backbone of almost all developing economies. The poorest part of developing country populations – living in the rural areas – depends for its income on the development of a sustainable and productive agricultural sector. Despite the low average export share, for nearly 50 developing economies, agriculture accounts for over one third of export earnings, and for nearly 40 of them it represents over half. Also, agriculture remains a surprisingly important export sector for some of the world's largest economies. The United States is the world's biggest exporter of agricultural products; its farm exports accounting for about 10% of total United States exports and about 12% of world market demand.
>
> Yet massive agricultural support in the OECD countries undercuts prices in developing countries and forces even the most efficient producers out of markets where they would otherwise be earning foreign exchange. A key element of a development agenda will therefore be to reduce substantially such support and to eliminate the specific export subsidies – although these are only a small fraction of total agricultural support payments which reach one billion dollars a day. In addition, the average OECD bound tariff on agricultural products is four times that on industrial products: action is needed on this front also if competitive producers are to benefit from access to global demand.

and agreement by 30 July, after which the US elections and the reappointment of the European Commission seemed likely to slow further progress in 2004. Throughout the last two weeks of July more-or-less continuous work in the negotiating committees and in informal groups massaged the text of a 'package' of modalities and other agreements that was finally settled shortly after midnight on 1 August 2004.

The August 2004 'package'[1] annexed agreements on modalities for negotiations on agriculture, trade facilitation and NAMA and recommendations on speeding up progress in services negotiations. It also

[1] WTO document WT/L/579.

detailed processes for responding to the Cotton Initiative, reaffirmed the central importance of development issues and the readiness of Members to reflect this in special and differential treatment of developing countries in the outcome of negotiations (without, however, making any new proposals) and took note of progress in other negotiating groups.

Finally, the Decision of the General Council reset the negotiating 'clock', extending the negotiations 'beyond the timeframe set out in paragraph 45 of the Doha Declaration', but not setting a new deadline for completion of the Round. It decided that the Ministers would meet again in Hong Kong in December 2005.

Director-General Supachai Panitchpakdi summed up the results of the 'package' agreed by Members:

> For the first time, member governments have agreed to abolish all forms of agricultural export subsidies by a date certain. They have agreed to substantial reductions in trade distorting domestic support in agriculture.
>
> As part of this agreement we have achieved a significant breakthrough in cotton trade which offers great opportunity for cotton farmers in West Africa and throughout the developing world.
>
> Governments have agreed to launch negotiations to set new rules streamlining trade and customs procedures. We have assigned ourselves ambitious guidelines for opening trade in manufactured products and we have set ourselves a clear agenda for improving rules that are of great benefit to developing countries.
>
> As importantly, WTO governments have sharpened the focus of the Doha round and provided a foundation which will enable negotiators to

---

THE G-20

The G-20 is a group of developing countries that formed after the EC and the US presented their 'joint text' on Agriculture for Cancún. The G-20 includes the largest and most active developing country Members of the WTO. It was immediately influential in the debates on agriculture. Two of its Members (Brazil and India) are among the 'five interested parties' that met on the margins of the July 2004 General Council meeting, to devise recommendations to the chairman of the Agriculture negotiations. The Members of the Group are: Argentina, Bolivia, Brazil, Chile, China, Cuba, Egypt, India, Indonesia, Mexico, Nigeria, Pakistan, Paraguay, Philippines, South Africa, Tanzania, Venezuela, Zimbabwe.

> **COTTON INITIATIVE**
>
> The governments of Benin, Burkina Faso, Chad and Mali raised this issue in June 2003 at the General Council. They claimed that domestic production subsidies for cotton in the EC, USA and China were depressing prices of cotton, an essential export from West and Central Africa, and called for the subsidies to be eliminated, and for compensation to be paid while the subsidies are being phased out to cover their economic losses.

continue these talks from a significantly higher level; greatly enhancing our chances for successful completion of these important talks.

The Agriculture Committee's Special Sessions (i.e. the negotiations) discussed the proposal in July 2003 and suggested that Ministers at Cancún should address the problem.

Members differed on whether to handle the Cotton initiative as a specific question or whether it should come under the broader heading of agricultural subsidies and domestic support. They also differed over the question of compensation, how it should be paid (for example whether it should be development assistance) and who should handle it – the WTO does not have development funding except for training officials in WTO affairs.

No conclusion was reached in Cancún but the 'Framework' decision of 1 August 2004 stipulates that cotton will be addressed 'ambitiously, expeditiously and specifically' within the agriculture negotiations.

14

Looking back, looking forward

Looking back at the first ten years of WTO, one thing that stands out much more strongly than the stumbles over the agenda and the protests in the streets is that every government in the world sees the WTO as part of its future. Even the governments of economies in a difficult transition from centrally-planned to market-organized make every effort to join the WTO as soon as possible. Even governments of the poorest or the most isolated economies are keen to become Members of the WTO. There can be no more sincere tribute to the value that WTO holds for its Members.

But the first ten years has been a difficult inauguration. The WTO struggled into being in 1995 at the end eight years of a long and difficult negotiation, equipped with complex new agreements, a massive book of national 'schedules', a powerful disputes and enforcement mechanism, and a queue of governments demanding admission. Although there were questions in the minds of many Members about the meaning (let alone the benefits) of the obligations they'd accepted they were already committed to an agenda of continuing negotiations to complete the Round that gave it birth.

The early signs of its capacity to manage these responsibilities were good. The first Ministerial Conference in Singapore (1996) was a success. A start was made on new agreements on access for technology, on financial and telecommunications markets. The WTO even addressed two excursions away from its 'core' agenda: trade and environment and trade and labour standards.

But within a year or so the agenda had started to grow again and to become more complicated. It was as if some of the Members had paused at the end of the Uruguay Round to take their breath and were now ready to move forward again. 'Globalization' and the spreading digital economy seemed to demand a hectic pace and to propose multilateral negotiation on additional domains of economic regulations such as e-commerce, investment, and competition policy.

But many other Members were not ready to adopt multilateral obligations in these areas. Their concerns about implementing the agreements already concluded under the Uruguay Round remained unresolved. Differences over the relative priority to attach to new issues became a friction point among Members. Other irritations grew: the price of accession to WTO seemed to inflate rapidly; heads of government and street protestors alike criticized the WTO for lack of openness and accountability; making decisions that included the whole membership demanded constant, difficult consultations; even organizational matters such as the appointment of a Director-General demanded ministerial attention and elaborate compromises. Given all this, it was a shock, but no surprise, that the high profile Third Ministerial Conference at Seattle ended in disarray.

As we have seen, the road from Seattle to Doha and on past Cancún was rocky. It looks that way ahead as well.[1]

Is the future of the 'multilateral' trading system assured?

The continuing strong growth of WTO membership seems a good reason to say that the future of multilateralism is assured. The WTO's membership of 148 Members by the close of the Cancún meeting is getting close to universal and the gap will narrow still further when the 31[2] economies negotiating accession – including Russia, Saudi Arabia, Iran and Viet Nam – actually become Members. When governments vote 'with their feet' can there be any doubt that the system is credible?

But discriminatory trade agreements ('regional' or 'preferential' trade agreements such as 'free trade areas') seem to be growing still more rapidly, posing a direct challenge to the multilateral trading system. Discrimination is the converse of multilateralism: a government that elects to be a member of several preferential agreements – as most do – must do so conscious of the basic derogation from WTO principles.

There were 300 of these agreements of which the WTO was aware up to the third quarter of 2004; almost every Member of the WTO is a member of at least one of them. Their numbers have more than doubled since 1995 when only 124 had been notified. By WTO Secretariat calculations,

---

[1] The Director-General of the WTO has recently been provided with a report with advice on how to reform and improve the WTO: 'The Future of the WTO', Report of the Director-General's Consultative Board, Chairman, Peter Sutherland.

[2] List of countries negotiating accession (1 June, 2005): Afghanistan, Algeria, Andorra, Azerbaijan, Bahamas, Belarus, Bhutan, Bosnia and Herzegovina, Cape Verde, Ethiopia, Iran, Iraq, Kazakhstan, Lao PDR, Lebanon, Libya, Russian Federation, Samoa, Sao Tomé, Saudi Arabia, Serbia, Montenegro, Seychelles, Sudan, Tajikistan, Tonga, Ukraine, Uzbekistan, Vanuatu, Viet Nam, Yemen.

more than half of all merchandise trade takes place between members of discriminatory agreements. Despite the strong demand for membership in WTO, therefore, the question remains: will the trading system remain based on the WTO's multilateral rules?

It's a nice irony, that the WTO's short, occasionally stormy, history may give us the best reason to be confident that the multilateral system still holds sway. During the first ten years of the WTO, when the numbers of preferential trade agreements grew so fast, there is no evidence that they distracted Members from the extension of WTO rules – for example in financial and telecommunications services – or from the extension of market access – for example, the free trade agreed on a multilateral basis in the Information Technology Agreement.[3]

There were, as we've acknowledged, a number of stumbles along the road to agreements – Seattle and Cancún being just two of the most prominent – but we haven't needed to refer to a lack of interest in multilateralism to explain those events. The challenges of reaching complex agreements among a diverse membership offer sufficient, plausible explanations for the various failures to reach consensus.

Nor is there any evidence from the past ten years that the growth of preferential trade agreements has weakened Members' interest in the effective application of the existing multilateral rules. The persistent and laborious efforts of the Members to resolve the implementation issues make this clear. The respect for the new dispute settlement system and the level of compliance with dispute settlement rulings seen so far is not what one would predict from a system in decline.[4]

If recent history provides little evidence that preferential trade agreements have undermined governments' support for the multilateral system, does it explain why they embraced preferential agreements so enthusiastically?

It's likely that the spread of discriminatory agreements reflects frustration with the slow and difficult pace of negotiations in the WTO. When the former US Trade Representative Robert Zoellick wrote in the *Financial Times* after Cancún that the US might not 'wait for the won't-do coun-

---

[3] The products covered by the ITA now account for 12% of world merchandise trade; more than the whole of the agriculture sector.

[4] Between 1 January 1995 and 31 December 2004, 323 complaints were notified to the Dispute Settlement Body (DSB); 162 resulted in panels, three quarters of which have resulted in appeals. 'Retaliatory' action failing full compliance has been authorized on only six cases and in four of those (involving the EC and USA), the threat of retaliation has been withdrawn or did not start.

tries' he was suggesting that the US would find ways to meet its goals in regional agreements. President-elect Clinton had made a similar suggestion toward the end of the Uruguay Round. He threatened that the US would focus on the extension of the North American Free Trade Agreement rather than on the multilateral system if agreement were not reached quickly on the remaining issues in the Uruguay Round.

In the event, neither threat was carried out and the nature of the alternative probably explains why. Three months after his article in the *Financial Times*, Ambassador Zoellick wrote to all Members, setting out some proposals for resolving the disagreements at Cancún that bear a close resemblance to the Decision eventually adopted in the July 2004 'framework' package. At the top of the United States' agenda, as Ambassador Zoellick's January letter acknowledged, was an agreement on the shape of future reforms to global agriculture policies and markets.

Not even the world's largest economy would have been able to achieve such global agreements by working with only a subset of the WTO's Members, no matter how 'can-do' they might have been. Even were it possible to reach such an agreement, few bilateral or even regional trade relationships have the depth and diversity needed to justify fundamental reforms in a 'sensitive' sector such as agriculture on a reciprocal basis among parties, nor to enforce them against even the largest economies in the powerful but non-contentious manner of the dispute settlement decisions of the WTO.[5] Nor is it likely that most of what the US and others sought in the NAMA[6] negotiations could be achieved in a series of bilateral agreements; still less in the complex domain of trade in services.

But WTO successes, as well as frustrations may also offer a reason for the rapid growth in preferential trade agreements over the past few years. Developing countries have used preferential trade agreements to protect their access to the markets of industrialized countries (and the largest developing country markets) as MFN tariff cuts reduce the value of non-reciprocal tariff preferences. The end of the discriminatory MFA garment and textile quotas in North America and Europe from 1 January 2005 has already led to renewed efforts by some developing and least-developed countries to seek agreements on a broader preferential basis with the industrialized markets.

---

[5] The customs union of the European Communities is the exception that tests this 'rule'. Its attractions have been known to overcome any objections of new members to compliance with the provisions of the Common Agricultural Policy.
[6] Non-Agricultural Market Access.

If there is no evidence that they are undermining support for multilateralism and there is nothing fundamental about the multilateral system that is giving rise to these inconsistent agreements, should the adherents of the multilateral trade system be concerned?

The Consultative Board to Director-General Supachai Panitchpakdi believed so. In its report 'The Future of the WTO' the Board pointed to possible 'wedge' effects that could lead the WTO in directions it had so far declined to go. Preferential agreements, in the Consultative Board's view, could be used to develop 'templates' for agreements on 'non-trade' issues that once accepted by a number of countries on a bilateral basis could be re-introduced to the multilateral agenda. Again, there is no evidence in the first ten years to support this suggestion, but that may be because the preferential agreement 'templates' are still under development.

What we have seen in the first ten years is a sophisticated and so-far successful approach by Members to managing the overlap of WTO rights and obligations with governments' obligations and interests in areas such as the global environmental 'commons', human rights including labour standards, animal welfare, consumer protection and the management of cultural and biological diversity. There are already many international, regional and bilateral agreements in all of these domains and the first ten years saw several proposals – even passionate demands from civil society – that they should be introduced into, or explicitly recognized by, the WTO Agreement. But WTO Members have shown no interest in extending the WTO's mandates in that direction. They rejected proposals to start negotiations on environment and labour in Singapore; they endorsed the findings of dispute panels and the Appellate Body that discovered in the WTO Agreement room for governments to take necessary action, including under other treaties, to protect the environment, and they decided to work out detailed plans for avoiding conflict with the multilateral environment agreements. Rather than being led into complex new territories, Members have recently narrowed their agenda to focus on completing their work on core issues related to 'market access' in agriculture, industrial products and services.

The evidence of the first ten years is that the processes of multilateral trade negotiation are exhausting, frustrating and, from the perspective of many Members, slow. The determination of Members to recover their perspective after every set-back, to restructure their agenda and to recommence the negotiations with the incentive of some historical concessions (e.g. on agricultural export subsidies) is surely confirmation of a shared conviction that the WTO system works and that it can and must be improved. The participation of all Members in the recovery in mid-2004, and especially the leadership shown by the largest developing economies in crafting the recovery, is further evidence that the system retains its credibility.

The problem of decision-making

> [One theory] suggests that we simply have to get up, brush ourselves down, remount the horse and press ahead regardless with the negotiations, perhaps with a decent down-payment of early concessions up-front to stress our bonne volonté, our determination to bring the Round, come what may, to an early conclusion. The second theory suggests that hard thinking is needed before you jump back on the horse, lest you fall off again, or ride off in the wrong direction. In all honesty, I suggest to you that some serious thinking is needed post-Cancún, and that all sides would benefit from some reflection.
>
> EC Trade Commissioner Pascal Lamy, speaking at the Journal of Common Market Studies, London, October 2003

The first ten years of the WTO has seen an uneven pace of agreement with some important accords (Marrakesh, Doha), some steady advances (Singapore) and some pauses or reversals (Seattle, Cancún). The variable pace can be seen in just the last year: there have been periods when nothing seemed to be happening (October 2003 to May 2004) followed by periods of constant meetings, consultations and intense debate (July 2004) and reversion to apparent quiet (September to December, 2004).

The sporadic pace is not new: it was a characteristic of the GATT for much of its 50 years and of many other multilateral forums – especially those that gave rise to complex legal regimes such as the UN Conferences on the Environment or the fifteen-year negotiation that culminated in the UN Convention on the Law of the Sea.

Essential characteristics of the WTO and of the trading system suggest that these ups and downs are unlikely to change. They reflect an environment where Members face many hurdles before reaching agreement and where each agreement must be shaped and re-shaped many times – and sometimes surrounded by contingent, complementary agreements – to eventually achieve consensus. The hurdles include: the greater number of Members who must be party to an agreement; their continued economic diversity; the more precise legal interpretation now given to the text of the WTO agreements by the disputes mechanism; the greater exposure of economies to global trade and the adjustment pressures that this brings, and; the increasing capacity of Members to participate in and influence the debates at all levels, and the heightened visibility of the WTO, that brings with it greater exposure to public scrutiny and pressures from civil society.

The appearance of uneven pace in this short history is also exaggerated by our focus on progress in the rounds of negotiations. The negotiations are created, and then punctuated by Ministerial Conferences that reach agreement on agendas and attempt to bridge the biggest 'gaps' in the debates in four- or five-day bursts every two years. They naturally have an episodic character.

The work of the WTO is much more than supporting the trade negotiations, and it continues throughout the year, mostly without much external profile (despite the publication of almost all of the documentation associated with it on the WTO internet site). This short history has referred to some of this work: the adjudication of disputes, the review of trade policies, the work of the Goods and Services and Intellectual Property Councils in managing the agreements, a large technical assistance and training program, the outreach and information activities for Members not represented in Geneva and for civil society organizations, the management of joint programs with the IMF and World Bank. But we have been able to convey only a slight impression of the level of continuing activity that is required to manage, day-to-day, the only regime governing international trade relations between almost every trading economy in the world.

The WTO is under constant pressure – probably felt most acutely by its top officials including the chairs of the General Council and its subsidiary bodies, the Director-General and the Secretariat – to take responsibility for moving the high profile negotiating rounds forward, bringing a wide range of matters to agreement as a 'single undertaking' on an abbreviated schedule. In the Doha negotiations the schedule was set at just four years; a period that in view of the characteristics of the WTO just mentioned, looks 'heroic'.

One explanation for this pressure for decisions appears to be that politicians in most democracies work with cycles much shorter than the eight years it took to complete the Uruguay Round. Many of them are frustrated by the length of time it takes to get things done in the multilateral system. Many of them are more used to the decisiveness of a parliamentary system where proposals are voted up or down 'on the numbers' and governments face 'sudden death' at the ballot box every three, or four, or five years. All of them are used to making decisions on difficult matters under the pressure of short deadlines. So it is not so surprising that they would want to keep the WTO under the pressure of short deadlines, forcing Members to focus on making decisions even on complex matters so that they can move on to the next issue.

'Brinkmanship' was a common tool of agenda management in the GATT for decades, and remains so in the WTO. Abbreviating time frames forces decisions by bringing issues sharply into focus and by limiting the opportunity for holding out on a compromise. All that is needed is a credible 'drop-dead' date for the negotiations and a reasonable fear of the consequences of failure. This technique has been part of GATT/WTO committee procedures at every level including the Ministerial level. The Uruguay Round had a four-year time frame when it was launched in 1986 with an explicit 'mid-term' review deadline for decisions within two years at the Ministerial meeting in Montreal.

Up to now, it has been the industrialized countries which have also had much greater capacity to manage complex issues in the multilateral arena and to set a pace of analysis and consultation needed to arrive at a detailed agreement – at least among themselves – within the short time frames adopted.

Until recently, developing countries have not had similar capacity for preparation and agenda management so, throughout the negotiations and when it came to the 'brink' of a decision, their options tended to be an 'up or down' decision – to join a consensus on terms set by the proponents or hold it up – rather than to develop and advocate alternative decisions. Developing countries did not generally have access to the same national analytical capacity – backstopped for the industrialized countries by the OECD – or to external sources of advice from experienced analysts and consultants.[7] Even if they had advice they did not have sufficient numbers of experienced officials to follow, let alone prosecute, an agenda in the GATT/WTO. Although a forced pace affected all Members, it tended to direct pressure more in one direction (toward developing country Members) than in the other (toward industrialized country Members). Throughout the Uruguay Round, when the developing countries first started to play a role that reflected their majority of membership, and up to the Ministerial Conference in Seattle, the pressure to agree at the last minute or accept the blame for 'failure' operated mostly on the developing countries. There can be no doubt, reading ministers' own interventions, that they resented it.

---

[7] UNCTAD provided some advice, but within the limits of fewer specialized resources and a more universal service obligation than the OECD.

The consequences of the 'single undertaking' hardened the developing countries to the pressure of this sort of brinkmanship. The African group of countries – displeased by the management of the parallel working groups at Seattle[8] and frustrated, like all others, by the lack of preparation – became the first to 'pull the plug' on a final communiqué. It appears they had learned from the still-expanding list of implementation issues arising from the Uruguay Round agreements that the single undertaking increased the risk of a negotiation that would not produce a balance of obligations and benefits for them, but that they would be committed to the final outcome as part of the 'single undertaking'. They realized they should either be ready to live with the consequences of agreements they might not have the resources to shape during the negotiations, or they should insist on a shorter agenda whose demands they could meet and, consequently, that responded only to their own priorities, such as agriculture, textiles, implementation and development issues. The dilemma they faced is that the shorter agenda would not have the breadth necessary to attract the participation of their industrialized trading partners.

The lesson from Seattle was not lost on the WTO, with the result that the Doha Ministerial Conference in 2001 – the second attempt at a compromise on the same issues discussed in Seattle – was much better prepared. There was a 'brink' reached in the final plenary after other compromises had been reached but it was arguably one managed by a developing country.[9]

The Cancún Ministerial in 2003 again revealed a 'brinksmanship' strategy in play. Ministers were unable to progress the Conference Chairman's revised draft decision for a variety of reasons including disagreements over the management of the cotton initiative. But the key problem appears to have been the attempt to secure a decision on the Singapore issues that clearly had not been brought to the point of a consensus, as indicated by the overlapping objections from African and least-developed countries before the meeting. The inclusion of proposed

---

[8] 'One African delegate told *Africa Recovery* that after the overwhelming majority of participants in one working group rejected European proposals for the addition of new issues to the WTO agenda, the chair nonetheless reported a consensus in favour of the EU position. The working groups, the delegate said furiously, "are toy telephones. You can talk into them but they're not connected to anything. Nobody is listening."' *Africa Recovery*, vol. 13 no. 4, December 1999. UN, New York.

[9] India, supported by members of the African group, was the last to hold out, in a successful attempt to postpone a decision to launch negotiation on the Singapore Issues. See 'WTO agrees to launch new global trade round', *Financial Times*, 14 Nov. 2001 and 'All-night haggling in Doha ends in agreement', *Financial Times*, 15 Nov. 2001.

decisions to begin developing modalities for negotiations on investment and competition policy and to start negotiations on government procurement and trade facilitation was interpreted by many developing country ministers as an effort to force all of these issues into the single undertaking, at the last minute, over their objections.

In the event the Cancún Ministerial ended without agreement. It is typical of the process of WTO negotiations that a compromise was worked out after Cancún through intensive efforts by the Director-General Supachai Panitchpakdi, the General Council and Secretariat officials. They were successful in brokering agreement on the 'July Package' to move the negotiations back onto a positive track. But it is difficult to avoid the conclusion that WTO decision-making is no longer as 'responsive' to deadline pressures as it once was. If longer deadlines and more detailed preparations are to become the norm, this will have implications for Members' expectations of the multilateral system for their approach to the management of the 'global commons' that is the trading system.

Global agreements

It is a commonplace of international relations that the open multilateral trading system is like a public good in whose benefits all share but in whose maintenance – absent the rules of GATT/WTO – individual economies are likely to under-invest. The value of this public good depends on its breadth: the good is greatest when all economies participate. Because the founders of GATT recognized this and wanted a universal system, smaller economies could get away with a certain amount of free-riding on the benefits of the MFN system during the first decades, enjoying access rights in larger markets without binding their own tariffs.

But public goods are not 'free', as the Uruguay Round's 'single undertaking' rule emphasized. There is a cost to the agreements that is equal at least to the cost of implementation (ignoring the mercantilist view that imports themselves are a cost). The long-running implementation debates in the first ten years of the WTO's history show, more than anything else, Members working through an understanding of these costs. Industrialized countries faced the realization that the rules imposed obligations that in some instances – for example in the Customs Valuation Agreement – were beyond the capacity of some developing countries to implement. Developing countries sought, retrospectively, to trim their obligations to increase the overall net benefits of the agreements.

As a close reading of the pre-Doha implementation decisions and the text of the Decision eventually adopted on Implementation and Related Concerns reveals, the results of this ten-year attempt to re-balance the accounts were meagre. Either developing countries have complied with their obligations or, if they are small economies, their non-compliance has not attracted objection.

The lesson of the past ten years is not, however, that re-balancing obligations in the single undertaking after the fact is frustrating and ineffective. The lesson is that, in a single undertaking, there should be an adequate assurance of the breadth of net benefits for Members and, consequently, of the priority that should attach to any proposed agreement *before* negotiations start. The decision to start a negotiation could be made on the basis of that assessment and of, any prior arrangements for, differential treatment of those Members (developing countries) whose net benefits would be smallest or whose development priorities are not served by the proposed agreement.[10]

'High policy' and the market access agenda

From the mid-1980s onwards the multilateral trading system embodied in the GATT/WTO turned gradually back towards its roots in the International Trade Organization (ITO), which set out on the 'high' road of international trade policy coordination in 1947 but never arrived at its destination.[11] For the first three decades or so, the GATT adopted a modest, conservative, 'low policy' agenda embodying broader policy principles only to the extent necessary to support its main market access objective: cutting tariffs.

Over the decades, GATT was expanded by the addition of Part IV (covering development in a 'best endeavours' way), by the extension of the Tokyo Round 'codes' and finally – massively – by the Uruguay Round agreements that encompassed services, intellectual property, trade-related investment barriers, as well as an unprecedented policy reform program in the agriculture sector.

---

[10] This could mean a stratification of obligations under an agreement in accordance with some objective criteria related to the circumstances of countries whose development priorities are not served by the agreement. Alexander Keck and Patrick Low of the WTO Secretariat discuss the application of objective differentiation criteria in future S&D provisions in their *Working Paper on Special and Differential Treatment* available on the WTO website (www.wto.org).

[11] 'High policy' here means politics as opposed to 'low' policy that is only administration or at most regulation subordinate to law.

The WTO skirted the borders of high policy right from the start. Although the WTO put behind it matters of labour standards and environmental regulation at the Singapore Ministerial, Members maintained preliminary support for a framework for investment exchanges and for competition policy that not even the OECD members had been able to agree among themselves.

A multilateral organization that wishes to reach binding agreements on matters that have broad social and economic impact and that engage governments at the highest level – not just trade ministers – is likely to find the path to agreement slow and difficult. The WTO, which has almost universal membership and requires that each Member bind itself to every rule under the threat of effective sanction, should expect hesitation on the part of its membership. When, furthermore, the WTO's most powerful Members demand that it act more openly and be more responsive to the concerns of citizens' groups on some of these same issues, it can only expect to be stymied occasionally by inconsistent political demands and impossible choices.

One way to manage this problem is for the WTO to shun issues of 'high' policy implicating matters outside the domain of market access regulations and return to resolving regulatory and technical problems of opening markets and safeguarding principles of fairness and due process such as those addressed by the GATT.

Ambassador Zoellick's January 2004 letter to Ministers, attempting to restart the negotiations after the Cancún debacle, contains echoes of this idea of 'sticking to our knitting'. He heads his proposals with a banner meant, probably, to reassure: 'A Suggested Focus: The Market Access Agenda'.

As the 10th anniversary of the WTO is celebrated, we've entered a period of retrenchment in its agenda. Since Cancún, Members have attempted to reduce the number of issues under negotiation and pull back to essentially those issues that continue the directions set in the Uruguay Round Agreements (agriculture, services, NAMA, TRIPS, development) or issues (trade facilitation) that can be represented as an extension of disciplines that already existed in GATT. Although it contains several breakthroughs and promises significant reform, there is little in the July 2004 'package' that could be described as politically 'adventurous'.

But the era when the old 'low policy' agenda was sufficient to deal with the most important conflicts between Members is long gone. Ambassador Zoellick characterized the next steps in agriculture, NAMA and trade facilitation as related to market access. But he also proposed work across a broader agenda on services and substantial further cuts to domestic support for agriculture (among other things). Neither of these essential components of the negotiations for almost twenty years can be divorced from 'high policy' issues such as rural incomes, food security, environment, public services, investment and the movement of people. It is no longer possible for modern government administration to avoid overlap between trade regulation and many other aspects of interaction between individuals and the global economy.

How well has WTO managed development issues?

> Recalling the Preamble to the Marrakesh Agreement, we shall continue to make positive efforts designed to ensure that developing countries, and especially the least-developed among them, secure a share in the growth of world trade commensurate with the needs of their economic development. In this context, enhanced market access, balanced rules, and well targeted, sustainably-financed technical assistance and capacity-building programmes have important roles to play.
>
> From Paragraph 2 of the Doha Declaration

A reasonable way to put this question in perspective is to ask what has happened to the trade of developing countries over that period of time and to what extent should the WTO take the credit, or the blame. A full evaluation is beyond the scope of this essay but a summary answer would be that WTO strongly serves the interests of its developing Members because it maintains a system that has secured significant trade opportunities for them rather than on account of any specific advantages that it has provided to them.

The WTO's efforts to increase direct assistance within its mandate on behalf of its developing country Members and on behalf of the least-developed of them (more than one-third of all WTO's technical assistance goes to Africa) has been exemplary. Directors-General have given the highest priority to expanding and making better use of the technical assistance resources of the WTO[12] including by leveraging its coordinating role with the IMF and World Bank and by making use of UNCTAD and ITC resources to help with the objective of 'mainstreaming' trade in the development policies of developing countries. They have also made

---

[12] Mostly through extra-budgetary resources since regular budget resources have not been increased much: they represent less than 20% of recent technical assistance expenditure.

> **DEVELOPING COUNTRY GROWTH, TRADE SINCE 1995**
>
> 1. The economic growth of developing countries as a group has not been stronger at any time since the 1980s than it was in the period since 1995: with the exception of a short plunge in rates during 1998, due to the impacts of the Asian financial crisis.
> 2. Developing country exports – excluding China – have outpaced those of developed countries; their shares of world markets have risen steadily throughout the 1990s to about 30% in 2004.
> 3. Africa's exports grew by an impressive 30% in 2004, after rising strongly in 2003. Attributable in significant measure to commodity price rises, this marks the highest growth in African exports since 1980. This trade growth has been associated with an improved expansion in production, which registered more than 4% growth for the continent in 2004.
> 4. At 7% and 8% respectively, developing Asia and the Commonwealth of Independent States (CIS) countries continued to report the strongest regional GDP growth worldwide. South America recorded GDP growth of 6%, which represented not only the strongest improvement against the preceding year among regions, but also the highest growth rate since 1986. Africa and the Middle East registered GDP growth of approximately 4% in 2004.
> 5. The export earnings of the poorest countries, especially in Sub-Saharan Africa, have fallen further behind the rest of the world due for the most part to the composition of their exports which are concentrated in the slowest growing sectors and to capacity constraints.
> 6. WTO has taken few decisions in that period that could be said to directly affect this trade growth (the ITA may have had an impact) but it has considerably expanded its program of technical assistance including efforts to 'mainstream' trade in the development policies of developing countries.

extraordinary efforts to maintain a flow of information and support to small delegations and to Members not represented in Geneva.

The WTO rules are not an algorithm for economic growth or development policy. The S&D provisions that modify the application of the rules do not directly affect the growth or development of developing countries either. At the margin, however, the rules can support or hinder the operation of policies that developing countries may consider offer them opportunities to improve development outcomes, so 'special and differential' provisions have been included in GATT/WTO rules and exceptions since the mid-1960s. It may be that these exceptional provisions have contributed to the overall growth of world trade that has been the main benefit of the system for developing and industrialized countries alike.

The WTO still faces a challenge, however, during a self-described 'Development Round' to come up with practical initiatives within its mandate that will promote development objectives and that Members will be willing to put into place. The 'modalities' for making development objectives more 'operational' in the WTO have not been decided. Some Members, as shown in the Doha Decision on Implementation, want the S&D provisions for developing countries to be the rule rather than the exception to the rules of the WTO. Others consider this is a constitutional change that would make a 'dead letter' of the WTO rules even for the beneficiaries of S&D.

Of all the issues that figure in the S&D debate, none has prompted more discussion than the availability and value of developing country preferences. At first sight they seem to be a 'win-win' idea: they marginally reduce protection in industrialized countries (to the benefit of their economies and their consumers) and offer competitive advantages to developing countries that seem to need the advantage most. Like any source of rents[13] they are the focus of an intense and sometimes expensive lobbying activity by potential beneficiaries and absorb hours of the formal agenda at most Ministerial Conferences. But in the past few years improvements in global trade data have allowed analysts to evaluate access to non-reciprocal preferences. It has become clear that they offer much smaller opportunities than might be expected from the 'headline' preference margins – mostly because of the rules of origin and other qualifications attached to the preferences.[14] Furthermore the preference margins are not secure against erosion over time by MFN trade liberalization.

Eroded preferences include, notably, the quota rents and preferential access opportunities that the Multifibre Agreement quotas may have

[13] The preference margin is potentially an unrequited transfer from an industrialized country government to developing country exporters in the form of taxes foregone, although many exporters see the value of the preference, more starkly, as the difference between sales and no sales.

[14] See, for example, *Improving Market Access for Least Developed Countries*, UNCTAD (2001).

offered. These were reduced and, on 1 January 2005, eliminated by the MFN liberalization of the garment and textile sectors under the WTO's Agreement on Textiles and Clothing. The erosion of these 'preferences' offered more growth opportunities, not fewer, because the removal of the barriers that gave rise to the preferences is expected to lead to more trade-led growth in developing countries, not less. 'On average', according to the IMF, 'each [textile or garment industry] job saved in developed countries by tariffs and quotas is . . . estimated to cost 35 jobs in developing countries'.[15] The difficulty facing several former textile and garment exporters, however, is that the distribution of opportunities from the elimination of the MFA quotas seems to be narrower than the distribution of the former quota rents. But, in principle, the same observations about the growth in trade opportunity can also be made about cuts in MFN tariff barriers that protect other industries.

Unilateral preferences for developing countries is an issue that may reveal even more differences among the membership in the future than it has in the past as the developing country group itself becomes more diverse and the preference 'rents' become smaller. Some of the largest developing countries will lose access to preferences and will gain more from cuts to MFN barriers, despite the erosion of preferences that this implies. Other developing countries, more dependent on preferences for access to export markets in industrialized countries, will find it more difficult to sustain a priority for preferences in the negotiations and to extract concessions to maintain the quality of the remaining preferences against specific rules of origin and other conditions.

This is not to say that it would not be possible to improve on the unilateral preferences that are offered to the poorest developing countries by, for example,

- broadening their coverage: several, but not all industrialized countries offer unconditional tariff and quota free access to least-developed countries; and
- removing restrictive rules of origin and other administrative resistances.

There is still every reason to look forward to more substantial results. The negotiations in the Doha Development Agenda are only half done. The debates since Doha on ways to make S&D provisions mandatory (in the terms of the Implementation Decision) or at least 'more operational' (in the more modest terms of the Doha Declaration itself) have not yet

---

[15] *Finance and Development*, vol. 39, no. 3, September 2002.

reached a conclusion. But finding ways to appropriately respond to the needs of developing countries without compromising the overall goals of the system remains a challenge.

What overcoming that challenge represents for the world was summarized by Director-General Supachai Panitchpakdi (2002–2005) at the WTO public symposium in April, 2005:

> Let us remember the urgency of the work we are engaged in. More than one billion people still live below the extreme poverty line of one dollar per day and, according to the UN Secretary-General, 20,000 people die from poverty each day. Trade is not the answer to all the world's problems, but it can make a powerful contribution to international efforts for development. We must ensure this contribution is realised and that the enormous potential of globalization is harnessed for the benefit of people the world over.

The WTO's greatest achievement

The WTO suffers from exaggerated or eccentric expectations that distract from the evaluation of its central mission. One of the most common complaints, even from well-informed analysts, is that joining the WTO does not necessarily result in a boost to any Member's trade.[16] But to expect that the rules that favour trade liberalization should always lead to growth in trade is a bit like expecting traffic laws to promote good driving or libel laws to promote truthfulness.

The WTO helps to create the right environment for trade and growth. Over the past decade it has accomplished this core task effectively across a much broader range of economic activities than its predecessor the GATT.

WTO has:

> Provided an effective forum for further trade liberalization and rule-making. Shortly after the Uruguay Round was concluded, agreements were reached on financial services, basic telecommunications and information technology products – all cutting edge sectors of today's global economy.
>
> Taken great strides towards universal membership. Already, 148 Members, representing more than 90% of world trade have committed to

---

[16] For example, *Do We Know that WTO Increases Trade?* Andrew Rose, CEPR Discussion Paper 3538 (London), available on line at http://ideas.repec.org/p/cpr/ceprdp/3538.html. Rose has produced several critical reviews of the impact of WTO membership along the same lines.

the rules and principles of the WTO. Since the creation of the WTO in January 1995 around 20 new Members have joined the system. Thirty-one countries are currently in the process of negotiating their accession.

Made a significant investment in technical assistance and capacity building to integrate developing countries more fully into the multilateral trading system, enabling them to benefit more from membership in the WTO.

Made a determined and ultimately successful effort to make its debates, processes and decisions more open to the outside world – through speedier and more automatic de-restriction of WTO official documents which can be easily accessed over the internet; through enhanced outreach activities with NGOs, parliamentarians, universities and other sectors of civil society.

But the WTO's greatest achievement in the past ten years has been to help maintain the peace through a period of economic turbulence marked by an historical advance in the globalization of markets that was liberating, absorbing and also deeply threatening to many governments, businesses and consumers.

Maintaining the peace – avoiding and resolving conflicts between the interests and policies of Members – may seem an unexciting goal, because we've become used to the idea that 'trade wars' don't leak into armed conflict as they did in the first half of the twentieth century.

But the tensions over trade continue almost as strongly today as they did in the 1930s. Ministers of the world's largest economies – industrialized and developing – still find themselves cornered into shouting matches over the protection of steel markets or subsidies to aircraft production or support for cotton farmers or discrimination in the distribution of preferences on banana imports or over national health programs to control the prices of imported drugs.

The difference is not only that there are now rules designed to minimize the opportunity for conflict, or that there is a system for the compulsory adjudication of notified disputes but also that this compulsory system now inhibits the use of unilateral action to resolve disputes through force.

After the first ten years of the WTO it is clear that without it the world market would be smaller, the opportunities poorer, the 'winners' from globalization fewer and the 'losers' left stranded with fewer alternatives.

ANNEX 1

List of WTO Members and Observers (1 June 2005)

WTO MEMBERS AND OBSERVERS, JUNE 2005

(148 governments, since 13 October 2004, with date of membership)

Albania 8 September 2000
Angola 23 November 1996
Antigua and Barbuda 1 January 1995
Argentina 1 January 1995
Armenia 5 February 2003
Australia 1 January 1995
Austria 1 January 1995
Bahrain, Kingdom of 1 January 1995
Bangladesh 1 January 1995
Barbados 1 January 1995
Belgium 1 January 1995
Belize 1 January 1995
Benin 22 February 1996
Bolivia 12 September 1995
Botswana 31 May 1995
Brazil 1 January 1995
Brunei Darussalam 1 January 1995
Bulgaria 1 December 1996
Burkina Faso 3 June 1995
Burundi 23 July 1995
Cambodia 13 October 2004
Cameroon 13 December 1995
Canada 1 January 1995
Central African Republic 31 May 1995
Chad 19 October 1996
Chile 1 January 1995
China 11 December 2001

Colombia 30 April 1995
Congo 27 March 1997
Costa Rica 1 January 1995
Côte d'Ivoire 1 January 1995
Croatia 30 November 2000
Cuba 20 April 1995
Cyprus 30 July 1995
Czech Republic 1 January 1995
Democratic Republic of the Congo 1 January 1997
Denmark 1 January 1995
Djibouti 31 May 1995
Dominica 1 January 1995
Dominican Republic 9 March 1995
Ecuador 21 January 1996
Egypt 30 June 1995
El Salvador 7 May 1995
Estonia 13 November 1999
European Communities 1 January 1995
Fiji 14 January 1996
Finland 1 January 1995
Former Yugoslav Republic of Macedonia (FYROM) 4 April 2003
France 1 January 1995
Gabon 1 January 1995
The Gambia 23 October 1996
Georgia 14 June 2000
Germany 1 January 1995
Ghana 1 January 1995

Greece 1 January 1995
Grenada 22 February 1996
Guatemala 21 July 1995
Guinea 25 October 1995
Guinea Bissau 31 May 1995
Guyana 1 January 1995
Haiti 30 January 1996
Honduras 1 January 1995
Hong Kong, China 1 January 1995
Hungary 1 January 1995
Iceland 1 January 1995
India 1 January 1995
Indonesia 1 January 1995
Ireland 1 January 1995
Israel 21 April 1995
Italy 1 January 1995
Jamaica 9 March 1995
Japan 1 January 1995
Jordan 11 April 2000
Kenya 1 January 1995
Korea, Republic of 1 January 1995
Kuwait 1 January 1995
Kyrgyz Republic 20 December 1998
Latvia 10 February 1999
Lesotho 31 May 1995
Liechtenstein 1 September 1995
Lithuania 31 May 2001
Luxembourg 1 January 1995
Macao, China 1 January 1995
Madagascar 17 November 1995
Malawi 31 May 1995
Malaysia 1 January 1995
Maldives 31 May 1995
Mali 31 May 1995
Malta 1 January 1995
Mauritania 31 May 1995
Mauritius 1 January 1995
Mexico 1 January 1995
Moldova 26 July 2001
Mongolia 29 January 1997
Morocco 1 January 1995
Mozambique 26 August 1995

Myanmar 1 January 1995
Namibia 1 January 1995
Nepal 23 April 2004
Netherlands – For the Kingdom in Europe and for the Netherlands Antilles 1 January 1995
New Zealand 1 January 1995
Nicaragua 3 September 1995
Niger 13 December 1996
Nigeria 1 January 1995
Norway 1 January 1995
Oman 9 November 2000
Pakistan 1 January 1995
Panama 6 September 1997
Papua New Guinea 9 June 1996
Paraguay 1 January 1995
Peru 1 January 1995
Philippines 1 January 1995
Poland 1 July 1995
Portugal 1 January 1995
Qatar 13 January 1996
Romania 1 January 1995
Rwanda 22 May 1996
Saint Kitts and Nevis 21 February 1996
Saint Lucia 1 January 1995
Saint Vincent & the Grenadines 1 January 1995
Senegal 1 January 1995
Sierra Leone 23 July 1995
Singapore 1 January 1995
Slovak Republic 1 January 1995
Slovenia 30 July 1995
Solomon Islands 26 July 1996
South Africa 1 January 1995
Spain 1 January 1995
Sri Lanka 1 January 1995
Suriname 1 January 1995
Swaziland 1 January 1995
Sweden 1 January 1995
Switzerland 1 July 1995
Chinese Taipei 1 January 2002

Tanzania 1 January 1995
Thailand 1 January 1995
Togo 31 May 1995
Trinidad and Tobago 1 March 1995
Tunisia 29 March 1995
Turkey 26 March 1995
Uganda 1 January 1995
United Arab Emirates 10 April 1996
United Kingdom 1 January 1995
United States of America 1 January 1995
Uruguay 1 January 1995
Venezuela (Bolivarian Republic of) 1 January 1995
Zambia 1 January 1995
Zimbabwe 5 March 1995

Observer governments

Afghanistan
Algeria
Andorra
Azerbaijan
Bahamas
Belarus
Bhutan
Bosnia and Herzegovina
Cape Verde
Equatorial Guinea
Ethiopia
Holy See (Vatican)
Iran
Iraq
Kazakhstan
Lao People's Democratic Republic
Lebanese Republic
Libya
Montenegro
Russian Federation
Samoa
Sao Tomé and Principe
Saudi Arabia
Serbia
Seychelles
Sudan
Tajikistan
Tonga
Ukraine
Uzbekistan
Vanuatu
Viet Nam
Yemen

Note: With the exception of the Holy See, observers must start accession negotiations within five years of becoming observers.

ANNEX 2

Agreement Establishing the World Trade Organization (1995)

AGREEMENT ESTABLISHING THE WORLD TRADE ORGANIZATION

The *Parties* to this Agreement,

Recognizing that their relations in the field of trade and economic endeavour should be conducted with a view to raising standards of living, ensuring full employment and a large and steadily growing volume of real income and effective demand, and expanding the production of and trade in goods and services, while allowing for the optimal use of the world's resources in accordance with the objective of sustainable development, seeking both to protect and preserve the environment and to enhance the means for doing so in a manner consistent with their respective needs and concerns at different levels of economic development,

Recognizing further that there is need for positive efforts designed to ensure that developing countries, and especially the least developed among them, secure a share in the growth in international trade commensurate with the needs of their economic development,

Being desirous of contributing to these objectives by entering into reciprocal and mutually advantageous arrangements directed to the substantial reduction of tariffs and other barriers to trade and to the elimination of discriminatory treatment in international trade relations,

Resolved, therefore, to develop an integrated, more viable and durable multilateral trading system encompassing the General Agreement on Tariffs and Trade, the results of past trade liberalization efforts, and all of the results of the Uruguay Round of Multilateral Trade Negotiations,

Determined to preserve the basic principles and to further the objectives underlying this multilateral trading system,

Agree as follows:

Article I

Establishment of the Organization

The World Trade Organization (hereinafter referred to as 'the WTO') is hereby established.

Article II

Scope of the WTO

1. The WTO shall provide the common institutional framework for the conduct of trade relations among its Members in matters related to the agreements and associated legal instruments included in the Annexes to this Agreement.
2. The agreements and associated legal instruments included in Annexes 1, 2 and 3 (hereinafter referred to as 'Multilateral Trade Agreements') are integral parts of this Agreement, binding on all Members.
3. The agreements and associated legal instruments included in Annex 4 (hereinafter referred to as 'Plurilateral Trade Agreements') are also part of this Agreement for those Members that have accepted them, and are binding on those Members. The Plurilateral Trade Agreements do not create either obligations or rights for Members that have not accepted them.
4. The General Agreement on Tariffs and Trade 1994 as specified in Annex 1A (hereinafter referred to as 'GATT 1994') is legally distinct from the General Agreement on Tariffs and Trade, dated 30 October 1947, annexed to the Final Act Adopted at the Conclusion of the Second Session of the Preparatory Committee of the United Nations Conference on Trade and Employment, as subsequently rectified, amended or modified (hereinafter referred to as 'GATT 1947').

Article III

Functions of the WTO

1. The WTO shall facilitate the implementation, administration and operation, and further the objectives, of this Agreement and of the Multilateral Trade Agreements, and shall also provide the framework for the implementation, administration and operation of the Plurilateral Trade Agreements.
2. The WTO shall provide the forum for negotiations among its Members concerning their multilateral trade relations in matters dealt with under the agreements in the Annexes to this Agreement. The WTO may also provide a forum for further negotiations among its Members concerning their multilateral trade relations, and a framework for the implementation of the results of such negotiations, as may be decided by the Ministerial Conference.
3. The WTO shall administer the Understanding on Rules and Procedures Governing the Settlement of Disputes (hereinafter referred to as the 'Dispute Settlement Understanding' or 'DSU') in Annex 2 to this Agreement.
4. The WTO shall administer the Trade Policy Review Mechanism (hereinafter referred to as the 'TPRM') provided for in Annex 3 to this Agreement.

5. With a view to achieving greater coherence in global economic policy-making, the WTO shall cooperate, as appropriate, with the International Monetary Fund and with the International Bank for Reconstruction and Development and its affiliated agencies.

Article IV

Structure of the WTO

1. There shall be a Ministerial Conference composed of representatives of all the Members, which shall meet at least once every two years. The Ministerial Conference shall carry out the functions of the WTO and take actions necessary to this effect. The Ministerial Conference shall have the authority to take decisions on all matters under any of the Multilateral Trade Agreements, if so requested by a Member, in accordance with the specific requirements for decision-making in this Agreement and in the relevant Multilateral Trade Agreement.
2. There shall be a General Council composed of representatives of all the Members, which shall meet as appropriate. In the intervals between meetings of the Ministerial Conference, its functions shall be conducted by the General Council. The General Council shall also carry out the functions assigned to it by this Agreement. The General Council shall establish its rules of procedure and approve the rules of procedure for the Committees provided for in paragraph 7.
3. The General Council shall convene as appropriate to discharge the responsibilities of the Dispute Settlement Body provided for in the Dispute Settlement Understanding. The Dispute Settlement Body may have its own chairman and shall establish such rules of procedure as it deems necessary for the fulfilment of those responsibilities.
4. The General Council shall convene as appropriate to discharge the responsibilities of the Trade Policy Review Body provided for in the TPRM. The Trade Policy Review Body may have its own chairman and shall establish such rules of procedure as it deems necessary for the fulfilment of those responsibilities.
5. There shall be a Council for Trade in Goods, a Council for Trade in Services and a Council for Trade-Related Aspects of Intellectual Property Rights (hereinafter referred to as the 'Council for TRIPS'), which shall operate under the general guidance of the General Council. The Council for Trade in Goods shall oversee the functioning of the Multilateral Trade Agreements in Annex 1A. The Council for Trade in Services shall oversee the functioning of the General Agreement on Trade in Services (hereinafter referred to as 'GATS'). The Council for TRIPS shall oversee the functioning of the

Agreement on Trade-Related Aspects of Intellectual Property Rights (hereinafter referred to as the 'Agreement on TRIPS'). These Councils shall carry out the functions assigned to them by their respective agreements and by the General Council. They shall establish their respective rules of procedure subject to the approval of the General Council. Membership in these Councils shall be open to representatives of all Members. These Councils shall meet as necessary to carry out their functions.

6. The Council for Trade in Goods, the Council for Trade in Services and the Council for TRIPS shall establish subsidiary bodies as required. These subsidiary bodies shall establish their respective rules of procedure subject to the approval of their respective Councils.

7. The Ministerial Conference shall establish a Committee on Trade and Development, a Committee on Balance-of-Payments Restrictions and a Committee on Budget, Finance and Administration, which shall carry out the functions assigned to them by this Agreement and by the Multilateral Trade Agreements, and any additional functions assigned to them by the General Council, and may establish such additional Committees with such functions as it may deem appropriate. As part of its functions, the Committee on Trade and Development shall periodically review the special provisions in the Multilateral Trade Agreements in favour of the least-developed country Members and report to the General Council for appropriate action. Membership in these Committees shall be open to representatives of all Members.

8. The bodies provided for under the Plurilateral Trade Agreements shall carry out the functions assigned to them under those Agreements and shall operate within the institutional framework of the WTO. These bodies shall keep the General Council informed of their activities on a regular basis.

Article V

Relations with Other Organizations

1. The General Council shall make appropriate arrangements for effective cooperation with other intergovernmental organizations that have responsibilities related to those of the WTO.

2. The General Council may make appropriate arrangements for consultation and cooperation with non-governmental organizations concerned with matters related to those of the WTO.

Article VI

The Secretariat

1. There shall be a Secretariat of the WTO (hereinafter referred to as 'the Secretariat') headed by a Director-General.
2. The Ministerial Conference shall appoint the Director-General and adopt regulations setting out the powers, duties, conditions of service and term of office of the Director-General.
3. The Director-General shall appoint the members of the staff of the Secretariat and determine their duties and conditions of service in accordance with regulations adopted by the Ministerial Conference.
4. The responsibilities of the Director-General and of the staff of the Secretariat shall be exclusively international in character. In the discharge of their duties, the Director-General and the staff of the Secretariat shall not seek or accept instructions from any government or any other authority external to the WTO. They shall refrain from any action which might adversely reflect on their position as international officials. The Members of the WTO shall respect the international character of the responsibilities of the Director-General and of the staff of the Secretariat and shall not seek to influence them in the discharge of their duties.

Article VII

Budget and Contributions

1. The Director-General shall present to the Committee on Budget, Finance and Administration the annual budget estimate and financial statement of the WTO. The Committee on Budget, Finance and Administration shall review the annual budget estimate and the financial statement presented by the Director-General and make recommendations thereon to the General Council. The annual budget estimate shall be subject to approval by the General Council.
2. The Committee on Budget, Finance and Administration shall propose to the General Council financial regulations which shall include provisions setting out:
   (a) the scale of contributions apportioning the expenses of the WTO among its Members; and
   (b) the measures to be taken in respect of Members in arrears.
   The financial regulations shall be based, as far as practicable, on the regulations and practices of GATT 1947.

3. The General Council shall adopt the financial regulations and the annual budget estimate by a two-thirds majority comprising more than half of the Members of the WTO.
4. Each Member shall promptly contribute to the WTO its share in the expenses of the WTO in accordance with the financial regulations adopted by the General Council.

Article VIII

Status of the WTO

1. The WTO shall have legal personality, and shall be accorded by each of its Members such legal capacity as may be necessary for the exercise of its functions.
2. The WTO shall be accorded by each of its Members such privileges and immunities as are necessary for the exercise of its functions.
3. The officials of the WTO and the representatives of the Members shall similarly be accorded by each of its Members such privileges and immunities as are necessary for the independent exercise of their functions in connection with the WTO.
4. The privileges and immunities to be accorded by a Member to the WTO, its officials, and the representatives of its Members shall be similar to the privileges and immunities stipulated in the Convention on the Privileges and Immunities of the Specialized Agencies, approved by the General Assembly of the United Nations on 21 November 1947.
5. The WTO may conclude a headquarters agreement.

Article IX

Decision-making

1. The WTO shall continue the practice of decision-making by consensus followed under GATT 1947.[1] Except as otherwise provided, where a decision cannot be arrived at by consensus, the matter at issue shall be decided by voting. At meetings of the Ministerial Conference and the General Council, each Member of the WTO shall have one vote. Where the European Communities exercise their right to vote, they shall have a number of votes equal to the number of their member States[2] which are

---

[1] The body concerned shall be deemed to have decided by consensus on a matter submitted for its consideration, if no Member, present at the meeting when the decision is taken, formally objects to the proposed decision.

[2] The number of votes of the European Communities and their member States shall in no case exceed the number of the member States of the European Communities.

Members of the WTO. Decisions of the Ministerial Conference and the General Council shall be taken by a majority of the votes cast, unless otherwise provided in this Agreement or in the relevant Multilateral Trade Agreement.[3]

2. The Ministerial Conference and the General Council shall have the exclusive authority to adopt interpretations of this Agreement and of the Multilateral Trade Agreements. In the case of an interpretation of a Multilateral Trade Agreement in Annex 1, they shall exercise their authority on the basis of a recommendation by the Council overseeing the functioning of that Agreement. The decision to adopt an interpretation shall be taken by a three-fourths majority of the Members. This paragraph shall not be used in a manner that would undermine the amendment provisions in Article X.

3. In exceptional circumstances, the Ministerial Conference may decide to waive an obligation imposed on a Member by this Agreement or any of the Multilateral Trade Agreements, provided that any such decision shall be taken by three fourths[4] of the Members unless otherwise provided for in this paragraph.

   (a) A request for a waiver concerning this Agreement shall be submitted to the Ministerial Conference for consideration pursuant to the practice of decision-making by consensus. The Ministerial Conference shall establish a time-period, which shall not exceed 90 days, to consider the request. If consensus is not reached during the time-period, any decision to grant a waiver shall be taken by three fourths of the Members.

   (b) A request for a waiver concerning the Multilateral Trade Agreements in Annexes 1A or 1B or 1C and their annexes shall be submitted initially to the Council for Trade in Goods, the Council for Trade in Services or the Council for TRIPS, respectively, for consideration during a time-period which shall not exceed 90 days. At the end of the time-period, the relevant Council shall submit a report to the Ministerial Conference.

4. A decision by the Ministerial Conference granting a waiver shall state the exceptional circumstances justifying the decision, the terms and conditions governing the application of the waiver, and the date on which the waiver shall terminate. Any waiver granted for a period of more than one year shall be reviewed by the Ministerial Conference not later than

---

[3] Decisions by the General Council when convened as the Dispute Settlement Body shall be taken only in accordance with the provisions of paragraph 4 of Article 2 of the Dispute Settlement Understanding.

[4] A decision to grant a waiver in respect of any obligation subject to a transition period or a period for staged implementation that the requesting Member has not performed by the end of the relevant period shall be taken only by consensus.

one year after it is granted, and thereafter annually until the waiver terminates. In each review, the Ministerial Conference shall examine whether the exceptional circumstances justifying the waiver still exist and whether the terms and conditions attached to the waiver have been met. The Ministerial Conference, on the basis of the annual review, may extend, modify or terminate the waiver.
5. Decisions under a Plurilateral Trade Agreement, including any decisions on interpretations and waivers, shall be governed by the provisions of that Agreement.

Article X

Amendments

1. Any Member of the WTO may initiate a proposal to amend the provisions of this Agreement or the Multilateral Trade Agreements in Annex 1 by submitting such proposal to the Ministerial Conference. The Councils listed in paragraph 5 of Article IV may also submit to the Ministerial Conference proposals to amend the provisions of the corresponding Multilateral Trade Agreements in Annex 1 the functioning of which they oversee. Unless the Ministerial Conference decides on a longer period, for a period of 90 days after the proposal has been tabled formally at the Ministerial Conference any decision by the Ministerial Conference to submit the proposed amendment to the Members for acceptance shall be taken by consensus. Unless the provisions of paragraphs 2, 5 or 6 apply, that decision shall specify whether the provisions of paragraphs 3 or 4 shall apply. If consensus is reached, the Ministerial Conference shall forthwith submit the proposed amendment to the Members for acceptance. If consensus is not reached at a meeting of the Ministerial Conference within the established period, the Ministerial Conference shall decide by a two-thirds majority of the Members whether to submit the proposed amendment to the Members for acceptance. Except as provided in paragraphs 2, 5 and 6, the provisions of paragraph 3 shall apply to the proposed amendment, unless the Ministerial Conference decides by a three-fourths majority of the Members that the provisions of paragraph 4 shall apply.
2. Amendments to the provisions of this Article and to the provisions of the following Articles shall take effect only upon acceptance by all Members:

Article IX of this Agreement;
Articles I and II of GATT 1994;
Article II:1 of GATS;
Article 4 of the Agreement on TRIPS.

3. Amendments to provisions of this Agreement, or of the Multilateral Trade Agreements in Annexes 1A and 1C, other than those listed in paragraphs 2 and 6, of a nature that would alter the rights and obligations of the Members, shall take effect for the Members that have accepted them upon acceptance by two-thirds of the Members and thereafter for each other Member upon acceptance by it. The Ministerial Conference may decide by a three-fourths majority of the Members that any amendment made effective under this paragraph is of such a nature that any Member which has not accepted it within a period specified by the Ministerial Conference in each case shall be free to withdraw from the WTO or to remain a Member with the consent of the Ministerial Conference.

4. Amendments to provisions of this Agreement or of the Multilateral Trade Agreements in Annexes 1A and 1C, other than those listed in paragraphs 2 and 6, of a nature that would not alter the rights and obligations of the Members, shall take effect for all Members upon acceptance by two-thirds of the Members.

5. Except as provided in paragraph 2 above, amendments to Parts I, II and III of GATS and the respective annexes shall take effect for the Members that have accepted them upon acceptance by two-thirds of the Members and thereafter for each Member upon acceptance by it. The Ministerial Conference may decide by a three-fourths majority of the Members that any amendment made effective under the preceding provision is of such a nature that any Member which has not accepted it within a period specified by the Ministerial Conference in each case shall be free to withdraw from the WTO or to remain a Member with the consent of the Ministerial Conference. Amendments to Parts IV, V and VI of GATS and the respective annexes shall take effect for all Members upon acceptance by two thirds of the Members.

6. Notwithstanding the other provisions of this Article, amendments to the Agreement on TRIPS meeting the requirements of paragraph 2 of Article 71 thereof may be adopted by the Ministerial Conference without further formal acceptance process.

7. Any Member accepting an amendment to this Agreement or to a Multilateral Trade Agreement in Annex 1 shall deposit an instrument of acceptance with the Director-General of the WTO within the period of acceptance specified by the Ministerial Conference.

8. Any Member of the WTO may initiate a proposal to amend the provisions of the Multilateral Trade Agreements in Annexes 2 and 3 by submitting such proposal to the Ministerial Conference. The decision to approve amendments to the Multilateral Trade Agreement in Annex 2 shall be made by consensus and these amendments shall take effect for all Members upon approval by the Ministerial Conference. Decisions to approve

amendments to the Multilateral Trade Agreement in Annex 3 shall take effect for all Members upon approval by the Ministerial Conference.
9. The Ministerial Conference, upon the request of the Members parties to a trade agreement, may decide exclusively by consensus to add that agreement to Annex 4. The Ministerial Conference, upon the request of the Members parties to a Plurilateral Trade Agreement, may decide to delete that Agreement from Annex 4.
10. Amendments to a Plurilateral Trade Agreement shall be governed by the provisions of that Agreement.

Article XI

Original Membership

1. The contracting parties to GATT 1947 as of the date of entry into force of this Agreement, and the European Communities, which accept this Agreement and the Multilateral Trade Agreements and for which Schedules of Concessions and Commitments are annexed to GATT 1994 and for which Schedules of Specific Commitments are annexed to GATS shall become original Members of the WTO.
2. The least-developed countries recognized as such by the United Nations will only be required to undertake commitments and concessions to the extent consistent with their individual development, financial and trade needs or their administrative and institutional capabilities.

Article XII

Accession

1. Any State or separate customs territory possessing full autonomy in the conduct of its external commercial relations and of the other matters provided for in this Agreement and the Multilateral Trade Agreements may accede to this Agreement, on terms to be agreed between it and the WTO. Such accession shall apply to this Agreement and the Multilateral Trade Agreements annexed thereto.
2. Decisions on accession shall be taken by the Ministerial Conference. The Ministerial Conference shall approve the agreement on the terms of accession by a two-thirds majority of the Members of the WTO.
3. Accession to a Plurilateral Trade Agreement shall be governed by the provisions of that Agreement.

Article XIII

Non-application of Multilateral Trade Agreements between Particular Members

1. This Agreement and the Multilateral Trade Agreements in Annexes 1 and 2 shall not apply as between any Member and any other Member if either of the Members, at the time either becomes a Member, does not consent to such application.
2. Paragraph 1 may be invoked between original Members of the WTO which were contracting parties to GATT 1947 only where Article XXXV of that Agreement had been invoked earlier and was effective as between those contracting parties at the time of entry into force for them of this Agreement.
3. Paragraph 1 shall apply between a Member and another Member which has acceded under Article XII only if the Member not consenting to the application has so notified the Ministerial Conference before the approval of the agreement on the terms of accession by the Ministerial Conference.
4. The Ministerial Conference may review the operation of this Article in particular cases at the request of any Member and make appropriate recommendations.
5. Non-application of a Plurilateral Trade Agreement between parties to that Agreement shall be governed by the provisions of that Agreement.

Article XIV

Acceptance, Entry into Force and Deposit

1. This Agreement shall be open for acceptance, by signature or otherwise, by contracting parties to GATT 1947, and the European Communities, which are eligible to become original Members of the WTO in accordance with Article XI of this Agreement. Such acceptance shall apply to this Agreement and the Multilateral Trade Agreements annexed hereto. This Agreement and the Multilateral Trade Agreements annexed hereto shall enter into force on the date determined by Ministers in accordance with paragraph 3 of the Final Act Embodying the Results of the Uruguay Round of Multilateral Trade Negotiations and shall remain open for acceptance for a period of two years following that date unless the Ministers decide otherwise. An acceptance following the entry into force of this Agreement shall enter into force on the 30th day following the date of such acceptance.
2. A Member which accepts this Agreement after its entry into force shall implement those concessions and obligations in the Multilateral Trade

Agreements that are to be implemented over a period of time starting with the entry into force of this Agreement as if it had accepted this Agreement on the date of its entry into force.
3. Until the entry into force of this Agreement, the text of this Agreement and the Multilateral Trade Agreements shall be deposited with the Director-General to the CONTRACTING PARTIES to GATT 1947. The Director-General shall promptly furnish a certified true copy of this Agreement and the Multilateral Trade Agreements, and a notification of each acceptance thereof, to each government and the European Communities having accepted this Agreement. This Agreement and the Multilateral Trade Agreements, and any amendments thereto, shall, upon the entry into force of this Agreement, be deposited with the Director-General of the WTO.
4. The acceptance and entry into force of a Plurilateral Trade Agreement shall be governed by the provisions of that Agreement. Such Agreements shall be deposited with the Director-General to the CONTRACTING PARTIES to GATT 1947. Upon the entry into force of this Agreement, such Agreements shall be deposited with the Director-General of the WTO.

Article XV

Withdrawal

1. Any Member may withdraw from this Agreement. Such withdrawal shall apply both to this Agreement and the Multilateral Trade Agreements and shall take effect upon the expiration of six months from the date on which written notice of withdrawal is received by the Director-General of the WTO.
2. Withdrawal from a Plurilateral Trade Agreement shall be governed by the provisions of that Agreement.

Article XVI

Miscellaneous provisions

1. Except as otherwise provided under this Agreement or the Multilateral Trade Agreements, the WTO shall be guided by the decisions, procedures and customary practices followed by the CONTRACTING PARTIES to GATT 1947 and the bodies established in the framework of GATT 1947.
2. To the extent practicable, the Secretariat of GATT 1947 shall become the Secretariat of the WTO, and the Director-General to the CONTRACTING PARTIES to GATT 1947, until such time as the Ministerial Conference has appointed a Director-General in accordance with paragraph 2 of Article VI of this Agreement, shall serve as Director-General of the WTO.

3. In the event of a conflict between a provision of this Agreement and a provision of any of the Multilateral Trade Agreements, the provision of this Agreement shall prevail to the extent of the conflict.
4. Each Member shall ensure the conformity of its laws, regulations and administrative procedures with its obligations as provided in the annexed Agreements.
5. No reservations may be made in respect of any provision of this Agreement. Reservations in respect of any of the provisions of the Multilateral Trade Agreements may only be made to the extent provided for in those Agreements. Reservations in respect of a provision of a Plurilateral Trade Agreement shall be governed by the provisions of that Agreement.
6. This Agreement shall be registered in accordance with the provisions of Article 102 of the Charter of the United Nations.

DONE at Marrakesh this fifteenth day of April one thousand nine hundred and ninety-four, in a single copy, in the English, French and Spanish languages, each text being authentic.

Explanatory Notes:

The terms 'country' or 'countries' as used in this Agreement and the Multilateral Trade Agreements are to be understood to include any separate customs territory Member of the WTO.

In the case of a separate customs territory Member of the WTO, where an expression in this Agreement and the Multilateral Trade Agreements is qualified by the term 'national', such expression shall be read as pertaining to that customs territory, unless otherwise specified.

LIST OF ANNEXES

ANNEX 1

ANNEX 1A: Multilateral Agreements on Trade in Goods
   General Agreement on Tariffs and Trade 1994
   Agreement on Agriculture
   Agreement on the Application of Sanitary and Phytosanitary Measures
   Agreement on Textiles and Clothing
   Agreement on Technical Barriers to Trade
   Agreement on Trade-Related Investment Measures
   Agreement on Implementation of Article VI of the General Agreement on Tariffs and Trade 1994
   Agreement on Implementation of Article VII of the General Agreement on Tariffs and Trade 1994
   Agreement on Preshipment Inspection

Agreement on Rules of Origin
Agreement on Import Licensing Procedures
Agreement on Subsidies and Countervailing Measures
Agreement on Safeguards
ANNEX 1B: General Agreement on Trade in Services and Annexes
ANNEX 1C: Agreement on Trade-Related Aspects of Intellectual Property Rights

ANNEX 2

Understanding on Rules and Procedures Governing the Settlement of Disputes

ANNEX 3

Trade Policy Review Mechanism

ANNEX 4

Plurilateral Trade Agreements

Agreement on Trade in Civil Aircraft
Agreement on Government Procurement
International Dairy Agreement
International Bovine Meat Agreement

ANNEX 3

Singapore Ministerial Declaration (1996)

WT/MIN(96)/DEC
18 December 1996
(96-5316)

WORLD TRADE
ORGANIZATION

MINISTERIAL CONFERENCE
Singapore, 9–13 December 1996

SINGAPORE MINISTERIAL DECLARATION

<u>Adopted on 13 December 1996</u>

1. We, the Ministers, have met in Singapore from 9 to 13 December 1996 for the first regular biennial meeting of the WTO at Ministerial level, as called for in Article IV of the Agreement Establishing the World Trade Organization, to further strengthen the WTO as a forum for negotiation, the continuing liberalization of trade within a rule-based system, and the multilateral review and assessment of trade policies, and in particular to:

   - assess the implementation of our commitments under the WTO Agreements and decisions;
   - review the ongoing negotiations and Work Programme;
   - examine developments in world trade; and
   - address the challenges of an evolving world economy.

Purpose

2. For nearly 50 years Members have sought to fulfil, first in the GATT and now in the WTO, the objectives reflected in the preamble to the WTO Agreement of conducting our trade relations with a view to raising standards of living worldwide. The rise in global trade facilitated by trade liberalization within the rules-based system has created more and better-paid jobs in many countries. The achievements of the WTO during its first two years bear witness to our

Trade and Economic Growth

desire to work together to make the most of the possibilities that the multilateral system provides to promote sustainable growth and development while contributing to a more stable and secure climate in international relations.

3. We believe that the scope and pace of change in the international economy, including the growth in trade in services and direct investment, and the increasing integration of economies offer unprecedented opportunities for improved growth, job creation, and development. These developments require adjustment by economies and societies. They also pose challenges to the trading system. We commit ourselves to address these challenges. **Integration of Economies; Opportunities and Challenges**

4. We renew our commitment to the observance of internationally recognized core labour standards. The International Labour Organization (ILO) is the competent body to set and deal with these standards, and we affirm our support for its work in promoting them. We believe that economic growth and development fostered by increased trade and further trade liberalization contribute to the promotion of these standards. We reject the use of labour standards for protectionist purposes, and agree that the comparative advantage of countries, particularly low-wage developing countries, must in no way be put into question. In this regard, we note that the WTO and ILO Secretariats will continue their existing collaboration. **Core Labour Standards**

5. We commit ourselves to address the problem of marginalization for least-developed countries, and the risk of it for certain developing countries. We will also continue to work for greater coherence in international economic policy-making and for improved coordination between the WTO and other agencies in providing technical assistance. **Marginalization**

6. In pursuit of the goal of sustainable growth and development for the common good, we envisage a world where trade flows freely. To this end we renew our commitment to: **Role of WTO**

- a fair, equitable and more open rule-based system;

- progressive liberalization and elimination of tariff and non-tariff barriers to trade in goods;
- progressive liberalization of trade in services;
- rejection of all forms of protectionism;
- elimination of discriminatory treatment in international trade relations;
- integration of developing and least-developed countries and economies in transition into the multilateral system; and
- the maximum possible level of transparency.

7. We note that trade relations of WTO Members are being increasingly influenced by regional trade agreements, which have expanded vastly in number, scope and coverage. Such initiatives can promote further liberalization and may assist least-developed, developing and transition economies in integrating into the international trading system. In this context, we note the importance of existing regional arrangements involving developing and least-developed countries. The expansion and extent of regional trade agreements make it important to analyse whether the system of WTO rights and obligations as it relates to regional trade agreements needs to be further clarified. We reaffirm the primacy of the multilateral trading system, which includes a framework for the development of regional trade agreements, and we renew our commitment to ensure that regional trade agreements are complementary to it and consistent with its rules. In this regard, we welcome the establishment and endorse the work of the new Committee on Regional Trade Agreements. We shall continue to work through progressive liberalization in the WTO as we are committed in the WTO Agreement and Decisions adopted at Marrakesh, and in so doing facilitate mutually supportive processes of global and regional trade liberalization. **Regional Agreements**

8. It is important that the 28 applicants now negotiating accession contribute to completing the accession process by accepting the WTO rules and by offering meaningful market access commitments. We will work to bring these applicants expeditiously into the WTO system. **Accessions**

9. The Dispute Settlement Understanding (DSU) offers a means for the settlement of disputes among Members that is unique in international agreements. We consider its impartial and transparent operation to be of fundamental importance in assuring the resolution of trade disputes, and in fostering the implementation and application of the WTO agreements. The Understanding, with its predictable procedures, including the possibility of appeal of panel decisions to an Appellate Body and provisions on implementation of recommendations, has improved Members' means of resolving their differences. We believe that the DSU has worked effectively during its first two years. We also note the role that several WTO bodies have played in helping to avoid disputes. We renew our determination to abide by the rules and procedures of the DSU and other WTO agreements in the conduct of our trade relations and the settlement of disputes. We are confident that longer experience with the DSU, including the implementation of panel and appellate recommendations, will further enhance the effectiveness and credibility of the dispute settlement system.   **Dispute Settlement**

10. We attach high priority to full and effective implementation of the WTO Agreement in a manner consistent with the goal of trade liberalization. Implementation thus far has been generally satisfactory, although some Members have expressed dissatisfaction with certain aspects. It is clear that further effort in this area is required, as indicated by the relevant WTO bodies in their reports. Implementation of the specific commitments scheduled by Members with respect to market access in industrial goods and trade in services appears to be proceeding smoothly. With respect to industrial market access, monitoring of implementation would be enhanced by the timely availability of trade and tariff data. Progress has been made also in advancing the WTO reform programme in agriculture, including in implementation of agreed market   **Implementation**

access concessions and domestic subsidy and export subsidy commitments.

11. Compliance with notification requirements has not been fully satisfactory. Because the WTO system relies on mutual monitoring as a means to assess implementation, those Members which have not submitted notifications in a timely manner, or whose notifications are not complete, should renew their efforts. At the same time, the relevant bodies should take appropriate steps to promote full compliance while considering practical proposals for simplifying the notification process.

12. Where legislation is needed to implement WTO rules, Members are mindful of their obligations to complete their domestic legislative process without further delay. Those Members entitled to transition periods are urged to take steps as they deem necessary to ensure timely implementation of obligations as they come into effect. Each Member should carefully review all its existing or proposed legislation, programmes and measures to ensure their full compatibility with the WTO obligations, and should carefully consider points made during review in the relevant WTO bodies regarding the WTO consistency of legislation, programmes and measures, and make appropriate changes where necessary.

13. The integration of developing countries in the multilateral trading system is important for their economic development and for global trade expansion. In this connection, we recall that the WTO Agreement embodies provisions conferring differential and more favourable treatment for developing countries, including special attention to the particular situation of least-developed countries. We acknowledge the fact that developing country Members have undertaken significant new commitments, both substantive and procedural, and we recognize the range and complexity of the efforts that they are making to comply with them. In order to assist them in these efforts, including those with respect to notification and legislative requirements, we will improve the availability of technical

Notifications and Legislation

Developing Countries

assistance under the agreed guidelines. We have also agreed to recommendations relative to the decision we took at Marrakesh concerning the possible negative effects of the agricultural reform programme on least-developed and net food-importing developing countries.

14. We remain concerned by the problems of the least-developed countries and have agreed to: **Least-Developed Countries**

   - a Plan of Action, including provision for taking positive measures, for example duty-free access, on an autonomous basis, aimed at improving their overall capacity to respond to the opportunities offered by the trading system;
   - seek to give operational content to the Plan of Action, for example, by enhancing conditions for investment and providing predictable and favourable market access conditions for LLDCs' products, to foster the expansion and diversification of their exports to the markets of all developed countries; and in the case of relevant developing countries in the context of the Global System of Trade Preferences; and
   - organize a meeting with UNCTAD and the International Trade Centre as soon as possible in 1997, with the participation of aid agencies, multilateral financial institutions and least-developed countries to foster an integrated approach to assisting these countries in enhancing their trading opportunities.

15. We confirm our commitment to full and faithful implementation of the provisions of the Agreement on Textiles and Clothing (ATC). We stress the importance of the integration of textile products, as provided for in the ATC, into GATT 1994 under its strengthened rules and disciplines because of its systemic significance for the rule-based, non-discriminatory trading system and its contribution to the increase in export earnings of developing countries. We attach importance to the implementation of this Agreement so as to ensure an effective transition to GATT 1994 by way of integration **Textiles and Clothing**

which is progressive in character. The use of safeguard measures in accordance with ATC provisions should be as sparing as possible. We note concerns regarding the use of other trade distortive measures and circumvention. We reiterate the importance of fully implementing the provisions of the ATC relating to small suppliers, new entrants and least-developed country Members, as well as those relating to cotton-producing exporting Members. We recognize the importance of wool products for some developing country Members. We reaffirm that as part of the integration process and with reference to the specific commitments undertaken by the Members as a result of the Uruguay Round, all Members shall take such action as may be necessary to abide by GATT 1994 rules and disciplines so as to achieve improved market access for textiles and clothing products. We agree that, keeping in view its quasi-judicial nature, the Textiles Monitoring Body (TMB) should achieve transparency in providing rationale for its findings and recommendations. We expect that the TMB shall make findings and recommendations whenever called upon to do so under the Agreement. We emphasize the responsibility of the Goods Council in overseeing, in accordance with Article IV:5 of the WTO Agreement and Article 8 of the ATC, the functioning of the ATC, whose implementation is being supervised by the TMB.

16. The Committee on Trade and Environment has made an important contribution towards fulfilling its Work Programme. The Committee has been examining and will continue to examine, *inter alia*, the scope of the complementarities between trade liberalization, economic development and environmental protection. Full implementation of the WTO Agreements will make an important contribution to achieving the objectives of sustainable development. The work of the Committee has underlined the importance of policy coordination at the national level in the area of trade and environment. In this connection, the work of the

Trade and Environment

Committee has been enriched by the participation of environmental as well as trade experts from Member governments and the further participation of such experts in the Committee's deliberations would be welcomed. The breadth and complexity of the issues covered by the Committee's Work Programme shows that further work needs to be undertaken on all items of its agenda, as contained in its report. We intend to build on the work accomplished thus far, and therefore direct the Committee to carry out its work, reporting to the General Council, under its existing terms of reference.

17. The fulfilment of the objectives agreed at Marrakesh for negotiations on the improvement of market access in services – in financial services, movement of natural persons, maritime transport services and basic telecommunications – has proved to be difficult. The results have been below expectations. In three areas, it has been necessary to prolong negotiations beyond the original deadlines. We are determined to obtain a progressively higher level of liberalization in services on a mutually advantageous basis with appropriate flexibility for individual developing country Members, as envisaged in the Agreement, in the continuing negotiations and those scheduled to begin no later than 1 January 2000. In this context, we look forward to full MFN agreements based on improved market access commitments and national treatment. Accordingly, we will:

Services Negotiations

- achieve a successful conclusion to the negotiations on basic telecommunications in February 1997; and
- resume financial services negotiations in April 1997 with the aim of achieving significantly improved market access commitments with a broader level of participation in the agreed time frame.

With the same broad objectives in mind, we also look forward to a successful conclusion of the negotiations on Maritime Transport Services in the next round of negotiations on services liberalization.

In professional services, we shall aim at completing the work on the accountancy sector by the end of 1997, and will continue to develop multilateral disciplines and guidelines. In this connection, we encourage the successful completion of international standards in the accountancy sector by IFAC, IASC, and IOSCO. With respect to GATS rules, we shall undertake the necessary work with a view to completing the negotiations on safeguards by the end of 1997. We also note that more analytical work will be needed on emergency safeguards measures, government procurement in services and subsidies.

18. Taking note that a number of Members have agreed on a Declaration on Trade in Information Technology Products, we welcome the initiative taken by a number of WTO Members and other States or separate customs territories which have applied to accede to the WTO, who have agreed to tariff elimination for trade in information technology products on an MFN basis as well as the addition by a number of Members of over 400 products to their lists of tariff-free products in pharmaceuticals. **ITA and Pharmaceuticals**

19. Bearing in mind that an important aspect of WTO activities is a continuous overseeing of the implementation of various agreements, a periodic examination and updating of the WTO Work Programme is a key to enable the WTO to fulfil its objectives. In this context, we endorse the reports of the various WTO bodies. A major share of the Work Programme stems from the WTO Agreement and decisions adopted at Marrakesh. As part of these Agreements and decisions we agreed to a number of provisions calling for future negotiations on Agriculture, Services and aspects of TRIPS, or reviews and other work on Anti-Dumping, Customs Valuation, Dispute Settlement Understanding, Import Licensing, Preshipment Inspection, Rules of Origin, Sanitary and Phyto-Sanitary Measures, Safeguards, Subsidies and Countervailing Measures, Technical Barriers to Trade, **Work Programme and Built-in Agenda**

Textiles and Clothing, Trade Policy Review Mechanism, Trade-Related Aspects of Intellectual Property Rights and Trade-Related Investment Measures. We agree to a process of analysis and exchange of information, where provided for in the conclusions and recommendations of the relevant WTO bodies, on the Built-in Agenda issues, to allow Members to better understand the issues involved and identify their interests before undertaking the agreed negotiations and reviews. We agree that:

- the time frames established in the Agreements will be respected in each case;
- the work undertaken shall not prejudge the scope of future negotiations where such negotiations are called for; and
- the work undertaken shall not prejudge the nature of the activity agreed upon (i.e. negotiation or review).

20. Having regard to the existing WTO provisions on matters related to investment and competition policy and the built-in agenda in these areas, including under the TRIMs Agreement, and on the understanding that the work undertaken shall not prejudge whether negotiations will be initiated in the future, we also agree to: **Investment and Competition**

- establish a working group to examine the relationship between trade and investment; and
- establish a working group to study issues raised by Members relating to the interaction between trade and competition policy, including anti-competitive practices, in order to identify any areas that may merit further consideration in the WTO framework.

These groups shall draw upon each other's work if necessary and also draw upon and be without prejudice to the work in UNCTAD and other appropriate intergovernmental fora. As regards UNCTAD, we welcome the work under way as provided for in the Midrand Declaration and the contribution it can make to the understanding of issues. In the conduct of the work of the working groups, we encourage cooperation with the above organizations to make the best use of available resources and to ensure that the development dimension is taken fully into account. The General Council will keep the work of each body under review, and will determine after two years how the work of each body should proceed. It is clearly understood that future negotiations, if any, regarding multilateral disciplines in these areas, will take place only after an explicit consensus decision is taken among WTO Members regarding such negotiations.

21. We further agree to:

    - establish a working group to conduct a study on transparency in government procurement practices, taking into account national policies, and, based on this study, to develop elements for inclusion in an appropriate agreement; and **Transparency in Government Procurement**
    - direct the Council for Trade in Goods to undertake exploratory and analytical work, drawing on the work of other relevant international organizations, on the simplification of trade procedures in order to assess the scope for WTO rules in this area. **Trade Facilitation**

22. In the organization of the work referred to in paragraphs 20 and 21, careful attention will be given to minimizing the burdens on delegations, especially those with more limited resources, and to coordinating meetings with those of relevant UNCTAD bodies. The technical cooperation programme of the Secretariat will be available to developing and, in particular, least-developed country Members to facilitate their participation in this work.

23. Noting that the 50th anniversary of the multilateral trading system will occur early in 1998, we instruct the General Council to consider how this historic event can best be commemorated.

* * * * *

Finally, we express our warmest thanks to the Chairman of the Ministerial Conference, Mr. Yeo Cheow Tong, for his personal contribution to the success of this Ministerial Conference. We also want to express our sincere gratitude to Prime Minister Goh Chok Tong, his colleagues in the Government of Singapore and the people of Singapore for their warm hospitality and the excellent organization they have provided. The fact that this first Ministerial Conference of the WTO has been held at Singapore is an additional manifestation of Singapore's commitment to an open world trading system.

ANNEX 4

Ministerial Declaration on Trade in Information Technology Products (1996)

WT/MIN(96)/16

WORLD TRADE ORGANIZATION

13 December 1996

(96-5438)

MINISTERIAL CONFERENCE
Singapore, 9–13 December 1996

MINISTERIAL DECLARATION ON TRADE IN INFORMATION TECHNOLOGY PRODUCTS

SINGAPORE, 13 DECEMBER 1996

Ministers,
Representing the following Members of the World Trade Organization ('WTO'), and States or separate customs territories in the process of acceding to the WTO, which have agreed in Singapore on the expansion of world trade in information technology products and which account for well over 80 per cent of world trade in these products ('parties'):

Australia
Canada
European Communities
Hong Kong
Iceland
Indonesia
Japan
Korea
Norway
Separate Customs Territory of Taiwan, Penghu, Kinmen and Matsu
Singapore
Switzerland[1]
Turkey
United States

Considering the key role of trade in information technology products in the development of information industries and in the dynamic expansion of the world economy,
Recognizing the goals of raising standards of living and expanding the production of and trade in goods;
Desiring to achieve maximum freedom of world trade in information technology products;

---
[1] On behalf of the customs union Switzerland and Liechtenstein.

Desiring to encourage the continued technological development of the information technology industry on a world-wide basis;

Mindful of the positive contribution information technology makes to global economic growth and welfare;

Having agreed to put into effect the results of these negotiations which involve concessions additional to those included in the Schedules attached to the Marrakesh Protocol to the General Agreement on Tariffs and Trade 1994, and

Recognizing that the results of these negotiations also involve some concessions offered in negotiations leading to the establishment of Schedules annexed to the Marrakesh Protocol,

Declare as follows:

1. Each party's trade regime should evolve in a manner that enhances market access opportunities for information technology products.
2. Pursuant to the modalities set forth in the Annex to this Declaration, each party shall bind and eliminate customs duties and other duties and charges of any kind, within the meaning of Article II:1(b) of the General Agreement on Tariffs and Trade 1994, with respect to the following:
   (a) all products classified (or classifiable) with Harmonized System (1996) ('HS') headings listed in Attachment A to the Annex to this Declaration; and
   (b) all products specified in Attachment B to the Annex to this Declaration, whether or not they are included in Attachment A;

   through equal rate reductions of customs duties beginning in 1997 and concluding in 2000, recognizing that extended staging of reductions and, before implementation, expansion of product coverage may be necessary in limited circumstances.

3. Ministers express satisfaction about the large product coverage outlined in the Attachments to the Annex to this Declaration. They instruct their respective officials to make good faith efforts to finalize plurilateral technical discussions in Geneva on the basis of these modalities, and instruct these officials to complete this work by 31 January 1997, so as to ensure the implementation of this Declaration by the largest number of participants.
4. Ministers invite the Ministers of other Members of the WTO, and States or separate customs territories in the process of acceding to the WTO, to provide similar instructions to their respective officials, so that they may participate in the technical discussions referred to in paragraph 3 above and participate fully in the expansion of world trade in information technology products.

Annex: Modalities and Product Coverage

> Attachment A: list of HS headings
> Attachment B: list of products

ANNEX

Modalities and Product Coverage

Any Member of the World Trade Organization, or State or separate customs territory in the process of acceding to the WTO, may participate in the expansion of world trade in information technology products in accordance with the following modalities:

1. Each participant shall incorporate the measures described in paragraph 2 of the Declaration into its schedule to the General Agreement on Tariffs and Trade 1994, and, in addition, at either its own tariff line level or the Harmonized System (1996) ('HS') 6-digit level in either its official tariff or any other published versions of the tariff schedule, whichever is ordinarily used by importers and exporters. Each participant that is not a Member of the WTO shall implement these measures on an autonomous basis, pending completion of its WTO accession, and shall incorporate these measures into its WTO market access schedule for goods.

2. To this end, as early as possible and no later than 1 March 1997 each participant shall provide all other participants a document containing (a) the details concerning how the appropriate duty treatment will be provided in its WTO schedule of concessions, and (b) a list of the detailed HS headings involved for products specified in Attachment B. These documents will be reviewed and approved on a consensus basis and this review process shall be completed no later than 1 April 1997. As soon as this review process has been completed for any such document, that document shall be submitted as a modification to the Schedule of the participant concerned, in accordance with the Decision of 26 March 1980 on Procedures for Modification and Rectification of Schedules of Tariff Concessions (BISD 27S/25).

   (a) The concessions to be proposed by each participant as modifications to its Schedule shall bind and eliminate all customs duties and other duties and charges of any kind on information technology products as follows:

   (i) elimination of such customs duties shall take place through rate reductions in equal steps, except as may be otherwise agreed by the participants. Unless otherwise agreed by the participants, each participant shall bind all tariffs on items listed in the Attachments no later than 1 July 1997, and shall make the first such rate reduction effective no later than 1 July 1997, the

second such rate reduction no later than 1 January 1998, and the third such rate reduction no later than 1 January 1999, and the elimination of customs duties shall be completed effective no later than 1 January 2000. The participants agree to encourage autonomous elimination of customs duties prior to these dates. The reduced rate should in each stage be rounded off to the first decimal; and

 (ii) elimination of such other duties and charges of any kind, within the meaning of Article II:1(b) of the General Agreement, shall be completed by 1 July 1997, except as may be otherwise specified in the participant's document provided to other participants for review.

(b) The modifications to its Schedule to be proposed by a participant in order to implement its binding and elimination of customs duties on information technology products shall achieve this result:

 (i) in the case of the HS headings listed in Attachment A, by creating, where appropriate, sub-divisions in its Schedule at the national tariff line level; and

 (ii) in the case of the products specified in Attachment B, by attaching an annex to its Schedule including all products in Attachment B, which is to specify the detailed HS headings for those products at either the national tariff line level or the HS 6-digit level.

Each participant shall promptly modify its national tariff schedule to reflect the modifications it has proposed, as soon as they have entered into effect.

3. Participants shall meet periodically under the auspices of the Council on Trade in Goods to review the product coverage specified in the Attachments, with a view to agreeing, by consensus, whether in the light of technological developments, experience in applying the tariff concessions, or changes to the HS nomenclature, the Attachments should be modified to incorporate additional products, and to consult on non-tariff barriers to trade in information technology products. Such consultations shall be without prejudice to rights and obligations under the WTO Agreement.

4. Participants shall meet as soon as practicable and in any case no later than 1 April 1997 to review the state of acceptances received and to assess the conclusions to be drawn therefrom. Participants will implement the actions foreseen in the Declaration provided that participants representing approximately 90 per cent of world trade[2] in information technology products have by then notified their acceptance, and provided that the staging has been agreed to the participants' satisfaction. In assessing whether to implement actions foreseen in the Declaration, if the percentage of world

---

[2] This percentage shall be calculated by the WTO Secretariat on the basis of the most recent data available at the time of the meeting.

trade represented by participants falls somewhat short of 90 per cent of world trade in information technology products, participants may take into account the extent of the participation of States or separate customs territories representing for them the substantial bulk of their own trade in such products. At this meeting the participants will establish whether these criteria have been met.
5. Participants shall meet as often as necessary and no later than 30 September 1997 to consider any divergence among them in classifying information technology products, beginning with the products specified in Attachment B. Participants agree on the common objective of achieving, where appropriate, a common classification for these products within existing HS nomenclature, giving consideration to interpretations and rulings of the Customs Co-operation Council (also known as the World Customs Organization or 'WCO'). In any instance in which a divergence in classification remains, participants will consider whether a joint suggestion could be made to the WCO with regard to updating existing HS nomenclature or resolving divergence in interpretation of the HS nomenclature.
6. The participants understand that Article XXIII of the General Agreement will address nullification or impairment of benefits accruing directly or indirectly to a WTO Member participant through the implementation of this Declaration as a result of the application by another WTO Member participant of any measure, whether or not that measure conflicts with the provisions of the General Agreement.
7. Each participant shall afford sympathetic consideration to any request for consultation from any other participant concerning the undertakings set out above. Such consultations shall be without prejudice to rights and obligations under the WTO Agreement.
8. Participants acting under the auspices of the Council for Trade in Goods shall inform other Members of the WTO and States or separate customs territories in the process of acceding to the WTO of these modalities and initiate consultations with a view to facilitate their participation in the expansion of trade in information technology products on the basis of the Declaration.
9. As used in these modalities, the term 'participant' shall mean those Members of the WTO, or States or separate customs territories in the process of acceding to the WTO, that provide the document described in paragraph 2 no later than 1 March 1997.
10. This Annex shall be open for acceptance by all Members of the WTO and any State or any separate customs territory in the process of acceding to the WTO. Acceptances shall be notified in writing to the Director-General who shall communicate them to all participants.

There are two attachments to the Annex.
Attachment A lists the HS headings or parts thereof to be covered.
Attachment B lists specific products to be covered by an ITA wherever they are classified in the HS.

Attachment A, Section 1

HS96		HS description
3818		Chemical elements doped for use in electronics, in form of discs, wafers or similar forms; chemical compounds doped for use in electronics
8469	11	Word processing machines
8470		Calculating machines and pocket-size data recording, reproducing and displaying machines with a calculating function; accounting machines, postage franking machines, ticket-issuing machines and similar machines, incorporating calculating devices; cash registers:
8470	10	Electronic calculators capable of operating without an external source of electric power and pocket size data recording, reproducing and displaying machines with calculating functions
8470	21	Other electronic calculating machines incorporating a printing device
8470	29	Other
8470	30	Other calculating machines
8470	40	Accounting machines
8470	50	Cash registers
8470	90	Other
8471		Automatic data processing machines and units thereof; magnetic or optical readers, machines for transcribing data onto data media in coded form and machines for processing such data, not elsewhere specified or included:
8471	10	Analogue or hybrid automatic data processing machines
8471	30	Portable digital automatic data processing machines, weighing no more than 10 kg, consisting of at least a central processing unit, a keyboard and a display

ANNEX 4

	HS96		HS description
	8471	41	Other digital automatic data processing machines comprising in the same housing at least a central processing unit and an input and output unit, whether or not combined
	8471	49	Other digital automatic data processing machines presented in the form of systems
	8471	50	Digital processing units other than those of subheading 8471 41 and 8471 49, whether or not in the same housing one or two of the following types of units: storage units, input units, output units
	8471	60	Input or output units, whether or not containing storage units in the same housing
	8471	70	Storage units, including central storage units, optical disk storage units, hard disk drives and magnetic tape storage units
	8471	80	Other units of automatic data processing machines
	8471	90	Other
ex	8472	90	Automatic teller machines
	8473	21	Parts and accessories of the machines of heading No 8470 of the electronic calculating machines of subheading 8470 10, 8470 21 and 8470 29
	8473	29	Parts and accessories of the machines of heading No 8470 other than the electronic calculating machines of subheading 8470 10, 8470 21 and 8470 29
	8473	30	Parts and accessories of the machines of heading No 8471
	8473	50	Parts and accessories equally suitable for use with machines of two or more of the headings Nos. 8469 to 8472
ex	8504	40	Static converters for automatic data processing machines and units thereof, and telecommunication apparatus
ex	8504	50	Other inductors for power supplies for automatic data processing machines and units thereof, and telecommunication apparatus
	8517		Electrical apparatus for line telephony or line telegraphy, including line telephone sets with cordless handsets and telecommunication apparatus for carrier-current line systems or for digital line systems; videophones:

	HS96		HS description
	8517	11	Line telephone sets with cordless handsets
	8517	19	Other telephone sets and videophones
	8517	21	Facsimile machines
	8517	22	Teleprinters
	8517	30	Telephonic or telegraphic switching apparatus
	8517	50	Other apparatus, for carrier-current line systems or for digital line systems
	8517	80	Other apparatus including entry-phone systems
	8517	90	Parts of apparatus of heading 8517
ex	8518	10	Microphones having a frequency range of 300 Hz to 3.4 KHz with a diameter of not exceeding 10 mm and a height not exceeding 3 mm, for telecommunication use
ex	8518	30	Line telephone handsets
ex	8518	29	Loudspeakers, without housing, having a frequency range of 300 Hz to 3.4 KHz with a diameter of not exceeding 50 mm, for telecommunication use
	8520	20	Telephone answering machines
	8523	11	Magnetic tapes of a width not exceeding 4 mm
	8523	12	Magnetic tapes of a width exceeding 4 mm but not exceeding 6.5 mm
	8523	13	Magnetic tapes of a width exceeding 6.5 mm
	8523	20	Magnetic discs
	8523	90	Other
	8524	31	Discs for laser reading systems for reproducing phenomena other than sound or image
ex	8524	39	Other : – for reproducing representations of instructions, data, sound, and image, recorded in a machine readable binary form, and capable of being manipulated or providing interactivity to a user, by means of an automatic data processing machine
	8524	40	Magnetic tapes for reproducing phenomena other than sound or image
	8524	91	Media for reproducing phenomena other than sound or image

ANNEX 4 191

	HS96		HS description
ex	8424	99	Other : – for reproducing representations of instructions, data, sound, and image, recorded in a machine readable binary form, and capable of being manipulated or providing interactivity to a user, by means of an automatic data processing machine
ex	8525	10	Transmission apparatus other than apparatus for radio-broadcasting or television
	8525	20	Transmission apparatus incorporating reception apparatus
ex	8525	40	Digital still image video cameras
ex	8527	90	Portable receivers for calling, alerting or paging
ex	8529	10	Aerials or antennae of a kind used with apparatus for radio-telephony and radio-telegraphy
ex	8529	90	Parts of: transmission apparatus other than apparatus for radio-broadcasting or television transmission apparatus incorporating reception apparatus digital still image video cameras, portable receivers for calling, alerting or paging
	8531	20	Indicator panels incorporating liquid crystal devices (LCD) or light emitting diodes (LED)
ex	8531	90	Parts of apparatus of subheading 8531 20
	8532		Electrical capacitors, fixed, variable or adjustable (pre-set):
	8532	10	Fixed capacitors designed for use in 50/60 Hz circuits and having a reactive power handling capacity of not less than 0.5 kvar (power capacitors)
	8532	21	Tantalum fixed capacitors
	8532	22	Aluminium electrolytic fixed capacitors
	8532	23	Ceramic dielectric, single layer fixed capacitors
	8532	24	Ceramic dielectric, multilayer fixed capacitors
	8532	25	Dielectric fixed capacitors of paper or plastics
	8532	29	Other fixed capacitors
	8532	30	Variable or adjustable (pre-set) capacitors
	8532	90	Parts

	HS96		HS description
	8533		Electrical resistors (including rheostats and potentiometers), other than heating resistors:
	8533	10	Fixed carbon resistors, composition or film types
	8533	21	Other fixed resistors for a power handling capacity not exceeding 20 W
	8533	29	Other fixed resistors for a power handling capacity of 20 W or more
	8533	31	Wirewound variable resistors, including rheostats and potentiometers, for a power handling capacity not exceeding 20 W
	8533	39	Wirewound variable resistors, including rheostats and potentiometers, for a power handling capacity of 20 W or more
	8533	40	Other variable resistors, including rheostats and potentiometers
	8533	90	Parts
	8534		Printed circuits
ex	8536	50	Electronic AC switches consisting of optically coupled input and output circuits (Insulated thyristor AC switches)
ex	8536	50	Electronic switches, including temperature protected electronic switches, consisting of a transistor and a logic chip (chip-on-chip technology) for a voltage not exceeding 1000 volts
ex	8536	50	Electromechanical snap-action switches for a current not exceeding 11 amps
ex	8536	69	Plugs and sockets for co-axial cables and printed circuits
ex	8536	90	Connection and contact elements for wires and cables
	8541		Diodes, transistors and similar semiconductor devices; photosensitive semiconductor devices, including photovoltaic cells whether or not assembled in modules or made up into panels; light-emitting diodes; mounted piezo-electric crystals:
	8541	10	Diodes, other than photosensitive or light-emitting diodes
	8541	21	Transistors, other than photosensitive transistors, with a dissipation rate of less than 1 W

ANNEX 4

	HS96		HS description
	8541	29	Transistors, other than photosensitive transistors, with a dissipation rate of 1 W or more
	8541	30	Thyristors, diacs and triacs, other than photosensitive devices
	8541	40	Photosensitive semiconductor devices, including photovoltaic cells whether or not assembled in modules or made up into panels; light emitting diodes
	8541	50	Other semiconductor devices
	8541	60	Mounted piezo-electric crystals
	8541	90	Parts
	8542		**Electronic integrated circuits and microassemblies**
	8542	12	Cards incorporating an electronic integrated circuit ('smart' cards)
	8542	13	Metal oxide semiconductors (MOS technology)
	8542	14	Circuits obtained by bipolar technology
	8542	19	Other monolithic digital integrated circuits, including circuits obtained by a combination of bipolar and MOS technologies (BIMOS technology)
	8542	30	Other monolithic integrated circuits
	8542	40	Hybrid integrated circuits
	8542	50	Electronic microassemblies
	8542	90	Part
	8543	81	Proximity cards and tags
ex	8543	89	Electrical machines with translation or dictionary functions
ex	8544	41	Other electric conductors, for a voltage not exceeding 80 V, fitted with connectors, of a kind used for telecommunications
ex	8544	49	Other electric conductors, for a voltage not exceeding 80 V, not fitted with connectors, of a kind used for telecommunications
ex	8544	51	Other electric conductors, for a voltage exceeding 80 V but not exceeding 1000 V, fitted with connectors, of a kind used for telecommunications
	8544	70	Optical fibre cables

	HS96		HS description
	9009	11	Electrostatic photocopying apparatus, operating by reproducing the original image directly onto the copy (direct process)
	9009	21	Other photocopying apparatus, incorporating an optical system
	9009	90	Parts and accessories
	9026		Instruments and apparatus for measuring or checking the flow, level, pressure or other variables of liquids or gases (for example, flow meters, level gauges, manometers, heat meters), excluding instruments and apparatus of heading No 9014, 9015, 9028 or 9032:
	9026	10	Instruments for measuring or checking the flow or level of liquids
	9026	20	Instruments and apparatus for measuring or checking pressure
	9026	80	Other instruments and apparatus for measuring or checking of heading 9026
	9026	90	Parts and accessories of instruments and apparatus of heading 9026
	9027	20	Chromatographs and electrophoresis instruments
	9027	30	Spectrometers, spectrophotometers and spectrographs using optical radiations (UV, visible, IR)
	9027	50	Other instruments and apparatus using optical radiations (UV, visible, IR) of heading No 9027
	9027	80	Other instruments and apparatus of heading No 9027 (other than those of heading No 9027 10)
ex	9027	90	Parts and accessories of products of heading 9027, other than for gas or smoke analysis apparatus and microtomes
	9030	40	Instruments and apparatus for measuring and checking, specially designed for telecommunications (for example, cross-talk meters, gain measuring instruments, distorsion factor meters, psophometers)

ANNEX 4

Attachment A, Section 2

Semiconductor manufacturing and testing equipment and parts thereof

	HS Code	Description	Comments
ex	7017 10	Quartz reactor tubes and holders designed for insertion into diffusion and oxidation furnaces for production of semiconductor wafers	For Attachment B
ex	8419 89	Chemical vapor deposition apparatus for semiconductor production	For Attachment B
ex	8419 90	Parts of chemical vapor deposition apparatus for semiconductor production	For Attachment B
ex	8421 19	Spin dryers for semiconductor wafer processing	
ex	8421 91	Parts of spin dryers for semiconductor wafer processing	
ex	8424 89	Deflash machines for cleaning and removing contaminants from the metal leads of semiconductor packages prior to the electroplating process	
ex	8424 89	Spraying appliances for etching, stripping or cleaning semiconductor wafers	
ex	8424 90	Parts of spraying appliances for etching, stripping or cleaning semiconductor wafers	
ex	8456 10	Machines for working any material by removal of material, by laser or other light or photo beam in the production of semiconductor wafers	
ex	8456 91	Apparatus for stripping or cleaning semiconductor wafers	For Attachment B
	8456 91	Machines for dry-etching patterns on semiconductor materials	
ex	8456 99	Focused ion beam milling machines to produce or repair masks and reticles for patterns on semiconductor devices	
ex	8456 99	Lasercutters for cutting contacting tracks in semiconductor production by laser beam	For Attachment B

	HS Code	Description	Comments
ex	8464 10	Machines for sawing monocrystal semiconductor boules into slices, or wafers into chips	For Attachment B
ex	8464 20	Grinding, polishing and lapping machines for processing of semiconductor wafers	
ex	8464 90	Dicing machines for scribing or scoring semiconductor wafers	
ex	8466 91	Parts for machines for sawing mono-crystal semiconductor boules into slices, or wafers into chips	For Attachment B
ex	8466 91	Parts of dicing machines for scribing or scoring semiconductor wafers	For Attachment B
ex	8466 91	Parts of grinding, polishing and lapping machines for processing of semiconductor wafers	
ex	8466 93	Parts of focused ion beam milling machines to produce or repair masks and reticles for patterns on semiconductor devices	
ex	8466 93	Parts of lasercutters for cutting contacting tracks in semiconductor production by laser beam	For Attachment B
ex	8466 93	Parts of machines for working any material by removal of material, by laser or other light or photo beam in the production of semiconductor wafers	
ex	8456 93	Parts of apparatus for stripping or cleaning semiconductor wafers	For Attachment B
ex	8466 93	Parts of machines for dry-etching patterns on semiconductor materials	
ex	8477 10	Encapsulation equipment for assembly of semiconductors	For Attachment B
ex	8477 90	Parts of encapsulation equipment	For Attachment B

ANNEX 4

	HS Code	Description	Comments
ex	8479 50	Automated machines for transport, handling and storage of semiconductor wafers, wafer cassettes, wafer boxes and other material for semiconductor devices	For Attachment B
ex	8479 89	Apparatus for growing or pulling monocrystal semiconductor boules	
ex	8479 89	Apparatus for physical deposition by sputtering on semiconductor wafers	For Attachment B
ex	8479 89	Apparatus for wet etching, developing, stripping or cleaning semiconductor wafers and flat panel displays	For Attachment B
ex	8479 89	Die attach apparatus, tape automated bonders, and wire bonders for assembly of semiconductors	For Attachment B
ex	8479 89	Encapsulation equipment for assembly of semiconductors	For Attachment B
ex	8479 89	Epitaxial deposition machines for semiconductor wafers	
ex	8479 89	Machines for bending, folding and straightening semiconductor leads	For Attachment B
ex	8479 89	Physical deposition apparatus for semiconductor production	For Attachment B
ex	8479 89	Spinners for coating photographic emulsions on semiconductor wafers	For Attachment B
ex	8479 90	Part of apparatus for physical deposition by sputtering on semiconductor wafers	For Attachment B
ex	8479 90	Parts for die attach apparatus, tape automated bonders, and wire bonders for assembly of semiconductors	For Attachment B
ex	8479 90	Parts for spinners for coating photographic emulsions on semiconductor wafers	For Attachment B
ex	8479 90	Parts of apparatus for growing or pulling monocrystal semiconductor boules	

	HS Code	Description	Comments
ex	8479 90	Parts of apparatus for wet etching, developing, stripping or cleaning semiconductor wafers and flat panel displays	For Attachment B
ex	8479 90	Parts of automated machines for transport, handling and storage of semiconductor wafers, wafer cassettes, wafer boxes and other material for semiconductor devices	For Attachment B
ex	8479 90	Parts of encapsulation equipment for assembly of semiconductors	For Attachment B
ex	8479 90	Parts of epitaxial deposition machines for semiconductor wafers	
ex	8479 90	Parts of machines for bending, folding and straightening semiconductor leads	For Attachment B
ex	8479 90	Parts of physical deposition apparatus for semiconductor production	For Attachment B
ex	8480 71	Injection and compression moulds for the manufacture of semiconductor devices	
ex	8514 10	Resistance heated furnaces and ovens for the manufacture of semiconductor devices on semiconductor wafers	
ex	8514 20	Inductance or dielectric furnaces and ovens for the manufacture of semiconductor devices on semiconductors wafers	
ex	8514 30	Apparatus for rapid heating of semiconductor wafers	For Attachment B
ex	8514 30	Parts of resistance heated furnaces and ovens for the manufacture of semiconductor devices on semiconductor wafers	
ex	8514 90	Parts of apparatus for rapid heating of wafers	For Attachment B
ex	8514 90	Parts of furnaces and ovens of Headings No 8514 10 to No 8514 30	

ANNEX 4

	HS Code	Description	Comments
ex	8536 90	Wafer probers	For Attachment B
	8543 11	Ion implanters for doping semiconductor materials	
ex	8543 30	Apparatus for wet etching, developing, stripping or cleaning semiconductor wafers and flat panel displays	For Attachment B
ex	8543 90	Parts of apparatus for wet etching, developing, stripping or cleaning semi-conductor wafers and flat panel displays	For Attachment B
ex	8543 90	Parts of ion implanters for doping semiconductor materials	
	9010 41 to 9010 49	Apparatus for projection, drawing or plating circuit patterns on sensitized semiconductor materials and flat panel displays	
ex	9010 90	Parts and accessories of the apparatus of Headings No 9010 41 to 9010 49	
ex	9011 10	Optical stereoscopic microscopes fitted with equipment specifically designed for the handling and transport of semiconductor wafers or reticles	For Attachment B
ex	9011 20	Photomicrographic microscopes fitted with equipment specifically designed for the handling and transport of semiconductor wafers or reticles	For Attachment B
ex	9011 90	Parts and accessories of optical stereoscopic microscopes fitted with equipment specifically designed for the handling and transport of semiconductor wafers or reticles	For Attachment B
ex	9011 90	Parts and accessories of photomicro-graphic microscopes fitted with equipment specifically designed for the handling and transport of semiconductor wafers or reticles	For Attachment B

	HS Code	Description	Comments
ex	9012 10	Electron beam microscopes fitted with equipment specifically designed for the handling and transport of semiconductor wafers or reticles	For Attachment B
ex	9012 90	Parts and accessories of electron beam microscopes fitted with equipment specifically designed for the handling and transport of semiconductor wafers or reticles	For Attachment B
ex	9017 20	Pattern generating apparatus of a kind used for producing masks or reticles from photoresist coated substrates	For Attachment B
ex	9017 90	Parts and accessories for pattern generating apparatus of a kind used for producing masks or reticles from photoresist coated substrates	For Attachment B
ex	9017 90	Parts of such pattern generating apparatus	For Attachment B
	9030 82	Instruments and apparatus for measuring or checking semiconductor wafers or devices	
ex	9030 90	Parts and accessories of instruments and apparatus for measuring or checking semiconductor wafers or devices	
ex	9030 90	Parts of instruments and appliances for measuring or checking semiconductor wafers or devices	
	9031 41	Optical instruments and appliances for inspecting semiconductor wafers or devices or for inspecting masks, photomasks or reticles used in manufacturing semiconductor devices	
ex	9031 49	Optical instruments and appliances for measuring surface particulate contamination on semiconductor wafers	

ANNEX 4

	HS Code	Description	Comments
ex	9031 90	Parts and accessories of optical instruments and appliances for inspecting semiconductor wafers or devices or for inspecting masks, photomasks or reticles used in manufacturing semiconductor devices	
ex	9031 90	Parts and accessories of optical instruments and appliances for measuring surface particulate contamination on semiconductor wafers	

Attachment B

Positive list of specific products to be covered by this agreement wherever they are classified in the HS.

Where parts are specified, they are to be covered in accordance with HS Notes 2(b) to Section XVI and Chapter 90, respectively.

Computers: automatic data processing machines capable of 1) storing the processing program or programs and at least the data immediately necessary for the execution of the program; 2) being freely programmed in accordance with the requirements of the user; 3) performing arithmetical computations specified by the user; and 4) executing, without human intervention, a processing program which requires them to modify their execution, by logical decision during the processing run.

The agreement covers such automatic data processing machines whether or not they are able to receive and process with the assistance of central processing unit telephony signals, television signals, or other analogue or digitally processed audio or video signals. Machines performing a specific function other than data processing, or incorporating or working in conjunction with an automatic data processing machine, and not otherwise specified under Attachment A or B, are not covered by this agreement.

Electric amplifiers when used as repeaters in line telephony products falling within this agreement, and parts thereof

---

Flat panel displays (including LCD, Electro Luminescence, Plasma and other technologies) for products falling within this agreement, and parts thereof.

Network equipment: Local Area Network (LAN) and Wide Area Network (WAN) apparatus, including those products dedicated for use solely or principally to permit the interconnection of automatic data processing machines and units thereof for a network that is used primarily for the sharing of resources such as central processor units, data storage devices and input or output units – including adapters, hubs, in-line repeaters, converters, concentrators, bridges and routers, and printed circuit assemblies for physical incorporation into automatic data processing machines and units thereof.

Monitors: display units of automatic data processing machines with a cathode ray tube with a dot screen pitch smaller than 0.4 mm not capable of receiving and processing television signals or other analogue or digitally processed audio or video signals without assistance of a central processing unit of a computer as defined in this agreement.

The agreement does not, therefore, cover televisions, including high definition televisions.[3]

Optical disc storage units, for automatic data processing machines (including CD drives and DVD-drives), whether or not having the capability of writing/recording as well as reading, whether or not in their own housings.

Paging alert devices, and parts thereof.

Plotters whether input or output units of HS heading No 8471 or drawing or drafting machines of HS heading No 9017.

Printed Circuit Assemblies for products falling within this agreement, including such assemblies for external connections such as cards that conform to the PCMCIA standard.

Such printed circuit assemblies consist of one or more printed circuits of heading 8534 with one or more active elements assembled thereon, with or without passive elements. 'Active elements' means diodes, transistors, and similar semiconductor devices, whether or not photosensitive, of heading 8541, and integrated circuits and micro assemblies of heading 8542.

Projection type flat panel display units used with automatic data processing machines which can display digital information generated by the central processing unit.

Proprietary format storage devices including media therefor for automatic data processing machines, with or without removable media and whether magnetic, optical or other technology, including Bernoulli Box, Syquest, or Zipdrive cartridge storage units.

Multimedia upgrade kits for automatic data processing machines, and units thereof, put up for retail sale, consisting of, at least, speakers and/or microphones as well as a printed circuit assembly that enables the ADP machines and units thereof to process audio signals (sound cards).

Set top boxes which have a communication function: a microprocessor-based device incorporating a modem for gaining access to the Internet, and having a function of interactive information exchange.

---

[3] Participants will conduct a review of this product description in January 1999 under the consultation provisions of paragraph 3 of the Declaration.

ANNEX 5

Geneva Ministerial Declaration (1998)

WORLD TRADE ORGANIZATION

WT/MIN(98)/DEC/1
25 May 1998
(98-2149)

MINISTERIAL CONFERENCE
Second Session
Geneva, 18 and 20 May 1998

MINISTERIAL DECLARATION

Adopted on 20 May 1998

1. This Second Session of the Ministerial Conference of the WTO is taking place at a particularly significant time for the multilateral trading system, when the fiftieth anniversary of its establishment is being commemorated. On this occasion we pay tribute to the system's important contribution over the past half-century to growth, employment and stability by promoting the liberalization and expansion of trade and providing a framework for the conduct of international trade relations, in accordance with the objectives embodied in the Preambles to the General Agreement on Tariffs and Trade and the World Trade Organization Agreement. We agree, however, that more remains to be done to enable all the world's peoples to share fully and equitably in these achievements.
2. We underline the crucial importance of the multilateral rule-based trading system. We reaffirm the commitments and assessments we made at Singapore, and we note that the work under existing agreements and decisions has resulted in significant new steps forward since we last met. In particular, we welcome the successful conclusion of the negotiations on basic telecommunications and financial services and we take note of the implementation of the Information Technology Agreement. We renew our commitment to achieve progressive liberalization of trade in goods and services.
3. The fiftieth anniversary comes at a time when the economies of a number of WTO Members are experiencing difficulties as a result of disturbances in financial markets. We take this opportunity to underline that keeping all markets open must be a key element in a durable solution to these difficulties. With this in mind, we reject the use of any protectionist

measures and agree to work together in the WTO as in the IMF and the World Bank to improve the coherence of international economic policy-making with a view to maximizing the contribution that an open, rule-based trading system can make to fostering stable growth for economies at all levels of development.

4. We recognize the importance of enhancing public understanding of the benefits of the multilateral trading system in order to build support for it and agree to work towards this end. In this context we will consider how to improve the transparency of WTO operations. We shall also continue to improve our efforts towards the objectives of sustained economic growth and sustainable development.

5. We renew our commitment to ensuring that the benefits of the multilateral trading system are extended as widely as possible. We recognize the need for the system to make its own contribution in response to the particular trade interests and development needs of developing-country Members. We welcome the work already underway in the Committee on Trade and Development for reviewing the application of special provisions in the Multilateral Trade Agreements and related Ministerial Decisions in favour of developing country Members, and in particular the least-developed among them. We agree on the need for effective implementation of these special provisions.

6. We remain deeply concerned over the marginalization of least-developed countries and certain small economies, and recognize the urgent need to address this issue which has been compounded by the chronic foreign debt problem facing many of them. In this context we welcome the initiatives taken by the WTO in cooperation with other agencies to implement in an integrated manner the Plan of Action for the least-developed countries which we agreed at Singapore, especially through the High-Level Meeting on Least-Developed Countries held in Geneva in October 1997. We also welcome the report of the Director-General on the follow-up of this initiative, to which we attach great importance. We commit ourselves to continue to improve market access conditions for products exported by the least-developed countries on as broad and liberal a basis as possible. We urge Members to implement the market-access commitments that they have undertaken at the High-Level Meeting.

7. We welcome the WTO Members who have joined since we met in Singapore: Congo, Democratic Republic of Congo, Mongolia, Niger and Panama. We welcome the progress made with 31 applicants currently negotiating their accession and renew our resolution to ensure that the accession processes proceed as rapidly as possible. We recall that accession to the WTO requires full respect of WTO rules and disciplines as well as meaningful market access commitments on the part of acceding candidates.

8. Full and faithful implementation of the WTO Agreement and Ministerial Decisions is imperative for the credibility of the multilateral trading system and indispensable for maintaining the momentum for expanding global trade, fostering job creation and raising standards of living in all parts of the world. When we meet at the Third Session we shall further pursue our evaluation of the implementation of individual agreements and the realization of their objectives. Such evaluation would cover, *inter alia*, the problems encountered in implementation and the consequent impact on the trade and development prospects of Members. We reaffirm our commitment to respect the existing schedules for reviews, negotiations and other work to which we have already agreed.

9. We recall that the Marrakesh Agreement Establishing the World Trade Organization states that the WTO shall provide the forum for negotiations among its Members concerning their multilateral trade relations in matters dealt with under the agreements in the Annexes to the Agreement, and that it may also provide a forum for further negotiations among its Members concerning their multilateral trade relations, and a framework for the implementation of the results of such negotiations, as may be decided by the Ministerial Conference. In the light of paragraphs 1–8 above, we decide that a process will be established under the direction of the General Council to ensure full and faithful implementation of existing agreements, and to prepare for the Third Session of the Ministerial Conference. This process shall enable the General Council to submit recommendations regarding the WTO's work programme, including further liberalization sufficiently broad-based to respond to the range of interests and concerns of all Members, within the WTO framework, that will enable us to take decisions at the Third Session of the Ministerial Conference. In this regard, the General Council will meet in special session in September 1998 and periodically thereafter to ensure full and timely completion of its work, fully respecting the principle of decision-making by consensus. The General Council's work programme shall encompass the following:

   (a) recommendations concerning:
      (i) the issues, including those brought forward by Members, relating to implementation of existing agreements and decisions;
      (ii) the negotiations already mandated at Marrakesh, to ensure that such negotiations begin on schedule;
      (iii) future work already provided for under other existing agreements and decisions taken at Marrakesh;
   (b) recommendations concerning other possible future work on the basis of the work programme initiated at Singapore;
   (c) recommendations on the follow-up to the High-Level Meeting on Least-Developed Countries;

(d) recommendations arising from consideration of other matters proposed and agreed to by Members concerning their multilateral trade relations.

10. The General Council will also submit to the Third Session of the Ministerial Conference, on the basis of consensus, recommendations for decision concerning the further organization and management of the work programme arising from the above, including the scope, structure and time-frames, that will ensure that the work programme is begun and concluded expeditiously.
11. The above work programme shall be aimed at achieving overall balance of interests of all Members.

ANNEX 6

Ministerial Declaration on Global Electronic Commerce (1998)

WORLD TRADE ORGANIZATION

WT/MIN(98)/DEC/2
25 May 1998
(98-2148)

MINISTERIAL CONFERENCE
Second Session
Geneva, 18 and 20 May 1998

DECLARATION ON GLOBAL ELECTRONIC COMMERCE

Adopted on 20 May 1998

Ministers,

Recognizing that global electronic commerce is growing and creating new opportunities for trade,

Declare that:

The General Council shall, by its next meeting in special session, establish a comprehensive work programme to examine all trade-related issues relating to global electronic commerce, including those issues identified by Members. The work programme will involve the relevant World Trade Organization ('WTO') bodies, take into account the economic, financial, and development needs of developing countries, and recognize that work is also being undertaken in other international fora. The General Council should produce a report on the progress of the work programme and any recommendations for action to be submitted at our third session. Without prejudice to the outcome of the work programme or the rights and obligations of Members under the WTO Agreements, we also declare that Members will continue their current practice of not imposing customs duties on electronic transmissions. When reporting to our third session, the General Council will review this declaration, the extension of which will be decided by consensus, taking into account the progress of the work programme.

ANNEX 7

Doha Ministerial Declaration (2001)

WT/MIN(01)/DEC/1
WORLD TRADE
ORGANIZATION
20 November 2001
(01-5859)

MINISTERIAL CONFERENCE
Fourth Session
Doha, 9–14 November 2001

MINISTERIAL DECLARATION

Adopted on 14 November 2001

1. The multilateral trading system embodied in the World Trade Organization has contributed significantly to economic growth, development and employment throughout the past fifty years. We are determined, particularly in the light of the global economic slowdown, to maintain the process of reform and liberalization of trade policies, thus ensuring that the system plays its full part in promoting recovery, growth and development. We therefore strongly reaffirm the principles and objectives set out in the Marrakesh Agreement Establishing the World Trade Organization, and pledge to reject the use of protectionism.

2. International trade can play a major role in the promotion of economic development and the alleviation of poverty. We recognize the need for all our peoples to benefit from the increased opportunities and welfare gains that the multilateral trading system generates. The majority of WTO Members are developing countries. We seek to place their needs and interests at the heart of the Work Programme adopted in this Declaration. Recalling the Preamble to the Marrakesh Agreement, we shall continue to make positive efforts designed to ensure that developing countries, and especially the least-developed among them, secure a share in the growth of world trade commensurate with the needs of their economic development. In this context, enhanced market access, balanced rules, and well targeted, sustainably financed technical assistance and capacity-building programmes have important roles to play.

3. We recognize the particular vulnerability of the least-developed countries and the special structural difficulties they face in the global economy. We are committed to addressing the marginalization of least-developed

countries in international trade and to improving their effective participation in the multilateral trading system. We recall the commitments made by Ministers at our meetings in Marrakesh, Singapore and Geneva, and by the international community at the Third UN Conference on Least-Developed Countries in Brussels, to help least-developed countries secure beneficial and meaningful integration into the multilateral trading system and the global economy. We are determined that the WTO will play its part in building effectively on these commitments under the Work Programme we are establishing.

4. We stress our commitment to the WTO as the unique forum for global trade rule-making and liberalization, while also recognizing that regional trade agreements can play an important role in promoting the liberalization and expansion of trade and in fostering development.

5. We are aware that the challenges Members face in a rapidly changing international environment cannot be addressed through measures taken in the trade field alone. We shall continue to work with the Bretton Woods institutions for greater coherence in global economic policy-making.

6. We strongly reaffirm our commitment to the objective of sustainable development, as stated in the Preamble to the Marrakesh Agreement. We are convinced that the aims of upholding and safeguarding an open and non-discriminatory multilateral trading system, and acting for the protection of the environment and the promotion of sustainable development can and must be mutually supportive. We take note of the efforts by Members to conduct national environmental assessments of trade policies on a voluntary basis. We recognize that under WTO rules no country should be prevented from taking measures for the protection of human, animal or plant life or health, or of the environment at the levels it considers appropriate, subject to the requirement that they are not applied in a manner which would constitute a means of arbitrary or unjustifiable discrimination between countries where the same conditions prevail, or a disguised restriction on international trade, and are otherwise in accordance with the provisions of the WTO Agreements. We welcome the WTO's continued cooperation with UNEP and other inter-governmental environmental organizations. We encourage efforts to promote cooperation between the WTO and relevant international environmental and developmental organizations, especially in the lead-up to the World Summit on Sustainable Development to be held in Johannesburg, South Africa, in September 2002.

7. We reaffirm the right of Members under the General Agreement on Trade in Services to regulate, and to introduce new regulations on, the supply of services.

8. We reaffirm our declaration made at the Singapore Ministerial Conference regarding internationally recognized core labour standards. We take note of work under way in the International Labour Organization (ILO) on the social dimension of globalization.

9. We note with particular satisfaction that this Conference has completed the WTO accession procedures for China and Chinese Taipei. We also welcome the accession as new Members, since our last Session, of Albania, Croatia, Georgia, Jordan, Lithuania, Moldova and Oman, and note the extensive market-access commitments already made by these countries on accession. These accessions will greatly strengthen the multilateral trading system, as will those of the 28 countries now negotiating their accession. We therefore attach great importance to concluding accession proceedings as quickly as possible. In particular, we are committed to accelerating the accession of least-developed countries.

10. Recognizing the challenges posed by an expanding WTO membership, we confirm our collective responsibility to ensure internal transparency and the effective participation of all Members. While emphasizing the intergovernmental character of the organization, we are committed to making the WTO's operations more transparent, including through more effective and prompt dissemination of information, and to improve dialogue with the public. We shall therefore at the national and multilateral levels continue to promote a better public understanding of the WTO and to communicate the benefits of a liberal, rules-based multilateral trading system.

11. In view of these considerations, we hereby agree to undertake the broad and balanced Work Programme set out below. This incorporates both an expanded negotiating agenda and other important decisions and activities necessary to address the challenges facing the multilateral trading system.

WORK PROGRAMME

Implementation-Related Issues and Concerns

12. We attach the utmost importance to the implementation-related issues and concerns raised by Members and are determined to find appropriate solutions to them. In this connection, and having regard to the General Council Decisions of 3 May and 15 December 2000, we further adopt the Decision on Implementation-Related Issues and Concerns in document WT/MIN(01)/17 to address a number of implementation problems faced by Members. We agree that negotiations on outstanding implementation issues shall be an integral part of the Work Programme we are establishing,

and that agreements reached at an early stage in these negotiations shall be treated in accordance with the provisions of paragraph 47 below. In this regard, we shall proceed as follows: (a) where we provide a specific negotiating mandate in this Declaration, the relevant implementation issues shall be addressed under that mandate; (b) the other outstanding implementation issues shall be addressed as a matter of priority by the relevant WTO bodies, which shall report to the Trade Negotiations Committee, established under paragraph 46 below, by the end of 2002 for appropriate action.

AGRICULTURE

13. We recognize the work already undertaken in the negotiations initiated in early 2000 under Article 20 of the Agreement on Agriculture, including the large number of negotiating proposals submitted on behalf of a total of 121 Members. We recall the long-term objective referred to in the Agreement to establish a fair and market-oriented trading system through a programme of fundamental reform encompassing strengthened rules and specific commitments on support and protection in order to correct and prevent restrictions and distortions in world agricultural markets. We reconfirm our commitment to this programme. Building on the work carried out to date and without prejudging the outcome of the negotiations we commit ourselves to comprehensive negotiations aimed at: substantial improvements in market access; reductions of, with a view to phasing out, all forms of export subsidies; and substantial reductions in trade-distorting domestic support. We agree that special and differential treatment for developing countries shall be an integral part of all elements of the negotiations and shall be embodied in the Schedules of concessions and commitments and as appropriate in the rules and disciplines to be negotiated, so as to be operationally effective and to enable developing countries to effectively take account of their development needs, including food security and rural development. We take note of the non-trade concerns reflected in the negotiating proposals submitted by Members and confirm that non-trade concerns will be taken into account in the negotiations as provided for in the Agreement on Agriculture.
14. Modalities for the further commitments, including provisions for special and differential treatment, shall be established no later than 31 March 2003. Participants shall submit their comprehensive draft Schedules based on these modalities no later than the date of the Fifth Session of the Ministerial Conference. The negotiations, including with respect to rules and disciplines and related legal texts, shall be concluded as part and at the date of conclusion of the negotiating agenda as a whole.

SERVICES

15. The negotiations on trade in services shall be conducted with a view to promoting the economic growth of all trading partners and the development of developing and least-developed countries. We recognize the work already undertaken in the negotiations, initiated in January 2000 under Article XIX of the General Agreement on Trade in Services, and the large number of proposals submitted by Members on a wide range of sectors and several horizontal issues, as well as on movement of natural persons. We reaffirm the Guidelines and Procedures for the Negotiations adopted by the Council for Trade in Services on 28 March 2001 as the basis for continuing the negotiations, with a view to achieving the objectives of the General Agreement on Trade in Services, as stipulated in the Preamble, Article IV and Article XIX of that Agreement. Participants shall submit initial requests for specific commitments by 30 June 2002 and initial offers by 31 March 2003.

MARKET ACCESS FOR NON-AGRICULTURAL PRODUCTS

16. We agree to negotiations which shall aim, by modalities to be agreed, to reduce or as appropriate eliminate tariffs, including the reduction or elimination of tariff peaks, high tariffs, and tariff escalation, as well as non-tariff barriers, in particular on products of export interest to developing countries. Product coverage shall be comprehensive and without *a priori* exclusions. The negotiations shall take fully into account the special needs and interests of developing and least-developed country participants, including through less than full reciprocity in reduction commitments, in accordance with the relevant provisions of Article XXVIII *bis* of GATT 1994 and the provisions cited in paragraph 50 below. To this end, the modalities to be agreed will include appropriate studies and capacity-building measures to assist least-developed countries to participate effectively in the negotiations.

TRADE-RELATED ASPECTS OF INTELLECTUAL PROPERTY RIGHTS

17. We stress the importance we attach to implementation and interpretation of the Agreement on Trade-Related Aspects of Intellectual Property Rights (TRIPS Agreement) in a manner supportive of public health, by promoting both access to existing medicines and research and development into new medicines and, in this connection, are adopting a separate Declaration.
18. With a view to completing the work started in the Council for Trade-Related Aspects of Intellectual Property Rights (Council for TRIPS) on the

implementation of Article 23.4, we agree to negotiate the establishment of a multilateral system of notification and registration of geographical indications for wines and spirits by the Fifth Session of the Ministerial Conference. We note that issues related to the extension of the protection of geographical indications provided for in Article 23 to products other than wines and spirits will be addressed in the Council for TRIPS pursuant to paragraph 12 of this Declaration.

19. We instruct the Council for TRIPS, in pursuing its work programme including under the review of Article 27.3(b), the review of the implementation of the TRIPS Agreement under Article 71.1 and the work foreseen pursuant to paragraph 12 of this Declaration, to examine, *inter alia*, the relationship between the TRIPS Agreement and the Convention on Biological Diversity, the protection of traditional knowledge and folklore, and other relevant new developments raised by Members pursuant to Article 71.1. In undertaking this work, the TRIPS Council shall be guided by the objectives and principles set out in Articles 7 and 8 of the TRIPS Agreement and shall take fully into account the development dimension.

RELATIONSHIP BETWEEN TRADE AND INVESTMENT

20. Recognizing the case for a multilateral framework to secure transparent, stable and predictable conditions for long-term cross-border investment, particularly foreign direct investment, that will contribute to the expansion of trade, and the need for enhanced technical assistance and capacity-building in this area as referred to in paragraph 21, we agree that negotiations will take place after the Fifth Session of the Ministerial Conference on the basis of a decision to be taken, by explicit consensus, at that Session on modalities of negotiations.

21. We recognize the needs of developing and least-developed countries for enhanced support for technical assistance and capacity building in this area, including policy analysis and development so that they may better evaluate the implications of closer multilateral cooperation for their development policies and objectives, and human and institutional development. To this end, we shall work in cooperation with other relevant intergovernmental organizations, including UNCTAD, and through appropriate regional and bilateral channels, to provide strengthened and adequately resourced assistance to respond to these needs.

22. In the period until the Fifth Session, further work in the Working Group on the Relationship Between Trade and Investment will focus on the clarification of: scope and definition; transparency; non-discrimination; modalities for pre-establishment commitments based on a GATS-type,

positive list approach; development provisions; exceptions and balance-of-payments safeguards; consultation and the settlement of disputes between Members. Any framework should reflect in a balanced manner the interests of home and host countries, and take due account of the development policies and objectives of host governments as well as their right to regulate in the public interest. The special development, trade and financial needs of developing and least-developed countries should be taken into account as an integral part of any framework, which should enable Members to undertake obligations and commitments commensurate with their individual needs and circumstances. Due regard should be paid to other relevant WTO provisions. Account should be taken, as appropriate, of existing bilateral and regional arrangements on investment.

INTERACTION BETWEEN TRADE AND COMPETITION POLICY

23. Recognizing the case for a multilateral framework to enhance the contribution of competition policy to international trade and development, and the need for enhanced technical assistance and capacity-building in this area as referred to in paragraph 24, we agree that negotiations will take place after the Fifth Session of the Ministerial Conference on the basis of a decision to be taken, by explicit consensus, at that Session on modalities of negotiations.
24. We recognize the needs of developing and least-developed countries for enhanced support for technical assistance and capacity building in this area, including policy analysis and development so that they may better evaluate the implications of closer multilateral cooperation for their development policies and objectives, and human and institutional development. To this end, we shall work in cooperation with other relevant intergovernmental organizations, including UNCTAD, and through appropriate regional and bilateral channels, to provide strengthened and adequately resourced assistance to respond to these needs.
25. In the period until the Fifth Session, further work in the Working Group on the Interaction between Trade and Competition Policy will focus on the clarification of: core principles, including transparency, non-discrimination and procedural fairness, and provisions on hardcore cartels; modalities for voluntary cooperation; and support for progressive reinforcement of competition institutions in developing countries through capacity building. Full account shall be taken of the needs of developing and least-developed country participants and appropriate flexibility provided to address them.

Transparency in Government Procurement

26. Recognizing the case for a multilateral agreement on transparency in government procurement and the need for enhanced technical assistance and capacity building in this area, we agree that negotiations will take place after the Fifth Session of the Ministerial Conference on the basis of a decision to be taken, by explicit consensus, at that Session on modalities of negotiations. These negotiations will build on the progress made in the Working Group on Transparency in Government Procurement by that time and take into account participants' development priorities, especially those of least-developed country participants. Negotiations shall be limited to the transparency aspects and therefore will not restrict the scope for countries to give preferences to domestic supplies and suppliers. We commit ourselves to ensuring adequate technical assistance and support for capacity building both during the negotiations and after their conclusion.

Trade Facilitation

27. Recognizing the case for further expediting the movement, release and clearance of goods, including goods in transit, and the need for enhanced technical assistance and capacity building in this area, we agree that negotiations will take place after the Fifth Session of the Ministerial Conference on the basis of a decision to be taken, by explicit consensus, at that Session on modalities of negotiations. In the period until the Fifth Session, the Council for Trade in Goods shall review and as appropriate, clarify and improve relevant aspects of Articles V, VIII and X of the GATT 1994 and identify the trade facilitation needs and priorities of Members, in particular developing and least-developed countries. We commit ourselves to ensuring adequate technical assistance and support for capacity building in this area.

WTO Rules

28. In the light of experience and of the increasing application of these instruments by Members, we agree to negotiations aimed at clarifying and improving disciplines under the Agreements on Implementation of Article VI of the GATT 1994 and on Subsidies and Countervailing Measures, while preserving the basic concepts, principles and effectiveness of these Agreements and their instruments and objectives, and taking into account the needs of developing and least-developed participants. In the initial phase of the negotiations, participants will indicate the provisions, including disciplines on trade distorting practices, that they seek to clarify and improve in

the subsequent phase. In the context of these negotiations, participants shall also aim to clarify and improve WTO disciplines on fisheries subsidies, taking into account the importance of this sector to developing countries. We note that fisheries subsidies are also referred to in paragraph 31.
29. We also agree to negotiations aimed at clarifying and improving disciplines and procedures under the existing WTO provisions applying to regional trade agreements. The negotiations shall take into account the developmental aspects of regional trade agreements.

Dispute Settlement Understanding

30. We agree to negotiations on improvements and clarifications of the Dispute Settlement Understanding. The negotiations should be based on the work done thus far as well as any additional proposals by Members, and aim to agree on improvements and clarifications not later than May 2003, at which time we will take steps to ensure that the results enter into force as soon as possible thereafter.

Trade and Environment

31. With a view to enhancing the mutual supportiveness of trade and environment, we agree to negotiations, without prejudging their outcome, on:
    (i) the relationship between existing WTO rules and specific trade obligations set out in multilateral environmental agreements (MEAs). The negotiations shall be limited in scope to the applicability of such existing WTO rules as among parties to the MEA in question. The negotiations shall not prejudice the WTO rights of any Member that is not a party to the MEA in question;
    (ii) procedures for regular information exchange between MEA Secretariats and the relevant WTO committees, and the criteria for the granting of observer status;
    (iii) the reduction or, as appropriate, elimination of tariff and non-tariff barriers to environmental goods and services.

We note that fisheries subsidies form part of the negotiations provided for in paragraph 28.

32. We instruct the Committee on Trade and Environment, in pursuing work on all items on its agenda within its current terms of reference, to give particular attention to:
    (i) the effect of environmental measures on market access, especially in relation to developing countries, in particular the least-developed among them, and those situations in which the elimination or

      reduction of trade restrictions and distortions would benefit trade, the environment and development;
- (ii) the relevant provisions of the Agreement on Trade-Related Aspects of Intellectual Property Rights; and
- (iii) labelling requirements for environmental purposes.

Work on these issues should include the identification of any need to clarify relevant WTO rules. The Committee shall report to the Fifth Session of the Ministerial Conference, and make recommendations, where appropriate, with respect to future action, including the desirability of negotiations. The outcome of this work as well as the negotiations carried out under paragraph 31(i) and (ii) shall be compatible with the open and non-discriminatory nature of the multilateral trading system, shall not add to or diminish the rights and obligations of Members under existing WTO agreements, in particular the Agreement on the Application of Sanitary and Phytosanitary Measures, nor alter the balance of these rights and obligations, and will take into account the needs of developing and least-developed countries.

33. We recognize the importance of technical assistance and capacity building in the field of trade and environment to developing countries, in particular the least-developed among them. We also encourage that expertize and experience be shared with Members wishing to perform environmental reviews at the national level. A report shall be prepared on these activities for the Fifth Session.

Electronic Commerce

34. We take note of the work which has been done in the General Council and other relevant bodies since the Ministerial Declaration of 20 May 1998 and agree to continue the Work Programme on Electronic Commerce. The work to date demonstrates that electronic commerce creates new challenges and opportunities for trade for Members at all stages of development, and we recognize the importance of creating and maintaining an environment which is favourable to the future development of electronic commerce. We instruct the General Council to consider the most appropriate institutional arrangements for handling the Work Programme, and to report on further progress to the Fifth Session of the Ministerial Conference. We declare that Members will maintain their current practice of not imposing customs duties on electronic transmissions until the Fifth Session.

Small Economies

35. We agree to a work programme, under the auspices of the General Council, to examine issues relating to the trade of small economies. The

objective of this work is to frame responses to the trade-related issues identified for the fuller integration of small, vulnerable economies into the multilateral trading system, and not to create a sub-category of WTO Members. The General Council shall review the work programme and make recommendations for action to the Fifth Session of the Ministerial Conference.

TRADE, DEBT AND FINANCE

36. We agree to an examination, in a Working Group under the auspices of the General Council, of the relationship between trade, debt and finance, and of any possible recommendations on steps that might be taken within the mandate and competence of the WTO to enhance the capacity of the multilateral trading system to contribute to a durable solution to the problem of external indebtedness of developing and least-developed countries, and to strengthen the coherence of international trade and financial policies, with a view to safeguarding the multilateral trading system from the effects of financial and monetary instability. The General Council shall report to the Fifth Session of the Ministerial Conference on progress in the examination.

TRADE AND TRANSFER OF TECHNOLOGY

37. We agree to an examination, in a Working Group under the auspices of the General Council, of the relationship between trade and transfer of technology, and of any possible recommendations on steps that might be taken within the mandate of the WTO to increase flows of technology to developing countries. The General Council shall report to the Fifth Session of the Ministerial Conference on progress in the examination.

TECHNICAL COOPERATION AND CAPACITY BUILDING

38. We confirm that technical cooperation and capacity building are core elements of the development dimension of the multilateral trading system, and we welcome and endorse the New Strategy for WTO Technical Cooperation for Capacity Building, Growth and Integration. We instruct the Secretariat, in coordination with other relevant agencies, to support domestic efforts for mainstreaming trade into national plans for economic development and strategies for poverty reduction. The delivery of WTO technical assistance shall be designed to assist developing and least-developed countries and low-income countries in transition to adjust to WTO rules and disciplines, implement obligations and exercise the rights of membership, including

drawing on the benefits of an open, rules-based multilateral trading system. Priority shall also be accorded to small, vulnerable, and transition economies, as well as to Members and Observers without representation in Geneva. We reaffirm our support for the valuable work of the International Trade Centre, which should be enhanced.

39. We underscore the urgent necessity for the effective coordinated delivery of technical assistance with bilateral donors, in the OECD Development Assistance Committee and relevant international and regional intergovernmental institutions, within a coherent policy framework and timetable. In the coordinated delivery of technical assistance, we instruct the Director-General to consult with the relevant agencies, bilateral donors and beneficiaries, to identify ways of enhancing and rationalizing the Integrated Framework for Trade-Related Technical Assistance to Least-Developed Countries and the Joint Integrated Technical Assistance Programme (JITAP).

40. We agree that there is a need for technical assistance to benefit from secure and predictable funding. We therefore instruct the Committee on Budget, Finance and Administration to develop a plan for adoption by the General Council in December 2001 that will ensure long-term funding for WTO technical assistance at an overall level no lower than that of the current year and commensurate with the activities outlined above.

41. We have established firm commitments on technical cooperation and capacity building in various paragraphs in this Ministerial Declaration. We reaffirm these specific commitments contained in paragraphs 16, 21, 24, 26, 27, 33, 38–40, 42 and 43, and also reaffirm the understanding in paragraph 2 on the important role of sustainably financed technical assistance and capacity-building programmes. We instruct the Director-General to report to the Fifth Session of the Ministerial Conference, with an interim report to the General Council in December 2002 on the implementation and adequacy of these commitments in the identified paragraphs.

LEAST-DEVELOPED COUNTRIES

42. We acknowledge the seriousness of the concerns expressed by the least-developed countries (LDCs) in the Zanzibar Declaration adopted by their Ministers in July 2001. We recognize that the integration of the LDCs into the multilateral trading system requires meaningful market access, support for the diversification of their production and export base, and trade-related technical assistance and capacity building. We agree that the meaningful integration of LDCs into the trading system and the global economy will involve efforts by all WTO Members. We commit ourselves to the objective of duty-free, quota-free market access for products

originating from LDCs. In this regard, we welcome the significant market access improvements by WTO Members in advance of the Third UN Conference on LDCs (LDC-III), in Brussels, May 2001. We further commit ourselves to consider additional measures for progressive improvements in market access for LDCs. Accession of LDCs remains a priority for the Membership. We agree to work to facilitate and accelerate negotiations with acceding LDCs. We instruct the Secretariat to reflect the priority we attach to LDCs' accessions in the annual plans for technical assistance. We reaffirm the commitments we undertook at LDC-III, and agree that the WTO should take into account, in designing its work programme for LDCs, the trade-related elements of the Brussels Declaration and Programme of Action, consistent with the WTO's mandate, adopted at LDC-III. We instruct the Sub-Committee for Least-Developed Countries to design such a work programme and to report on the agreed work programme to the General Council at its first meeting in 2002.

43. We endorse the Integrated Framework for Trade-Related Technical Assistance to Least-Developed Countries (IF) as a viable model for LDCs' trade development. We urge development partners to significantly increase contributions to the IF Trust Fund and WTO extra-budgetary trust funds in favour of LDCs. We urge the core agencies, in coordination with development partners, to explore the enhancement of the IF with a view to addressing the supply-side constraints of LDCs and the extension of the model to all LDCs, following the review of the IF and the appraisal of the ongoing Pilot Scheme in selected LDCs. We request the Director-General, following coordination with heads of the other agencies, to provide an interim report to the General Council in December 2002 and a full report to the Fifth Session of the Ministerial Conference on all issues affecting LDCs.

SPECIAL AND DIFFERENTIAL TREATMENT

44. We reaffirm that provisions for special and differential treatment are an integral part of the WTO Agreements. We note the concerns expressed regarding their operation in addressing specific constraints faced by developing countries, particularly least-developed countries. In that connection, we also note that some Members have proposed a Framework Agreement on Special and Differential Treatment (WT/GC/W/442). We therefore agree that all special and differential treatment provisions shall be reviewed with a view to strengthening them and making them more precise, effective and operational. In this connection, we endorse the work programme on special and differential treatment set out in the Decision on Implementation-Related Issues and Concerns.

ORGANIZATION AND MANAGEMENT OF THE WORK PROGRAMME

45. The negotiations to be pursued under the terms of this Declaration shall be concluded not later than 1 January 2005. The Fifth Session of the Ministerial Conference will take stock of progress in the negotiations, provide any necessary political guidance, and take decisions as necessary. When the results of the negotiations in all areas have been established, a Special Session of the Ministerial Conference will be held to take decisions regarding the adoption and implementation of those results.
46. The overall conduct of the negotiations shall be supervised by a Trade Negotiations Committee under the authority of the General Council. The Trade Negotiations Committee shall hold its first meeting not later than 31 January 2002. It shall establish appropriate negotiating mechanisms as required and supervise the progress of the negotiations.
47. With the exception of the improvements and clarifications of the Dispute Settlement Understanding, the conduct, conclusion and entry into force of the outcome of the negotiations shall be treated as parts of a single undertaking. However, agreements reached at an early stage may be implemented on a provisional or a definitive basis. Early agreements shall be taken into account in assessing the overall balance of the negotiations.
48. Negotiations shall be open to:
    (i) all Members of the WTO; and
    (ii) States and separate customs territories currently in the process of accession and those that inform Members, at a regular meeting of the General Council, of their intention to negotiate the terms of their membership and for whom an accession working party is established.

Decisions on the outcomes of the negotiations shall be taken only by WTO Members.

49. The negotiations shall be conducted in a transparent manner among participants, in order to facilitate the effective participation of all. They shall be conducted with a view to ensuring benefits to all participants and to achieving an overall balance in the outcome of the negotiations.
50. The negotiations and the other aspects of the Work Programme shall take fully into account the principle of special and differential treatment for developing and least-developed countries embodied in: Part IV of the GATT 1994; the Decision of 28 November 1979 on Differential and More Favourable Treatment, Reciprocity and Fuller Participation of Developing Countries; the Uruguay Round Decision on Measures in Favour of Least-Developed Countries; and all other relevant WTO provisions.

51. The Committee on Trade and Development and the Committee on Trade and Environment shall, within their respective mandates, each act as a forum to identify and debate developmental and environmental aspects of the negotiations, in order to help achieve the objective of having sustainable development appropriately reflected.
52. Those elements of the Work Programme which do not involve negotiations are also accorded a high priority. They shall be pursued under the overall supervision of the General Council, which shall report on progress to the Fifth Session of the Ministerial Conference.

ANNEX 8

Ministerial Declaration on the TRIPS Agreement and Public Health (2001)

WT/MIN(01)/DEC/2
20 November 2001
(01-5860)

WORLD TRADE ORGANIZATION

MINISTERIAL CONFERENCE
Fourth Session
Doha, 9–14 November 2001

DECLARATION ON THE TRIPS AGREEMENT AND PUBLIC HEALTH

Adopted on 14 November 2001

1. We recognize the gravity of the public health problems afflicting many developing and least-developed countries, especially those resulting from HIV/AIDS, tuberculosis, malaria and other epidemics.
2. We stress the need for the WTO Agreement on Trade-Related Aspects of Intellectual Property Rights (TRIPS Agreement) to be part of the wider national and international action to address these problems.
3. We recognize that intellectual property protection is important for the development of new medicines. We also recognize the concerns about its effects on prices.
4. We agree that the TRIPS Agreement does not and should not prevent Members from taking measures to protect public health. Accordingly, while reiterating our commitment to the TRIPS Agreement, we affirm that the Agreement can and should be interpreted and implemented in a manner supportive of WTO Members' right to protect public health and, in particular, to promote access to medicines for all.

    In this connection, we reaffirm the right of WTO Members to use, to the full, the provisions in the TRIPS Agreement, which provide flexibility for this purpose.
5. Accordingly and in the light of paragraph 4 above, while maintaining our commitments in the TRIPS Agreement, we recognize that these flexibilities include:

    (a) In applying the customary rules of interpretation of public international law, each provision of the TRIPS Agreement shall be read in the

light of the object and purpose of the Agreement as expressed, in particular, in its objectives and principles.
(b) Each Member has the right to grant compulsory licences and the freedom to determine the grounds upon which such licences are granted.
(c) Each Member has the right to determine what constitutes a national emergency or other circumstances of extreme urgency, it being understood that public health crises, including those relating to HIV/AIDS, tuberculosis, malaria and other epidemics, can represent a national emergency or other circumstances of extreme urgency.
(d) The effect of the provisions in the TRIPS Agreement that are relevant to the exhaustion of intellectual property rights is to leave each Member free to establish its own regime for such exhaustion without challenge, subject to the MFN and national treatment provisions of Articles 3 and 4.

6. We recognize that WTO Members with insufficient or no manufacturing capacities in the pharmaceutical sector could face difficulties in making effective use of compulsory licensing under the TRIPS Agreement. We instruct the Council for TRIPS to find an expeditious solution to this problem and to report to the General Council before the end of 2002.
7. We reaffirm the commitment of developed-country Members to provide incentives to their enterprises and institutions to promote and encourage technology transfer to least-developed country Members pursuant to Article 66.2. We also agree that the least-developed country Members will not be obliged, with respect to pharmaceutical products, to implement or apply Sections 5 and 7 of Part II of the TRIPS Agreement or to enforce rights provided for under these Sections until 1 January 2016, without prejudice to the right of least-developed country Members to seek other extensions of the transition periods as provided for in Article 66.1 of the TRIPS Agreement. We instruct the Council for TRIPS to take the necessary action to give effect to this pursuant to Article 66.1 of the TRIPS Agreement.

INDEX

Afghanistan, 14
Agreement on Textiles and Clothing
   abolition of preferential access, 140–1
   approach, 7, 10
   Article 6.10, 108–9
   implementation problems, 54
   notification requirements, 24
   US – combed cotton yarn dispute, 108–9
   US – cotton underwear dispute, 74–5
agriculture
   Agreement on Agriculture, 7, 8, 9–10, 88
   barriers, 51
   built-in agenda, 8, 50, 64, 66
   Cancún Conference, 118
   continuing negotiations, 50, 63, 80, 91, 92, 116–17
   Doha Declaration, 100–1
   growth set-back, 42
   new members, 14
   protectionism, 82
   significance, 123
   subsidies, 123
Albania, 14, 22, 79
Algeria, 14, 22
amicus curiae briefs, 57, 107–8
Andorra, 14, 22
annual reports
   1995, 24
   1996, 38
   1997, 32
   1998, 57
   1999, 42
   2000, 90
   2001, 40
anti-dumping measures, 90, 103, 106
Appellate Body
   amicus curiae briefs, 57, 107–8
   number of appeals, 12
   procedures, 56
   Rules of Conduct, 28
Argentina, 11, 124
Armenia, 22
asbestos, 107–8
ASEAN, 33
Asia Pacific Economic Cooperation (APEC), 33
Australia, 73
Azerbaijan, 14, 22

Bahamas, 14
Barshefsky, Charlene, 70
Belarus, 14, 22
Benin, 118, 125
Berne Convention, 106, 107
Bhutan, 14, 22
Blair, Tony, 46
Bolivia, 124
Bosnia, 14
Botswana, 118
Brazil, 11, 62, 124
Bretton Woods institutions, 16–18, 27
Bretton Woods system, 4–5
Brittan, Leon, 50
budget, 157–8
Bulgaria, 14, 22, 71
Burkina Faso, 125

Cambodia, 14, 22, 120
Canada, 11, 37, 73, 84–5, 107
Cancún Ministerial Conference 2003
    accessions, 120
    aftermath, 120–5
    agriculture, 118
    failure, 120–2, 128, 134–5
    generally, 117–19
    key issues, 121
    Ministerial Statement, 120
    post-Cancún package, 123–5, 135
    Singapore issues, 118–19
    stock taking, 110, 121
Cape Verde, 14
Cardoso, Fernando Henrique, 46
Castillo, Perez del, 117, 118
Castro, Fidel, 46
Chad, 125
chemical products, 60–1, 77–8
Chile, 11, 124
China
    accession, 14, 22, 45, 49, 79, 105
    cotton subsidies, 125
    G-20 member, 124
    trade policy reviews, 73
Clinton, Bill, 46, 47, 48, 50–1, 56–7, 63, 129
communication technologies, 4
competition negotiations, 37, 63, 91, 119
continuing negotiations
    agriculture, 50, 64, 66, 91, 92, 116–17
    basis for consensus, 90–2
    built-in agenda, 25, 50, 63–4
    Doha Round, 115–17
    financial services, 29–30
    and implementation issues, 126–7
    methodology, 69
    post-Doha, 103–4, 104–5
    post-Seattle, 79, 80
    reduction of issues, 137
    services, 29–31, 63, 64, 80–1, 91, 93
    Singapore issues, 63, 64
cooperation, 87, 156
copyright, United States, 106–7
Costa Rica, 67, 74–5
Cotti, Flavio, 46

Cotton Initiative, 121, 125
cotton underwear dispute, 74–5
cotton yarn dispute, 108–9
Council on Goods, 15
Croatia, 22, 79
Cuba, 124
customs duties, decrease, 87–8
customs unions, 83
Customs Valuation Agreement, 39, 135

decision-making, 97–9, 131–5, 158–60
Derbez, Luis Ernesto, 118, 121
developing countries
    accession negotiations, 21
    and continuing negotiations, 63–4
    and decision-making at WTO, 98, 133–4
    G-20, 124
    implementation problems, 25, 54, 88
    least-developed. *See* least-developed countries
    notification requirements, 24
    patents, 61, 77
    post-1995 growth, 139
    preferential trade agreements, 129–30, 140–1
    shrinking market share, 42
    special and different treatment, 113–14
    technical assistance, 86–7, 117, 138
    TRIPS and public health, 89–90
    use of dispute settlement mechanisms, 11
    WTO membership, 19
development
    1999 symposium, 48
    Development Round, 99–100, 138, 140, 141
    international financial institutions, 16–17
    WTO management of, 138–42
directors-general, 67–8
dispute resolution
    achievements, 45
    developing countries, 11
    Dispute Settlement Body, 11, 15, 28, 56, 114

Dispute Settlement Understanding
   (DSU), 72, 103, 110, 114
  early period, 28
  principles, 11
  procedures, 28, 56
  transparency, 56
disputes
  EC – asbestos, 107–108
  EC – bananas, 60, 76–7
  EC – beef hormones, 59–60, 75–6
  India – patent protection, 26, 60–1, 77–8
  numbers, 11–12, 28, 128^n
  US – Anti-Dumping Act, 106
  US – combed cotton yarn, 108–9
  US – Copyright Act, 106–7
  US – cotton underwear, 74–5
  US – shrimp/turtles, 47, 56, 58–9
  US – tuna dispute, 34
documents, access to, vii, 27, 48, 56, 132
Doha Ministerial Conference 2001
  accessions, 105
  agriculture, 100–1
  continuing negotiations, 104–5
  deadlines, 110
  decision-making, 97–9
  Declaration, 100–5, 138, 217–31
  developing countries, 104
  Development Round, 99–100, 138, 140, 141–2
  Dispute Settlement Understanding, 103, 110
  expectations, 90
  generally, 96–105
  implementation issues, 100
  NGOs, 105
  Non-Agricultural Market Access (NAMA), 101
  preparations, 94–5, 134
  regional agreements, 103
  services, 101
  Singapore issues, 102–3
  TRIPS and Public Health Declaration, 102, 110, 235–6
Doha Round
  continuing negotiations, 115–17
  developing countries, 112–14
  dispute settlement, 114–15
  duration, 124, 132
  generally, 110–17
  TRIPS, 110–13
dot.com boom/bubble, 36, 83, 92, 96

East Asia, 3, 41–3, 45, 47, 52, 62–3
Ecuador, 14, 60, 71, 76
Egypt, 124
electronic commerce, 55–6, 71–2, 92, 213
enforcement mechanisms, 11
environmental protection
  1999 symposium, 48
  Committee on Trade and Environment (CTE), 35
  debate, 33–4
  and European Union, 50
  protesters, 57
  shrimp/turtle dispute, 47, 56, 58–9
  Singapore Conference, 33, 35, 130
  sustainable development, 34, 35
  tuna dispute, 34
establishment phase 1995–96, 19–31
Estonia, 14, 22, 71
Ethiopia, 14, 22
European Union
  agenda, 63
  asbestos dispute, 57
  bananas disputes, 60, 76–7
  beef hormones dispute, 59–60, 75–6
  Cancún Conference, 118
  cotton subsidies, 125
  economic downturn, 83
  environmental protection, 50
  Information Technology Agreement, 37
  Internet use, 55
  labour issues, 50
  and LDCs, 84–5
  post-Cancún, 122
  regional trade agreements, 84
  trade policy reviews, 73
  and US Anti-Dumping Act, 106
  and US Copyright Act, 106–7
  use of dispute settlement mechanisms, 11
  WTO membership, 12^n
exchange rates, 4–5, 17

financial services, 29–30, 45
France, 107

G-8, 45
G-15, 45
G-20, 124
GATS
   See also services
   Article II, 60, 77
   Article XVII, 60, 77
   Article XIX, 80
   Council on Services, 15
   and electronic commerce, 71–2
   entry into force, 29
   nature, 8
   negotiations, 19
   notification requirements, 24
   requirements, 29
GATT
   50th anniversary, 46–51, 57
   achievements, 2
   Article I:1, 60, 76, 77
   Article III, 60, 77, 107, 108
   Article VI, 103
   Article XIII, 60
   Article XIII:1, 60
   Article XX(b), 7, 107–8
   Article XX(g), 59
   change to WTO, 7–18
   contracting states, 3
   creation, 2
   diplomat's agreement, 10
   limitations, 3–6
   members, 13
   structures, 4
   and trade policies, 9
General Council, 15
Geneva Conference 1982, 5–6, 7
Geneva Conference 1993, 1
Geneva Conference 1998
   50th anniversary celebrations, 46–51, 57
   Declaration, 64, 207–10
   Declaration on Electronic Commerce, 55–6
   generally, 52–61
   implementation issues, 53–5

   post-Geneva debate, 62–3
   protests, 46–8, 56, 57
Geneva Week, 82, 86
geographical indications, 94, 110
Georgia, 14, 22, 79
globalization, 2–6, 47
gold standard, 4–5, 16
goods. *See* trade in goods
green room, 98–9
Guatemala, 60, 76

Harbinson, Stuart, 94–5, 116, 118
Havana Charter 1947, 10
high policy, 136–8
HIV/AIDS, 89
Holy See, 149
Honduras, 60, 76
Hong Kong, 67, 73
Hungary, 67

IMF, 16, 17, 40, 43, 44, 47, 85, 141
implementation issues, 25, 53–5, 87–9, 100, 126–7
implementation phase
   'built-in agenda', 25
   continuing services negotiations, 29–31
   dispute settlement, 28
   generally, 19–31
   new membership, 20–1
   notifications, 23–6
   setting up, 21–3
   transparency, 26–8
import licensing, 39, 60
India
   financial services agreements, 30
   G-20 member, 124
   needs of developing countries, 54
   patent protection dispute, 26, 60–1, 77–8
   Singapore issues, 134[n]
   and TRIPS, 26, 54, 60–1, 77–8
   US – shrimp/turtle dispute, 58
   use of dispute mechanism, 11
Indonesia, 47, 73, 124
information technology, 36, 83, 96
Information Technology Agreement 1996, 36–7, 45, 92, 183–203

intellectual property. *See* TRIPS
International Federation of Free Trade Unions, 48^n
international financial institutions, 16–18, 27
International Labour Organization, 36, 48^n
International Trade Centre (ITC), 40, 85, 138
International Trade Organization (ITO), proposals, 2
Internet, 55–6, 71–2, 82
investment, 37, 38, 39, 53, 63, 91
　See also TRIMS
Iran, 14
Iraq, 14

Japan, 11, 37, 73, 83, 84–5, 106
Jordan, 14, 22, 79

Kazakhstan, 14, 22
Kenya, 67, 118
Korea, 11
Kyrgyz Republic, 14, 22, 71

labour standards, 35–6, 48^n, 50, 92, 130
Lamy, Pascal, 121, 131
Lao PDR, 14, 22
Latvia, 14, 22, 71
least-developed countries (LDCs)
　Doha Declaration, 104
　Geneva Conference, 52
　High-Level Meeting 1997, 43, 44, 64
　Integrated Framework, 43–4, 85, 86
　post-Seattle programs, 84–6
　Singapore issues, 118–19
　Singapore Plan, 40, 43
　sub-committee, 43
　UN Conference 2001, 86
　WTO commitment, 33
　WTO membership, 21, 120
Lebanon, 14, 22
Libya, 14
Lithuania, 14, 22, 105
logo, 40

Macedonia, 14, 22
malaria, 89
Malaysia, 58
Mali, 125
Mandela, Nelson, 46, 51
maritime transport, 29
market access agenda, 122, 136–8
Marrakesh Agreement
　Annexes, 165–6
　Article I, 1
　Article III, 1
　Article V:2, 73–4
　Article XIV.1, 12
　continuing negotiations, 63
　entry into force, 163–4
　legal consistency, 10–12
　preamble, 138
　ratification, 13
　signing, 19, 163
　single undertaking, 12–13, 69, 134, 135–6
　text, 153–65
　TPRM, 9, 15–16, 73, 86
　withdrawal from, 164
Marrakesh Decision on Coherence, 17
Mauritius, 118
members
　2000 accessions, 79
　accession process, 20–1, 22–3, 162
　bilateral negotiations, 14, 21
　Cancún accessions, 120
　Doha accessions, 105
　least-developed countries, 21, 120
　list, 147–9
　new membership, 13–14, 20–1
　original members, 20, 162
　Seattle accessions, 71
　transition economies, 21
MERCOSUR, 33
Mexico, 11, 34, 60, 76, 124
Millennium Development Goals, 97
Millennium Round, 46, 50, 64
ministerial conferences, 15, 50, 65, 69
Moldova, 14, 22, 105
Mongolia, 14, 22, 71
Montreal Ministerial Meeting 1988, 9^n

Moore, Mike
  2000 annual report, 90
  appointment, 68
  Development Round, 99–100
  Doha preparations, 94–5, 96–7
  implementation issues, 53
  protectionism, 82
  and Seattle, 67, 79
  succession, 112
  technical cooperation funds, 87
most favoured nation treatment, 60
movement of persons, 29, 30, 101
Multifibre Agreement, 140–1
multilateral trading system, 127–31, 135–6

NAFTA, 33, 129
national treatment, 15, 60
negotiations. *See* continuing negotiations
Nepal, 14, 22, 120
NGOs
  criticism of WTO, 62
  demonstrations, 48, 69
  and dispute procedures, 56
  Doha Conference, 105
  relations with WTO, 28, 48, 73–4
  and shrimp/turtle dispute, 47, 58
  and TRIPS, 90
Nicaragua, 60
Nigeria, 118, 124
Non-Agricultural Market Access (NAMA), 101, 115, 119
non-discrimination principle, 2, 12, 58–9
North–South division, 3
notification requirements, 10, 23–6

observer governments, 149
OECD, 39, 53, 82, 133
Oman, 14, 22, 79
Origin, Rules of, 39

Pakistan, 58, 108–9, 124
Panama, 14, 22, 71
Panitchpakdi, Supachai
  2004 package, 124
  agriculture negotiations, 116–17
  appointment, 68, 112
  Consultative Board, 130
  Doha Round, 112
  TNC Chair, 115, 116
  trade and poverty, 142
  TRIPS deadlock, 112
Paraguay, 124
participation, 73–4, 81–2
  See also NGOs
patents, 60–1, 77–8, 89–90
pharmaceutical products, 37, 45, 60–1, 77–8, 89–90, 110, 235–6
Philippines, 124
Poland, 67
preferential trade agreements, 128–9, 129–30, 140–1
Preparatory Committee, 21, 23, 28
preshipment inspections, 39
public health, and TRIPS, 89–90, 110–12, 112–13, 235–6

regional trade agreements, 83–4, 103, 127
Rose, Andrew, 142[n]
Ruggiero, Renato, 31, 32, 37, 38–9, 48[n], 49, 68
Russia, 14, 22, 41, 42, 45, 49, 82

Safeguards Agreement, 8, 108–9
Samoa, 14
Sanitary and Phytosanitary Measures. *See* SPS Agreement
Santer, Jacques, 46, 50
Sao Tomé, 14
Saudi Arabia, 14, 22
SCM Agreement, 8, 23–4
Seattle Ministerial Conference 1999
  accessions, 71
  agenda, 69–70
  demonstrations, 69, 79
  DSU review, 72
  electronic commerce, 71–2
  expectations, 64
  failure, 65, 69, 79–80, 128, 134
  NGO access, 73–4
  post-Seattle program, 79–82

preparations, 65–7, 94, 134
   TPRM review, 73
Secretariat, 157
Senegal, 118
Serbia and Montenegro, 14, 22
services
   See also GATS
   continuing negotiations, 29–31, 50, 63, 64, 80–1, 91, 93
   Doha Declaration, 101
Seychelles, 14, 22
shrimp/turtle dispute, 47, 56, 58–9
Sierra Leone, 118
Singapore, 67
Singapore issues, 63, 64, 67, 91, 102–3, 118–19, 135
Singapore Ministerial Conference 1996
   achievements, 45
   Declaration, 41, 169–80
   environmental debate, 33, 35, 130
   information technology, 36–7
   labour standards, 35–6, 36, 130
   and least-developed countries, 40
   new working groups, 37
   optimism, 32
   pre-Singapore period, 32–40
   preparation, 20
   success, 126
South Africa, 89, 124
SPS Agreement, 7, 9, 39, 59–60, 75–6
structures, 7, 14–16, 155–6
Su Yeang, 40
subsidies
   Doha Conference, 103
   export subsidies, meaning, 8
   SCM Agreement, 8, 23–4
Sudan, 14, 23
Sutherland, Peter, 1, 24, 67–8

Taipei, 14, 23, 79, 105
Tajikistan, 14, 23
Tanzania, 118, 124
tariff barriers, 2
technical assistance, 86–7, 117, 138
technical barriers to trade, 39
technical cooperation funds, 87
technology, and trade, 4

telecommunications
   agreements, 45
   GATS Annex, 9
   negotiations, 29, 30, 30–1
Thailand, 11, 30, 58, 73
Tokyo Round, Codes, 10, 136
Tonga, 14, 23
trade
   1998–99 decline, 62
   2001–2 decline, 83, 96
   East Asian set-back, 41–3
   and globalization, 2–6
   growth, 3, 13, 19–20, 33, 41, 82–3
   peace, 143
trade in goods
   barriers, 91
   Doha Declaration, 101
   multilateral agreements, 165–6
   NAMA negotiations, 101, 115, 129
   simplification, 38, 39–40
trade in services. *See* GATS; services
Trade Policy Review Body, 15
Trade Policy Review Mechanism (TPRM), 8–9, 15–16, 73, 86
transition economies, 21, 71
transparency
   decision-making, 98–9
   Geneva Conference 1998, 56–7
   government procurement, 63, 91
   and implementation phase, 26–8
   post-Seattle, 81
   secretiveness of WTO processes, 48
   and shrimp/turtle dispute, 56
TRIMS, 24–5, 38, 88
TRIPS
   approach, 9
   Article 9(1), 106, 107
   Article 13, 107
   Article 70.8(a), 77
   Council on TRIPS, 15
   disputes, 93
   Doha Declaration, 102, 110, 235–6
   and drugs, 60–1, 77–8, 89–90, 110–13, 235–6
   geographical indications, 94, 110
   implementation, 93
   and India, 54, 60–1, 77–8
   notification requirements, 24–5

TRIPS (cont.)
　review, 81
tuna dispute, 34

Uganda, 118
Ukraine, 14, 23
UNCTAD, 39, 40, 43, 44, 48^n, 55, 85, 138
UNDP, 40, 43, 44, 85
United Nations, 86, 89, 97
United States
　agenda, 63
　agricultural exports, 123
　Anti-Dumping Act 1961, 106
　Cancún Conference, 118
　combed cotton yarn dispute, 108–9
　Copyright Act, 106–7
　cotton subsidies, 125
　cotton-underwear dispute, 74–5
　EC – bananas dispute, 60, 76
　economic downturn, 83
　financial services agreements, 30
　growth, 63, 82–3
　India dispute, 26, 60–1, 77–8
　Information Technology Agreement, 36–7
　and LDCs, 84–5
　negotiating authority, 46, 63
　post-Cancún, 122, 128–9
　shrimp/turtle dispute, 47, 56, 58–9
　trade policy reviews, 73
　tuna dispute, 34
　use of dispute settlement mechanisms, 11
　weak dollar, 62
Uruguay Round
　agreements, 7
　approach, 7–18
　dispute resolution, 11
　ending, 1, 19
　number of agreements, 7
　separation of subjects, 15
Uzbekistan, 14, 23

Vanuatu, 14, 23
Venezuela, 67, 124
Viet Nam, 14, 23

website, vii, 27, 48, 132
World Bank, 16, 39, 40, 43, 44, 85, 96, 112
World Customs Organization (WCO), 39
World Health Organization, 89
WTO
　achievement, 142–3
　establishment, 1, 153–4
　functions, 1–2, 154–5
　future of multilateral trading system, 127–31, 135–6
　and GATT, 7–18
　goals, 17–18
　legal consistency, 10–12
　reform capacity, 8–10, 160–2
　scope, 1, 154
　sporadic pace, 131–2
　status, 158
　structures, 7, 14–16, 155–6
　website, vii, 27, 48, 132
　withdrawal from, 164
WTO agreements
　entry into force, 19
　intellectual property. See TRIPS
　list, 165–6
　numbers, 7
　Safeguards Agreement, 8, 108–9
　SCM Agreement, 8, 23–4
　services. See GATS
　single undertaking, 12–13, 69, 134, 135–6
　SPS Agreement, 7, 9, 39, 59–60, 75–6
　Textiles. See Agreement on Textiles and Clothing
　TRIMS, 24–5, 38, 88
　WTO Agreement. See Marrakesh Agreement

Yemen, 14, 23

Zambia, 118
Zimbabwe, 118, 124
Zoellick, Robert, 121, 122, 128–9, 137–8